The Haverford Discussions

THE HAVERFORD DISCUSSIONS

A BLACK INTEGRATIONIST MANIFESTO FOR RACIAL JUSTICE

Edited by
MICHAEL LACKEY
Assisted by Rachel Balzar

Afterword by Alfred E. Prettyman

UNIVERSITY OF VIRGINIA PRESS
CHARLOTTESVILLE AND LONDON

University of Virginia Press

Printed in the United States of America on acid-free paper

First published 2013

9 8 7 6 5 4 3 2 1

LIBRARY OF CONGRESS CATALOGING-IN-PUBLICATION DATA

The Haverford discussions : a black integrationist manifesto for racial justice / edited by Michael Lackey ; assisted by Rachel Balzar.

pages cm

Includes bibliographical references and index.

ISBN 978-0-8139-3486-0 (cloth : alk. paper)—ISBN 978-0-8139-3487-7 (e-book)

1. Hastie Group. 2. African Americans—Race identity. 3. African Americans—Cultural assimilation. 4. Black nationalism—United States. 5. United States—Race relations. I. Lackey, Michael. II. Balzar, Rachel, 1992–

E185.625.H386 2013

305.896′073—dc23

2013004567

To Bill Eckerle, a master historian

Contents

Acknowledgments

There are many people and organizations that have made this project possible. Let me start by thanking the original editor, Alfred E. Prettyman. Alfred's generosity and insight have made my job much easier and more rewarding. I feel immense gratitude for his encouragement and support. For many of my generation, Arnold Rampersad is the model scholar, the person many of us hope to emulate. I want to thank Arnold for supporting me and this project and for answering all my questions. Other people who have assisted me in more ways than they can imagine include Charles W. Mills, John Ernest, Dana Nelson, Bill Maxwell, Adelaide M. Cromwell, Eddie N. Williams, Chris Douglas, Roland Guyotte, Scott Michaelsen, Arne Kildegaard, Ramsay Bohm, Julie Eckerle, and Brook Miller. A special word of thanks goes to Roger Wareham. In all my years doing research, I have never met a person in grants development who more passionately, tirelessly, and aggressively secures funding for faculty research. My university is lucky to have Roger.

Much of the work for this project relied upon the good will and professional expertise of library archivists. In particular, I want to thank Janet C. Olson, Assistant University Archivist at Northwestern University Library; John Anderies and Diana Franzusoff Peterson, archivists at Haverford College; the archivists and library staff at Brown University's John Hay Library and the Library of Congress (Manuscript Division); and Sandy Kill, interlibrary loan manager at the University of Minnesota, Morris.

My biggest thanks go to Rachel Balzar, a research assistant who far exceeded my extremely high expectations. Never have I met such a responsible, competent, and reliable student.

I would also like to thank all the organizations that have provided generous financial support for this project. First is the University of Minnesota, Morris, which funded the visit to Brown University's John Hay Library, where I first discovered the manuscript of the Haverford Discussions. Second, I would like to thank the University of Minnesota for a grant-in-aid, which enabled me to visit a number of libraries.

Third, I would like to thank the National Endowment for the Humanities, which supported this project with a summer stipend. That funding enabled me to bring the project to completion.

Finally, I want to thank my editor, Cathie Brettschneider. From the very beginning, she believed in this project and in me.

A Brief History of the Haverford Group

The late sixties and early seventies were a time for race-inflected manifestos, agendas in support of black power, black liberation, black nationalism, and black aesthetics. Prominent works that had a significant impact include *The Autobiography of Malcolm X* (1965), Stokely Carmichael and Charles Hamilton's *Black Power* (1967), Harold Cruse's *Rebellion or Revolution?* (1968), Eldridge Cleaver's *Soul on Ice* (1968), and Addison Gayle's *The Black Aesthetic* (1971). In addition to the urgency and militancy of their message, what unified vocal advocates of black liberation was their critique of the "pro-integrationists,"[1] for most of these writers considered integration an incoherent fiction that had effectively duped the masses into accepting their inferior condition in the irredeemably racist United States. H. Rap Brown puts the matter best in his 1969 book *Die Nigger Die!*: "Integration is impractical." For Brown, it is "White people" who have "got hung up on integration." Black people, he asserts, were not opposed to the separate in separate but equal. "It was the unequal nature of segregation that Black people protested against in the South, not segregation itself."[2]

What has been conspicuously absent from this militant story of the late sixties and early seventies has been a systematic counter-narrative, a multi-black-authored work that not only offers a substantive critique of black separatist philosophies but also articulates a comprehensive pro-integrationist agenda. The contents of this volume, originally referred to as the Haverford Discussions, is that alternative narrative, a counter-testament of sorts to LeRoi Jones (Amiri Baraka) and Larry Neal's 1968 anthology *Black Fire,* which admonishes the black person in the United States to reject "assumptions based on white models" and to construct "his own culture—on definite black values."[3] It is my

1. James Boggs, "Black Power—a Scientific Concept Whose Time Has Come," in *Black Fire,* 106.

2. Brown, *Die Nigger Die!,* 55, 124.

3. James T. Stewart, "The Development of the Black Revolutionary Artist," in *Black Fire,* 3, 10.

contention that had the Haverford Discussions been published in 1969 or 1970, as was intended, it would have contributed significantly to our understanding of the assumptions underwriting separatist and integrationist agendas.

It was the Haverford Group that produced the Haverford Discussions, and the first leader of the group was Kenneth B. Clark, a psychologist who did studies using black and white dolls to document how segregation damaged black children; his findings were used in the 1954 *Brown v. Board of Education* case. From 1966 until 1975, Clark was the president of the Metropolitan Applied Research Center (MARC), a solutions- and action-oriented research center based in New York City with the mission of improving the living conditions of the urban poor. With regard to the Haverford Group, MARC was important because it funded the first meeting and provided the secretarial staff to produce the edited transcription of the Haverford Discussions.

Most of the materials, including an original manuscript of the Haverford Discussions, are in the Papers of Kenneth B. Clark at the Library of Congress (Manuscript Division).[4] The first document in the Haverford Folder of General Correspondence, dated November 2, 1967—an indication of when Clark became seriously concerned about the rise of black separatist political agendas—is a letter to Dr. Homer A. Jack (see appendix 3 for a transcription of this letter), director of the Unitarian Universalist Association and one of the founders of CORE (Congress of Racial Equality). Responding to the Black Caucus's call "for a racially separatist system," Clark tells Jack: "If the U.U.A. were to concede to such demands and give official sanction to an organization such as a Black Affairs Council or Black Unitarian Universalists for Radical Reform, it would be taking a regressive step." This Clark cannot accept, for he insists that he is "committed to a struggle for a racially integrated American society." He has adopted this position because he believes "that racial segregation in its subtle or flagrant forms is dehumanizing to both Negroes and whites." Indeed, he argues "that racially

4. There are also copies of the manuscript at the New York Public Library's Schomburg Center, the Special Collections at Haverford College, and in the J. Saunders Redding Papers at Brown University's John Hay Library. I first discovered the manuscript at the John Hay Library. But of all the collections, the Kenneth Clark Papers contain the most information about the group, including notes, memos, drafts, and correspondence.

segregated communities perpetuate intolerable forms of social pathology," and the primary victims are "Negro children."[5]

By the spring of 1969, black separatist ideologies and movements were proliferating so rapidly, especially among young college blacks, that it was simply impossible to ignore them, so Clark invited a number of prominent African American intellectuals to meet at Haverford College in Pennsylvania in order to identify flaws in the black separatist philosophy, to define a black integrationist position, and to formulate a comprehensive program of action.[6] The coordinator of the meeting and one of the participants was Anne Cooke Reid, a professor of drama and the wife of Ira De A. Reid (1901–68), a sociology professor at Haverford. By any standard of judgment, the list of participants is impressive: St. Clair Drake, Stanford University professor and coauthor of *Black Metropolis;* Ralph Ellison, author of *Invisible Man;* John Hope Franklin, University of Chicago professor and author of *From Slavery to Freedom* (among many other books); William Hastie, chief judge of the U.S. Court of Appeals for the Third Circuit; Robert C. Weaver, the first African American to hold a cabinet-level position (he was the secretary of housing and urban development); Adelaide M. Cromwell, director of the African Studies Program at Boston University and author of *An African Victorian Feminist: The Life and Times of Adelaide Smith Casely Hayford, 1868–1960* (among other books); and J. Saunders Redding, author of numerous books and the first African American to hold an

5. This letter is in the Kenneth Clark Papers, Box 318, Folder 11 (Hastie Group: General Correspondence, November 1967–July 1969). There is a problem referring to the Haverford Group as the Hastie Group. The initial meeting took place at Haverford College, so the original manuscript was titled the "Haverford Discussions," and the group was referred to as the Haverford Group until 1972. As discussed in the text below, at the third meeting, on May 29–31, 1972, the group decided to change its name to the Hastie Group, after William Hastie. When I refer to the Haverford Group, I am referring to the group that met at the first three meetings. When I refer to the Hastie Group, I am referring to the group that met at the fourth and final meeting, in 1975.

6. At the third Haverford Group meeting, when giving newcomers a brief history of the group, William Hastie says that Clark originated the idea of the Haverford Group, but that Anne Reid "took the effective initiative in suggesting that she would be very pleased to have some people meet with her at her home on the Haverford campus to talk over the separatist movement—versus the integration movement that preceded it." Kenneth Clark Papers, Box 320, Folder 3 (Hastie Group Meetings, 29–31 May 1972).

endowed chair at an Ivy League university, to name only a notable few.[7] The group met on May 30 and 31, 1969, and their meeting was taped. The transcription of that meeting was dubbed the Haverford Discussions, and it is here available for the first time.

On the surface, it would seem that the Haverford Group would have a relatively easy task in opposing militant black separatists, since its members were well-established intellectuals who could strategically place an article in the *New York Times* or get a meeting with the president of Princeton University. The most prominent black separatists, by contrast, had only recently become known and were surprisingly young at the time of the first Haverford meeting: H. Rap Brown was only twenty-five, Stokely Carmichael twenty-seven, Larry Neal thirty-one, and Eldridge Cleaver thirty-three. By referencing intellectual debates from the past, using rigorous forms of logic, and foregrounding their stellar achievements, members of the Haverford Group believed that they could successfully expose the flaws and limitations in the black separatists' philosophy and agenda. But as the members of the group would conclude within only a couple years after its first meeting, the black separatist agenda overshadowed the black integrationist approach.

The dominance of black separatism is one reason why the group not only failed to publish the Haverford Discussions after its 1969 meeting but also started to unravel after 1972. On October 8–9, 1969, the group convened its second meeting (which was titled "Follow-up Meeting to Haverford Discussions"), and based on a transcript of that meeting, there was considerable optimism about their agenda as well as their ability to counter black separatism. By this point, the Haverford Discussions had been transcribed, circulated to all the members, and subsequently edited; most members had contributed a position statement about the first meeting and black separatism (these are included in this volume after the Discussions); Kenneth Clark had commissioned the editor Alfred E. Prettyman to ready the manuscript for publication with Harper & Row; and the group was planning a strategy for publicizing and marketing its pro-integrationist agenda and

7. The first list of potential participants included James Baldwin, Julian Bond, Gwendolyn Brooks, Ralph Bunche, Harold Cruse, and Percy Julian. Kenneth Clark Papers, Box 319, Folder 1 (Hastie Group Meetings).

manuscript. In order to generate enthusiasm for the publication of the Haverford Discussions in book form, the group decided to put out a "pamphlet-position paper,"[8] a one-page statement defining the group's positions and objectives.

It was Prettyman who drafted the position paper, which was never published. Prettyman did not attend the first meeting, and Ellison considered this an asset, because it meant Prettyman could offer a more objective perspective of the manuscript's quality and significance. In response to Ellison's question about the manuscript's value, Prettyman claimed that it was "very good material," but he made an important qualification, saying that there was something missing. Without a more clearly defined focus or agenda, the Haverford Discussions would be seen as "a curiosity, a sort of window into how selected black intellectuals engage one another and what they're thinking, but as it stands, it doesn't lead to anything actual afterward."[9] What was needed to complete the manuscript were supplementary materials, which I have included in this volume. In an outline of the one-page position statement (dated October 27, 1969), which tentatively titles the project "Afro-American Studies & Black Power," Prettyman offers a systematic way of understanding the Haverford Discussions. Haverford Group members clarify "the social processes which have brought about the nascence of black studies and the quest for black power." The two things that have contributed significantly to the rise and popularity of Black Power movements have been the "deficiencies of western scholarship" and the "essential schizophrenia of American life and politics." Careful, however, not to focus primarily on the negative, Prettyman urges the group to foreground "individual statements of the positive goals to be achieved in the proper development of Afro-American Studies and the maximization of black authority and power in this society."[10] Put succinctly, if the project is going to have an enduring intellectual impact, then it needs to have a positive and clearly defined objective, which would justify and lead to a pro-integrationist agenda and movement. Such was the optimistic view at the 1969 meeting and shortly thereafter,

8. Kenneth Clark Papers, Box 320, Folder 2 (8–9 Oct. 1969, Jamaica, N.Y.), 30.

9. Kenneth Clark Papers, Box 320, Folder 2 (8–9 Oct. 1969, Jamaica, N.Y.), 15.

10. Kenneth Clark Papers, Box 318, Folder 11 (Hastie Group: General Correspondence).

which led members to believe that the Haverford Discussions would be published and that they would have a significant impact.[11]

By the third meeting in 1972 (May 29–31), however, the mood of the group was very different. At the 1969 meetings, the general consensus was that the rise of black separatism was a temporary development, something that would wane because it was driven by only a vocal minority of militant blacks. In the Haverford Discussions, Eddie N. Williams, vice president for public affairs and director of the Center for Policy Study at the University of Chicago, casually dismisses the black separatist movement as a "fad," something that "will pass." By the third meeting, however, Clark grimly observes: "The problem which we thought at our last meeting was probably going to recede, had not receded at all but was quietly proliferating." Indeed, Clark goes on to claim that students as well as institutions "now have given up on the possibilities or promises of integration in our society and are coming back aided and abetted by important forces in the white society toward 'separate but equal.'"[12]

So turbulent were the times that the Haverford Group had to change its name, which it did at the 1972 meeting. Mamie Phipps Clark, an educational psychologist and the wife of Kenneth Clark, disclosed what necessitated the change: "The group seems to have gotten attached to the label 'The Haverford Group' but Haverford has been in very deep trouble on this issue and it just doesn't seem appropriate any more."[13]

Haverford College would have seemed an unlikely place in the late 1960s to host a meeting of African American intellectuals. Established in 1833, Haverford is a Quaker-affiliated college that prides itself on its tradition of tolerance and respect. But like most colleges and universities in the United States, it experienced considerable turmoil in the late sixties and early seventies because of massive shifts in racial demographics. Until the 1950s and 1960s, "Haverford was almost exclusively

11. In a phone conversation with Prettyman, I asked him why the Discussions did not get published. He said that one of the main reasons was that "the funding dried up."

12. Kenneth Clark Papers, Box 320, Folder 3 (Hastie Group Meetings, 29–31 May 1972), 5, 10.

13. Kenneth Clark Papers, Box 320, Folder 3 (Hastie Group Meetings, 29–31 May 1972), 24.

white, Protestant and upperclass." The fifties and sixties witnessed a change, but only a minor one, for as Adolphus Williams and Cynthia Farr Brown claim, "one Black student represented racial diversity" during this period. It was only in 1968 that a significant number of minority students started to attend Haverford. According to Williams and Brown, "During the College's first 135 years there were fewer Black students than arrived in the fall of 1968–71. By the time these students were seniors, there were over 70 minority students in the College, well over 10% of the student body."[14]

The newly arrived students were certainly vocal, for they charged Haverford College with being inattentive and inhospitable to non-whites, and on March 18, 1970, four students "demanded a Black Cultural Center."[15] But it was in 1972 that minority students became more aggressive and coordinated. After pressuring Haverford in the late sixties to increase the number of minority students, administrators, and faculty, black and Hispanic students staged in the spring of 1972 well-coordinated boycotts and confrontations in order to achieve their objectives. So tense was the situation at this time that several nonwhite students had "been asked to leave College for academic reasons, but the Committee on Student Standings and Programs, which recommended the dismissals, also issued a statement saying, in effect, that the problem was not academic but racial: the strains of life at Haverford were making it impossible for many minority students to succeed academically."[16] This was the environment in which the group decided to change its name to the Hastie Group.

Ironically, it was when the group started to fall apart that it produced its only multiauthored publication. The renamed Hastie Group held its last meeting at MARC on May 16–18, 1975. Hastie's death almost a year later, on April 14, 1976, certainly contributed to the group's collapse, but there were already indications by the 1975 meeting to suggest that the group was in serious decline. For the first three meetings, there are typed transcriptions of the discussions, and there are usually many follow-up documents assessing the meeting and formulating a sub-

14. Adolphus L. Williams Jr. and Cynthia Farr Brown, "Minorities at Haverford," in *The Spirit and the Intellect,* 109, 110.

15. Robert G. Schwartz, "The Center Holds: Haverford in the Sixties," in *The Spirit and the Intellect,* 105.

16. Williams and Brown, "Minorities at Haverford," 112.

sequent strategy. The fourth meeting is the only one without a transcription, and there are no follow-up letters.[17] While Clark stopped leading the group after the second meeting in 1969,[18] he was nonetheless extremely active throughout, especially between 1972 and 1975 when he took an active role in producing *Black Separatism: A Bibliography,* which was published in 1976.[19] This volume contains Ellison's original statement, which was intended for publication in the Haverford Discussions and is published in this volume, as well as the revised statements of five participants from the first meeting and two statements from new members.[20] It also contains an extremely valuable introduction from Clark, which sheds light on the Haverford Group's philosophy and agenda.

In his introduction to the *Black Separatism* volume, Clark claims that the Haverford Group came together in order to "discuss the precipitous rise of black separatist thought and activity among Negro college

17. Clark was careful to save all documents from the meetings. Because Hastie became the leader of the group after the second 1969 meeting, it is possible that he was in charge of saving all documents. But this is unlikely. I have examined the Hastie Papers, which are housed at the Harvard Law School Library, and there was nothing relevant to the Haverford or the Hastie Group. Clark attended the 1975 meeting, and there are only a few documents from the 1975 meeting in his Papers. The folder for the 1975 meeting includes a copy of the letter of invitation, a list of members to whom the letter was sent, an agenda of the meeting, and a copy of an April 28, 1975, *New York Times* article titled "Black Intellectuals Divided over Ideological Direction." Kenneth Clark Papers, Box 320, Folder 4 (Hastie Group Meetings, 16–18 May 1975).

18. Given his commitments to MARC, Clark thought it best to step down as chairman of the Haverford Group. At the second meeting, he stressed that MARC staff would still do the bulk of the secretarial work. Near the end of the meeting, Clark basically appointed Hastie chairman: "One of the things that we will put in the minutes is that the group by consensus asked Judge Hastie to consider the chairmanship and he had not good reason to refuse." Kenneth Clark Papers, Box 320, Folder 2 (Hastie Group Meetings, 8–9 October 1969, Jamaica, N.Y.), 110.

19. In a letter dated March 23, 1973, addressed "To the Members of the Hastie Group," Clark indicates that the *Black Separatism* volume was "prepared at the suggestion of the Hastie Group at its last meeting," which would have been the third meeting, in 1972. Kenneth Clark Papers, Box 318, Folder 8 (Hastie Group: Bibliography on Black Separatism by Betty Jenkins and Susan Phillis, Drafts).

20. I am referring to Hylan Lewis as one of the new members. While he was present at the first 1969 meeting, he was not named as one of the participants, nor did he contribute a position paper.

students." For Clark, what united the members was their shared "conviction that racial integration was essential to racial progress and justice in America."[21] While it is certainly true that there was general consensus among the members of the group, there were also some significant points of divergence. For instance, when brainstorming about strategies for countering black separatist movements, Clark, Ellison, and Redding focused their attention primarily on life at the university, while Phyllis Wallace and M. Carl Holman saw the need to consider "pressing problems originating outside the campus gates."

These differences speak to some of the virtues and weaknesses of the group. On the one hand, the group certainly valued and encouraged dissent, for the members realized that engaging multiple and contrasting views could only strengthen their own arguments and positions. On the other hand, the group seemed to be out of touch with the younger generation, which perhaps explains why it was not as successful as it would have liked. Holman makes this point very nicely when he tells the members during the Friday evening session that their silence about the Vietnam War indicates a "great disparity between what we [university students] were sensitive to and concerned about and what they [university professors] were sensitive to and concerned about."

It was this generational gap that left some members of the group quite puzzled by crucial developments in the sixties, thus rendering them less effective in reaching the younger generation. These were some of the most accomplished people in the country, and most of them had spent more than twenty years formulating sophisticated models of sociocultural analysis to expose overt and covert structures of racism, utilizing rigorous forms of logic to identify contradictions between American constitutional ideals and America's antidemocratic practices, and charting a path toward the realization of a multiracial democracy. In response to the superior quality of their works and actions, they had been recognized and honored in the United States and overseas. So how could they explain the meteoric rise of Carmichael, Jones (Baraka), Neal, and Cleaver? For these black intellectuals, the problem was not simply a matter of differing ideologies and agendas. The problem was that they considered the work of these young black

21. Clark, "Some Personal Observations on Black Separatism," in *Black Separatism,* xiii.

militants to be historically uninformed and intellectually unsound. And yet, their work was getting widespread attention throughout the country. In the original version of the Haverford Discussions, some parts were expurgated, and it is these exchanges that most reveal the group's confusion.

For instance, when discussing why so many young college students have renounced integration and embraced separatism, the members note that black youth favor charismatic figures rather than wise elders. This leads them to wonder: what appeals to the young black students? To answer this question, they have a conversation about Sterling Brown, which is at times petty and mean-spirited. They describe Brown as a poet and a "great teacher" but not a "scholar."[22] What puzzles the group is that Brown connects with young blacks. But Franklin suggests that Brown succeeds because there is "an absence of a kind of organization and a discipline" in his work, which is considered a virtue among young blacks, for as Franklin says, "If there is control and if there is discipline, they are not interested in it." To illustrate his point, Franklin tells a story about how Brown presented a paper at a conference but had no prepared script. His extemporaneous presentation, Franklin continues, was a "sort of shuffling, disorganization,"[23] which is what the young generation likes about Brown. For Franklin, the younger generation prefers the non-scripted, inspirational speaker over the stodgy old scholar, whose methods and ideas are considered conservative and obsolete.

These comments about Sterling Brown indicate how the group considered itself so different from black separatists with regard to cultural analysis. While H. Rap Brown asserts in *Die Nigger Die!* that blacks in large measure support segregation, Clark makes the exact opposite claim: "During this period of intense and much publicized separatist activity on the campuses, the vast majority of the folk Negro did not themselves become advocates of black separatism. According to surveys of opinion among Negroes, no more than 15 per cent of a representative sample of Negroes ever expressed any sustained rejection of the goals of racial integration. Nor did they accept black separatism

22. Kenneth Clark Papers, Box 319, Folder 3 (Hastie Group Meetings, 30–31 May 1969), "Haverford Discussions" Transcripts (drafts), second session, 16, 8. This exchange occurred during the dinner discussion on May 30.

23. Kenneth Clark Papers, Box 319, Folder 3 (Hastie Group Meetings, 30–31 May 1969), "Haverford Discussions" Transcripts (drafts), second session, 7, 8.

as an effective approach to racial justice in America."[24] On the surface, separatists and integrationists had opposing conceptions of the most effective approach to racial justice. But actually, what differentiates the two was their method of analysis. Brown appeals to personal experience in order to justify his positions and advance his arguments, while Clark makes use of empirical evidence, such as a survey and statistics. Consequently, they draw contradictory conclusions. For members of the Haverford Group, the black separatists simply did not have a mastery of the most rigorous forms of scholarly analysis.

Throughout the Haverford Discussions, there are numerous subtextual references that strategically seek to expose the incoherent content as well as the flawed method of the black separatists. Let me briefly discuss only one example in order to illustrate how these references function. At one point in the Haverford Discussions, Ellison refers to Coleman Hawkins (1904–69), one of the first and most innovative saxophonists who had a decisive impact on the evolution of jazz. Although Ellison does not mention Lindsay Barrett's essay "The Tide Inside, It Rages!" which is in the 1968 anthology *Black Fire,* anyone familiar with the essay would realize that Ellison is mocking Barrett and his followers. Barrett makes a plea for a pure black aesthetic, one that effectively shuffles off the mortal coils of all things white. According to Barrett, the problem with many contemporary blacks is that they have been brainwashed with a white ideology and system of analysis, which explains why blacks could easily overlook the message of great black musicians. Put simply, the judgments of contemporary blacks have been "clouded by white Western thoughts." For Barrett, what is needed in 1968 is "the full recognition of the black light that illuminates the shapes contained in" black music, and Barrett specifically mentions Coleman Hawkins, because his work evinces "a need for the elimination of the whiteness of the social normalities that surround him." Indeed, Barrett claims that Hawkins has significantly contributed "to the historic drama of our urgent reality and desire to be free of the white sensibility that ropes its way about the alleys of our brain."[25]

In the Haverford Discussions, Ellison expresses frustration with black youth who use a Barrett-type critique to condemn him for his

24. Clark, "Some Personal Observations on Black Separatism," xiv. In the Haverford Discussions, Clark cited a similar statistic, which suggests that his view remained consistent on this point from 1969 to 1976.

25. Lindsay Barrett, "The Tide Inside, It Rages!," in *Black Fire,* 149, 151, 152.

integrationist stance. They say that Ellison has been brainwashed. To clarify why the stance of the young black separatists is incoherent, Ellison strategically mentions Hawkins, and specifically the multiracial origins of his musical innovations. Barrett's claim that Hawkins's music is free of the white sensibility is only possible because of historical ignorance, for, as Ellison observes, Hawkins learned to play the saxophone at the "racially integrated Washburn College, out in Kansas." Moreover, Hawkins "was a conscious musician who was trained in Western musical techniques and tradition and he took what he learned and extended it and created something startlingly new and uniquely his own and uniquely Negro-American." Ellison is not denying that Hawkins's racial background and experiences played a role in the evolution of his music. Rather, he is clarifying why it is impossible to disentangle black and white when it comes to his music, for Hawkins "integrated his knowledge with his inherited musical tradition and, like it or not, whites were involved in the process." To say that whites were involved does not minimize Hawkins's contribution. But providing information about the history of music, and Hawkins's history in particular, effectively exposes the black separatist representation of Barrett as incoherent. In essence, Ellison tacitly debunks Barrett's essay as uninformed nonsense, and thereby suggests that those young blacks who have adopted Barrett's ideas lack a basic grasp of history, have formulated implausible definitions of racial designators such as white and black, and have adopted faulty forms of thinking.

Given the Haverford Group's dismissive treatment of the black separatists, it would be wrong to conclude that the black integrationists were always right and that the black separatists were always wrong, and it is certainly not my intention to make such a case. The tragedy is that the black separatist ideology got so much attention in the late sixties and early seventies that it overshadowed the coordinated work of prominent black integrationists, such as the Haverford Group. Publishing the Haverford Discussions today is an attempt not simply to recover the coordinated thought of a powerful group of African American intellectuals. It is an attempt to contribute some relevant arguments to an ongoing discussion about race that could have and should have been addressed more than forty years ago.[26] To provide a context for this

26. Eddie S. Glaude has also adopted a less ideological approach to the debates between the black separatists and black integrationists. In his introduction to *Is It*

conversation, let me briefly identify some of the issues that at the time divided so many of the country's most famous black intellectuals.

Intellectual Contexts for the Haverford Discussions

There was a specter haunting the first 1969 Haverford meeting. It was Harold Cruse. Author of the controversial 1967 study *The Crisis of the Negro Intellectual,* Cruse eviscerated prominent black thinkers of the 1950s and 1960s, claiming that "the Negro intellectual is a retarded child whose thinking processes are still geared to piddling intellectual civil writism and racial integrationism."[27] For Cruse, the position of then-contemporary black leaders has been significantly compromised, because the "Negro leadership generally functions, even during protest, with one foot out and the other foot inside the Establishment."[28] Black leaders want to be a part of America's legal, political, and academic establishment, so they are forced to fight against the very social system that they want to join. This, however, places them in a tricky position, since they are "not really fighting *against* the system, but against being *left out of it.*"[29] Consequently, black intellectuals have, in large measure, become pawns of the establishment, which is why Cruse concludes that the black intellectual "plays second and third fiddle to white intellectuals in all the establishments—Left, Center, and Right." Indeed, "white intellectuals in these establishments do not recognize the Negro intellectual as a man who can speak both for himself and for the best interests of the nation, but only as someone who must be spoken for and on behalf of."[30]

In 1967 Cruse was not the lone critic of the black establishment. In *Black Power: The Politics of Liberation in America,* Carmichael and Hamilton developed a Fanonian model of "political colonialism" in order to demonstrate how black American leaders unwittingly sup-

---

Nation Time?, titled "Black Power Revisited," Glaude discusses the strengths and weaknesses of black power and black nationalism. For Glaude, "failure to examine seriously the period's accomplishments and deficiencies, its internal fissures, and its effect on the form and content of our contemporary political languages dooms us to continuously misunderstand the complex political and cultural desires of black America" (2). My approach in this volume is in the same tradition as Glaude's.

27. Cruse, *The Crisis of the Negro Intellectual,* 475.

28. Cruse, *The Crisis of the Negro Intellectual,* 371.

29. Cruse, *The Crisis of the Negro Intellectual,* 371; Cruse's emphasis.

30. Cruse, *The Crisis of the Negro Intellectual,* 475.

port a "white power structure." They conclude: "When one talks of a 'Negro Establishment' in most places in this country, one is talking of an Establishment resting on a white power base; of hand-picked blacks whom that base projects as showpieces out front. These black 'leaders' are, then, only as powerful as their white kingmakers will permit them to be."[31] Put simply, black establishment leaders are "no more than puppets."[32] Carmichael and Hamilton's critique was certainly nasty and brutish, but it was short, which is why members of the Haverford Group would not have felt particularly threatened by it.[33] But Cruse's critique was another matter altogether, for it was relentless, systematic, and comprehensive; and consequently, a cause for concern.[34]

In fact, during the first Haverford session, Hastie indicates the degree to which the critique of the establishment had already taken

31. Carmichael and Hamilton, *Black Power,* 10–11.

32. Carmichael and Hamilton, *Black Power,* 10.

33. In an influential 1964 essay titled "The Black Establishment," Lerone Bennett defined the black establishment and identified specific members. Bennett's critique is not as mean-spirited as the one found in Cruse's *The Crisis of the Negro Intellectual,* but it is still quite damning. While Bennett acknowledges that some establishment whites have contributed to the project of black liberation, he ultimately concludes that "Whites, as a group, have served as a brake rather than as an accelerator of the Freedom Movement" (88). This is the case because the establishment is founded on a contradiction: "The Establishment is both militant and conservative. Its pronouncements, in other words, are militant; but its actions are cautious and conciliatory" (89). In the 1960s "rebellious students" became extremely critical of the black establishment because there was a growing belief that "the Negro power structure has been more active in accommodating the masses to misery than in organizing them for an attack on the forces responsible for the misery" (90). In his article, Bennett mentions three members of the Haverford Group, Robert Weaver (84), Ralph Bunche (87–88), and William Hastie (92–93), but what he says about them is more positive than negative. Bunche was a member of the Haverford Group, but he never attended any of the meetings. Clark, however, did inform him about the content of the meetings.

34. In the preface to the 1976 MARC-sponsored book *Black Separatism,* Betty Lanier Jenkins and Susan Phillis write that the first Haverford Group meeting focused on "the changing role of the Negro intellectual" (ix). Since Jenkins and Phillis thank Kenneth Clark and Hylan Lewis for their "sensitive criticism" (x) of the book, it appears that prominent members of the group agreed with this assessment. Adelaide M. Cromwell, who changed her name to Adelaide Cromwell Gulliver by 1976, confirms this approach to the Discussions in a brief introductory statement about "the focus played on the role and responsibility of the black intellectual" (xviii) at the first meeting.

hold by 1969. At a Legal Day event at Howard University in 1968, a student told Hastie, who was the first African American appellate judge (1949–61) and was the chief judge of the Third Circuit in 1968, that he was a lackey "of the establishment." Hastie retorted that he could not be a lackey of the establishment because he was the establishment. Despite Hastie's humorous qualification, Holman confirmed later in the first session what many Haverford Group members probably suspected when he told his fellow discussants that he considered them "the establishment, or a part of it." Holman clearly believed this to be a problem, because, as he claims, the "establishment has been very seriously called in question, not just by black students, but by a great number of other people and forces in this country at this time."

What should strike readers of the Haverford Discussions is the degree to which black separatists and black integrationists define words in totally contradictory ways, and this is one reason why these discussions are so valuable. When Cruse refers to establishment intellectuals, here is what he means: The American judicial, political, and university systems are white-dominated institutions, which function to empower whites and disempower blacks. Some blacks have made it into the elite ranks of these institutions, but they are mere pawns of the dominant white power structure. By stark contrast, black integrationists think that, as members of the establishment, they are autonomous decision makers, which explains Hastie's comical quip about the impossibility of being a lackey.

In the introduction to his 1968 book *Rebellion or Revolution?*, a collection of his writings from 1950 through 1968, Cruse singled out Redding as a member "of the Negro intellectual establishment." A staunch opponent of integration, specifically as Marxists understood it, Cruse considered black establishment intellectuals even worse, for "integrationists such as Redding present a greater liability in terms of an intellectual renaissance in black thought than the Marxist integrationists." According to Cruse, "the Reddings are handicaps out of a traditional past that preserved in its own way but was never able to break the custom barriers to any kind of originality."[35] This charge, that Redding is in thrall to an outdated tradition of thinking, has been repeated by prominent writers such as Baraka, Faith Berry, and Henry Louis Gates Jr., and in one way or another it has significantly damaged the reputa-

35. Cruse, *Rebellion or Revolution?*, 21, 23, 23–24.

tion of Redding as well as other members of the Haverford Group.[36] But there is something ironic about the critique of Redding and the Haverford Group, especially given the postmodern claim that race is a constructed fiction, an idea that has come to dominate the academy since the 1980s. To clarify the nature of this irony, let me briefly discuss Lawrence P. Jackson's recent discussion of a crucial exchange between Cruse and Redding.

In the December 1957/January 1958 issue of *Présence Africaine,* Cruse published "An Afro-American's Cultural Views," an essay that viciously criticizes black "leaders, professionals, and intellectuals" because of their devotion to "racial integration." Cruse acknowledges that the American black's "racial and cultural experience as a group is distinctly American," because he or she has been raised in the United States and has had virtually no contact with Africa or his/her African heritage. But this has been the crux of the problem, for black leaders have failed to understand that the "American Negro cannot be understood culturally unless he is seen as a member of a detached ethnic bloc of people of African descent."[37] Until African Americans recover and embrace their distinctly African roots, they are not going to flourish and thrive in the United States.

In a 1960 issue of *The New Leader,* Redding published "Negro Writing in America," which offers two separate critiques of Cruse's position. According to Redding, the "American Negro people are not a *people* in Cruse's sense of the word,"[38] and the reason why is contained in a subtle reversal. Cruse gives primacy to the concept of race when he refers to himself as an "Afro-American," which, according to Redding, is a misnomer. Most Americans who happen to be black have been raised primarily, and often exclusively, in the United States. Therefore, America has, in a sociocultural sense, determined the identity of most American blacks far more than Africa, which is why Redding refers to the black American as an "American Negro" rather than an "Afro-American." To clarify the faulty logic implicit in Cruse's position, Redding contrasts black and Jewish Americans: "No ancient tradition that is kept visible by practice, by language, by institutions, dogmas and dreams, as in the case of the Jewish people, has sustained the American Negro and

36. I will discuss Baraka's and Gates's critiques of Redding later in this introduction. For Berry's critique, see her introduction to *A Scholar's Conscience,* 11.

37. Cruse, *Rebellion or Revolution?,* 50, 49.

38. Redding, "Negro Writing in America," 8; Redding's emphasis.

pushed him toward an ingenuous identification with Negroes native to other parts of the world."[39] Jews can lay claim to an identity connection with people in Israel, not because there is some sort of mystical link transmitted through a common bloodstream, but because there are empirical traditions that have led Jews in the United States and Israel to develop similar forms of behavior, establish comparable institutions, and formulate analogous belief systems. Most black Americans, by contrast, have been so severed from their African heritage that their identity has been determined far more by American cultural and political forms than by Cruse's imagined detached African ethnicity.

Redding's second critique of Cruse, which is even more profound than the first, foregrounds an epistemic slippage in the usage of the term Afro-American. When Redding writes about racial identity, he privileges sociological and anthropological theories. Moreover, he adamantly opposes genetic, biological, or metaphysical explanations. For Redding, the distinctions "between writing by black Americans on the one hand and white Americans on the other hand are the function of American socio-cultural history, and not of race." Because most black Americans have been raised in the United States and not Africa, "American socio-cultural history" determines their identity far more than either the continent of Africa or African sociocultural structures. The problem with black separatists such as Cruse is that they use the word Afro in a metaphysical sense and the word American in a sociocultural sense, and it is this slippage that has caused all kinds of confusion and problems. As Redding says of Cruse, he develops, in all sincerity, "the metaphysical argument that being black confers a special grace under the dispensation of which American Negroes can and should disclaim and reject their history in America and be born again as 'pure blacks . . . nationalistic in terms of the ethnic and cultural attributes of art expression.' "[40] For black separatists, African is a metaphysical signifier, which is different from and superior to the word American, which is merely a sociocultural signifier. Therefore, if blacks in the United States want to discover their true selves, they must give primacy to and embrace their racial metaphysical essence, which effectively supersedes their sociocultural heritage. Within this framework, the metaphysical

39. Redding, "Negro Writing in America," 9.

40. Redding, "The Black Arts Movement: A Modest Dissent," in *A Scholar's Conscience*, 214, 215.

(African) is more real and legitimate than the sociocultural (American). But for Redding, metaphysics is an obsolete concept of a bygone era, and consequently intellectually incoherent.[41] Within Redding's framework, therefore, the words African and American are epistemically equivalent as sociocultural signifiers, and since American blacks have been immersed in the sociocultural norms and forms of the United States and not those of Africa, they are, as a matter of sociocultural fact, primarily American.

In *The Indignant Generation* (2011), a massive study of the complex theories and debates about racial empowerment from the 1930s through the 1960s,Jackson briefly summarizes the Cruse/Redding exchange. More importantly, he suggests that Cruse was the victor by noting how, starting in the 1960s, Redding's writing languished while Cruse's flourished. His primary evidence is that Cruse's work contributed significantly to "the essential framework of thought and the historical events behind the LeRoi Jones–led Black Arts Movement of the second half of the 1960s and 1970s."[42] The irony, of course, is that the Cruse victory, if we can now call it that, could only be categorized as short-lived, for as it turns out, the metaphysical model of race underwriting Cruse's black cultural nationalism and the Black Arts Movement would be considered by today's standards profoundly misguided. Since the 1980s most academics have rejected the idea of race as an ontological fact of being and accepted the postmodern view of race as a sociopolitical invention. Given that Redding and most Haverford Group members considered the metaphysics of race an untenable and even dangerous political construction, their views regarding race are much more compelling today than those of the black separatists of the sixties and the seventies. I reference Jackson's recent discussion of this exchange for two reasons. First, he uses the same kind of rhetorical strategies that were deployed in the sixties and the seventies to misrepresent Haverford Group members. Second, his triumphalist approach prohibits us from getting a clear understanding of the central axioms animating the views of black integrationists. It is my contention that if we take seriously the core ideas of Haverford Group members, we will find their positions to be

41. For an extensive analysis of Redding's career-long assault on metaphysics, see my essay "Redeeming the Post-Metaphysical Promise."

42. Jackson, *The Indignant Generation*, 469.

philosophically prescient and politically empowering, which stands in stark contrast to the way black separatists represented their views.

We know very little today about the Haverford Group because prominent black separatists successfully utilized manipulative rhetorical strategies, which effectively distorted the group's position. We get a clear sense of these strategies through an exchange between Redding and Baraka. After the first formal meeting of the Haverford Group, the members agreed to publish essays that would clarify why black separatist philosophies were premised on intellectually faulty and even politically dangerous assumptions. Redding was one of the first to get an essay into print, which was titled "The Black Revolution in American Studies." In the first paragraph, Redding faults black separatists, who presume "no less than the universal social, cultural, and literary history of blacks from pre-Islamic times to the present and the biological and anthropological linkage of all black people." Redding opposes this view because it is premised on the idea of "a genetic constant, although the theory of a genetic constant has been repudiated by the best scientific minds for a hundred years." What is really behind Redding's critique is his rejection of metaphysics, the idea that there exists an immutable essence that transcends cultural context. Black separatists, Redding charges, believe that race is a metaphysical signifier. Consequently, twentieth-century American black separatists believe that they can trace their heritage and identity to the "blacks from pre-Islamic times."[43] Moreover, they believe that their American identities cannot be linked in any substantive way with eighteenth-century white Frenchmen or nineteenth-century white Brits.

Baraka was furious with Redding, and in "A Reply to Saunders Redding's 'The Black Revolution in American Studies,'" he formulated a view that would seriously damage Redding's reputation.[44] Baraka opens his essay by claiming that Redding's views are "conservative" and, therefore, "supportive of the oppression of the Afro-American nation and white chauvinism in general." According to Baraka, Redding's work

43. Redding, "The Black Revolution in American Studies," 8.

44. In the introduction to the reissue of *To Make a Poet Black,* Gates uses Baraka's critique in order to clarify why Redding's writings were considered limited by later generations of black writers. The problem, however, is that Gates does not examine all the errors in logic and fact in Baraka's essay. See Gates, "'. . . and bid him sing,'" ix–x.

is predicated on the idea "that the Afro-American people do not exist as a people at all, but in some servile non-person relationship to their white masters."[45] Baraka offers neither a clarification nor an argument to justify this view, but it is important to note that he does not even consider such a justification necessary. For Baraka, the measured approach of the scholar fails to generate the necessary kind of passion for cultural and societal transformation. If the black community were to wait for the scholar's patient and methodical approach to take cultural and political effect, nothing would get done. What accounts for the rise of black studies in the United States, Baraka asserts, has been the enthusiasm of students: "The inclusion of black studies on these campuses came only as a result of student struggle, and if some of the rhetoric which accompanied these struggles was overblown, even metaphysical and idealistic, the revolutionary core of those struggles was correct."[46] Notice how Baraka acknowledges that metaphysical discourse is overblown, a tacit admission that it is inaccurate. In essence, he subordinates scholarly rigor and intellectual precision to the rightness of a socially just political cause. His position could be stated thus: given the systemic antiblack racism rampant in the United States, blacks need to band together in order to secure their dignity and rights. Thus, in order to mobilize the masses in support of their race-based national agenda, which is basically correct, distortions and misrepresentations might prove useful and even necessary. In other words, falsehoods would not be incorrect were they to serve the correct objective.

Members of the Haverford Group knew that black separatists would use deceptive rhetorical strategies in order to advance their agenda or to destroy their opponents. As Ellison claims: "We can expect them to try to put us on the defensive with charges of being brainwashed and with epithets of Uncle Tom and so on." Less charitable is Franklin, who says that black separatists will utilize tactics that "involve the destruction of your position and of your right to have a position." Given the black separatist approach, Clark states directly "that we are against their tactics."

This focus on tactics is certainly important. But the Haverford Group consisted of serious intellectuals, who were more concerned

45. Baraka, "A Reply to Saunders Redding's 'The Black Revolution in American Studies,'" 15.

46. Baraka, "A Reply," 18.

with the deep-level philosophy underwriting the agendas of separatism and integrationism than with mere tactics. As Robert Weaver says in the Discussions, "It's been my experience that once you get tactics and philosophy mixed up, you end up with lousy philosophy and horrible tactics." For Weaver, once the group clearly defines its philosophy, then it "can turn to the tactics." Weaver's desire to privilege philosophy over tactics is not just an effort to bring clarity and rigor to their analysis. It is also an attempt to shift the conversation to the intellectual terrain where Haverford Group members had the decisive advantage, for they were convinced that most black separatists deployed faulty forms of logic, based their views on feeling rather than thinking, and lacked a grasp of history. Furthermore, they believed that their more historically aware, philosophically informed, and intellectually accurate approach would win the day. Unfortunately, given the rage against the systemic racism saturating every level of the American polity and "the disproportionate and uncritical coverage of student demonstrations by the media,"[47] the black separatists received far more attention than the black integrationists, which led many scholars to overlook the nuance and complexity in the writings of some prominent Haverford Group members. This explains why Jackson can so easily dismiss Redding's works as "irredeemable."[48] Let me indicate how a nuanced understanding of the Haverford Group's agenda effectively renders one of the black separatist critiques incoherent.

Baraka faults Redding for rejecting black studies programs. But this is not quite accurate, and the Haverford Discussions clarify precisely why. Members of the Haverford Group rejected black studies programs *only when* they presupposed a metaphysical approach to the concept of race. Here is how Franklin puts the matter:

> It is very important that in these days of heated debate we do not lose sight of the fact that the integrity of Afro-American studies rests on its validity as an intellectual discipline and not on its importance as a rallying point for some abstract proposed rendering of society. If it has value in the reordering of society, as I very much believe that it has, its claim must be argued from the position that it tells the truth and does not engage in

47. Clark, "Some Personal Observations on Black Separatism," in *Black Separatism*, xiv.

48. See Jackson's essay "Irredeemable Promise."

> myth-making. The ground for Afro-American Studies is weak, if not altogether untenable, if it operates on the premise that persons of African descent possess some mystical qualities that are denied to others.

According to many prominent black separatists, there exists within people of African descent a racial metaphysical essence that makes them distinctly what they are and that nonblacks can never really understand or appreciate. There are two reasons why members of the Haverford Group rejected this position. First, they considered it unrealistic. In a 1978 essay Redding explains that the black-separatist race-based approach is founded on a monolithic (and, therefore, totally unrealistic) conception of Africa and that which is African:

> The misconception is that the African continent is the seat of a homogeneous culture, which American blacks must reclaim as exclusively theirs—and they think they can do this, for instance, by wearing their hair in African style, not realizing that there are as many African hair styles as there are African tribes. They study the Swahili language, ignorant of the fact that there are at least five hundred spoken tribal languages in Africa and that Hausa comes nearest to being the lingua franca of the African continent. They change their names and convert to Islam, unmindful that some Africans are ancestor worshippers, some totemist, some Judaists, some animist, and that a fourth of Africa's 350,000,000 natives are Christians of various denominations, including hard-shell Baptists.[49]

For Redding, an American black who reclaimed his or her African heritage would suffer from a serious form of multiple personality disorder.

The Haverford Group's second objection was based on the members' view regarding the availability of knowledge. Given the logic of the black-separatist position, only black people could either understand or teach black studies courses, because only blacks have epistemological access to black reality. But this violates the theory of knowledge implicit within a democratic socio-intellectual order, which holds that knowledge must be universally accessible to all people irrespective of race. As Franklin insists, "Real knowledge should be universal in its acquisition and in its dissemination." If black studies becomes something that only

49. Redding, "Black Chauvinism and Black Culture: A Modest Dissent," 17.

black people can do, then Franklin would adamantly reject it, and he would do so, not because he is a self-loathing or white-brainwashed establishment black, but because he champions the ideals of radical democracy.

In her post–Haverford Discussions statement, Adelaide M. Cromwell articulates the group's position most clearly: "Afro-American Studies should take its rightful place in the body of knowledge available to all those who seek a complete education." Cromwell acknowledges that courses in Afro-American studies will probably have radically different meanings for blacks and whites, but she insists that "the acquisition of the knowledge of Afro-American Studies does not differ." All people, irrespective of race, should be able to do African American studies, so long as they are mentally equipped and intellectually disciplined to master the "techniques of scholarly inquiry" distinctive to the field of study. If the black separatists are right, then black studies would be useless not just in the American university system but in every democracy, because the whole premise of the movement is based on the existence of a knowable reality (a metaphysical kernel of racial truth) that is epistemologically accessible to certain people and inaccessible to all others. Put simply, for the Haverford Group what is really at stake with the rise of black separatism is the legitimacy and viability of democracy as an intellectual and political ideal. And for the members of the Haverford Group the black separatist position is, in its very essence, antidemocratic.

To bring into sharper focus the nature of the group's qualified objections to black studies, let me briefly discuss a section deleted from the Haverford Discussions. Clark describes that he was invited to Columbia University for a strategy session about "a black studies institute." The students at the meeting wanted "a solid, substantive black studies institute and they made a very good case for their point of view." But Clark asked them to clarify how they defined black studies: "Does this mean that this will be an autonomous unit within the University for black students only?"[50] Clark received a striking response from Wilfred Carty, who was then teaching at Columbia and soon to become the head of "the black studies institute at City College."[51] Carty said that

50. Kenneth Clark Papers, Box 319, Folder 3 (Hastie Group Meetings, 30–31 May 1969), "Haverford Discussions" Transcripts (drafts), 42.

51. Kenneth Clark Papers, Box 319, Folder 3 (Hastie Group Meetings, 30–31 May 1969), "Haverford Discussions" Transcripts (drafts), 40.

"yes, to all intents and purposes, this would be an institute for Negroes," but he went on to claim "that this could be done without articulating it." This, of course, upset Clark a great deal, but it was a follow-up comment that sent him spiraling out of control. According to Clark, someone then said, "No one is naïve enough to write this down."[52] Secretly, privately, it is agreed that the black studies institute is for blacks only. Obviously, Carty and others realized that this was dishonest, which is why they would not publicly acknowledge it and why they did not want anybody recording the conversation. But for members of the Haverford Group, this secret policy of discrimination merely replicated the pernicious forms of inclusion and exclusion that have dominated the United States and undermined America's credibility as a democratic nation, which is why Clark stormed out of the meeting at this point.

Given Clark's rejection of the secretive and exclusionary approach adopted by the strategy-session participants at Columbia, people could wrongly assume that he opposed black studies or that he refused to address the concept of race. And indeed, this is precisely the critique that black separatists lodged against scholars like Clark. For instance, in "An Afro-American's Cultural Views," Cruse faults black establishment intellectuals because they refuse to address "anything that smacks of 'racial culture,'"[53] a critique that can be found in the pages of both *Black Fire* and *The Black Aesthetic.* But for anyone who has read the writings of Drake, Ellison, Cromwell, Redding, Franklin, and Clark, this charge sounds totally uninformed. So how can we make sense of it? Throughout the Discussions, the members make a tacit distinction regarding race that black separatists never really understood or appreciated. For instance, when discussing the nature of their critique of separatism, Franklin says, "We do not subscribe to a kind of separatist ideology that seeks an endowment of special racial talents." Franklin clearly supports certain types of separatist activities, as he makes clear in his essay "The Future of Negro American History," which he delivered as the first annual Martin Luther King Jr. Memorial Lecture at the New School for Social Research on April 4, 1969, just eight weeks before the first meeting of the Haverford Group. He only rejects those that are premised on a principle of an intrinsic inferiority or superiority. He goes

52. Kenneth Clark Papers, Box 319, Folder 3 (Hastie Group Meetings, 30–31 May 1969), "Haverford Discussions" Transcripts (drafts), 43.

53. Cruse, *Rebellion or Revolution?*, 49.

on to denounce those approaches that lay claim to "some special body of knowledge." As a staunch proponent of a democratic epistemology, Franklin insists "that what we have to say we have to say to the whole world and not to this little jim crow bunch of Negro kids." Franklin would support certain kinds of black separatist activity, such as black studies and the meeting of the Haverford Group, so long as they are not premised on a metaphysical and, hence, antidemocratic approach to race.

Redding sheds additional light on the Haverford Group position when he suggests that black separatists have adopted the same approach to race as prominent white separatists, such as Arthur de Gobineau and Houston Stewart Chamberlain.[54] In a moment of clear frustration, Redding says that he has had "enough of the rah, rah, us blacks." What motivates this comment is his conviction that black separatists are merely adopting a nineteenth-century approach to race: "Just go back to the end of the 19th century. You've got Gobineau, you've got Houston Chamberlain. You've got all these people who are saying rah, rah, us whites, you see. So I don't think we can counteract that with rah, rah, us blacks. I don't think we can, but I think that kids should feel that they're in a position to say rah, rah, us blacks." At first glance, it seems that Redding contradicts himself. But actually, he has the same nuanced position as Franklin. When black separatists, like white separatists, presuppose a "special body of knowledge" that is only accessible to the epistemologically privileged, then the members of the Haverford Group reject the approach. As Redding argues in his essay "The Black Arts Movement," instead of moving forward by recognizing the degree to which concepts such as race are human constructions, supporters of black separatism are moving backward by adopting a metaphysical approach to race: "The Black Arts Movement is predicated on the assumption that black people are *inherently* different from people of other races and that the difference, quite apart from the influence of learning and experience, embraces emotional, spiritual and intellectual incitement and response."[55]

Put succinctly, Redding rejects race-based movements when they are premised on a metaphysical or essentialist foundation. But just

54. For a more extensive discussion of the race theories of Chamberlain and Gobineau as Redding understood them, see his novel *Stranger and Alone,* 41–48.

55. Redding, "The Black Arts Movement," in *A Scholar's Conscience,* 214–15.

because he rejects the metaphysics of race, it does not follow that he refuses to discuss race or that he opposes blacks coming together to celebrate their common heritage. Indeed, Redding wrote books about the African American literary tradition (*To Make a Poet Black*), black perspectives of slavery (*They Came in Chains: Americans from Africa*), and the extraordinary contributions of blacks to the making of the United States (*The Lonesome Road: The Story of the Negro's Part in America*), and he coedited an anthology of black literature (*Cavalcade: Negro American Writing from 1760 to the Present*). In other words, not only did he participate in racially segregated forums, but he also defined and celebrated black achievements. He only objected to the "urge to segregate" when it was premised on an "abstruse metaphysic" or a "genetic constant."

For the sake of clarity, let me briefly differentiate the way black separatists and black integrationists use the concept of race. In the *Black Fire* essay "The Development of the Revolutionary Artist," James T. Stewart faults black artists for crafting artworks that are "based on the wrong models," that is, "based on white models." To correct the problem, Stewart urges black writers to produce new models, which are "consistent with a black style, our natural aesthetic styles, and our moral and spiritual styles." In this instance, race signifies an essential characteristic inherent within black people, which is clearly different from and incompatible with an essential characteristic inherent within white people. Thus, Stewart concludes that the methodology of spirit that he promotes is easy to demarcate along racial lines: "That spirit is black. / That spirit is non-white."[56] Stewart clearly opposes theories of racial and ethnic crossing and passing that feature so prominently in the writings of Charles W. Chesnutt, James Weldon Johnson, Jean Toomer, Jessie Redmon Fauset, Nella Larsen, Zora Neale Hurston, James Baldwin, Lorraine Hansberry, Alice Walker, and so many others.

Members of the Haverford Group reject the idea of race as an ontological fact of being. Indeed, Franklin admonishes the group to formally denounce "the false ideologies that really feed on a specious kind of racism." Specifically, he calls on the group to condemn the view that "because they're black they have to feel that they have certain qualities that are inherent to their blackness." To illustrate what he means, Franklin mentions an incident that occurred in 1925, when a white man

56. Stewart, "The Development of the Revolutionary Artist," in *Black Fire*, 3, 6.

told Franklin that he could dance a jig because he was black. By 1969 the situation was reversed. Blacks have internalized and even embraced the metaphysical view of race, Franklin claims, so "now Negroes say they can, you know, they can dance a jig better than those [white] people." The implication of the position is that black people possess a jig gene, which means that jigness is a quality (a genetic constant) inherent within both thirteenth-century Africans and twentieth-century American blacks. Moreover, the quality of jigness is lacking in white people, so no matter how hard white people try, they will never really be able to dance a jig as well as a black person. When black separatists such as Gayle fault black integrationists for negating "race either by integrating the racial idiom with that of whites, or by obliterating racial characteristics altogether,"[57] as he says of Ellison, it is because the black integrationists refuse to use race as a metaphysical signifier in order to define the nature of black people.

The famous 1963/64 exchange between Irving Howe and Ellison best illustrates the distinct approach to race among Haverford Group members. In his essay "Black Boys and Native Sons," Howe extolled the writings of Richard Wright and faulted writers such as Ellison and Baldwin who were insufficiently indignant about their oppressed condition in the racist United States. Ellison objected to the essay for many reasons, but foremost was Howe's tendency to make "of 'Negroness' a metaphysical condition, one that is a state of irremediable agony which all but engulfs the mind."[58] Not all blacks have had the same experiences as Wright, and not all take their ideological and aesthetic cue from the same sources. When rejecting Howe's metaphysical view of race, therefore, Ellison lashes out not just at Howe but also at the primary precursors of black separatism: "My view of 'Negroness,'" Ellison insists, "is neither his [Howe's] nor that of the exponents of *negritude*." What links Howe, supporters of negritude, and black separatists is the view of Negroness as a metaphysical condition, an immutable essence or a genetic constant that makes blacks distinctly what they are. In the Haverford Discussions, Ellison refers to the black separatist approach to identity as "an oversimplified pseudo-identity based upon a mystique of blackness." Ellison, by contrast, adopts a nonmetaphysical approach to

57. Gayle, "The Function of Black Literature at the Present Time," in *The Black Aesthetic*, 414.

58. Ellison, "The World and the Jug," in *Shadow and Act*, 130–31.

race, which he clearly defines: "It is not skin color which makes a Negro American but cultural heritage as shaped by the American experience, the social and political predicament; a sharing of that 'concord of sensibilities' which the group expresses through historical circumstance and through which it has come to constitute a subdivision of the larger American culture."[59] In other words, social, political and cultural realities have shaped the identities of American blacks, and while race may have played an important role in the nature of that shaping, it has done so in a sociocultural and not a metaphysical sense. Consequently, it is impossible to take a monolithic approach to black Americans, for as Ellison claims in the Haverford Discussions, "We have various political objectives, we have a variety of origins, we have a variety of class backgrounds, we have a variety of values and personal traditions and scholarly traditions, regional and religious."

While it is certainly true that black integrationists do not use race as a metaphysical signifier in order to define the nature of blackness or to explain black motivation, it is wrong to suggest, as the black separatists do, that black integrationists do not use the concept of race to make systematic sense of American history and culture. The question is not whether black separatists and black integrationists use race to illuminate history and culture—both groups do. The question is how they use the concept of race. For instance, in the introduction to *The Black Aesthetic,* Gayle calls on blacks to initiate "a process of de-Americanization,"[60] for as John O'Neal claims later in the volume, "We are an African People. We are not an American People."[61] O'Neal acknowledges that blacks "have made an identity between" themselves "and America," but he considers this a horrible mistake, because blacks have African blood within them, which makes them incapable of discovering their true identity in the West: "We cannot find our essence in the West, for we are not of the west. We come from different blood—from our roots will come our sustaining flow. From those roots only, can we relate positively to the West. We are an African People."[62] Black is separate and distinct from white, and any attempt to mingle the two can only have disastrous consequences, especially for blacks. There-

59. Ellison, "The World and the Jug," 131.
60. Gayle, introduction to *The Black Aesthetic,* xxii.
61. O'Neal, "Black Arts: Notebook," in *The Black Aesthetic,* 50.
62. O'Neal, "Black Arts: Notebook," 47, 56.

fore, to recover their racial identity, O'Neal encourages blacks to de-Americanize themselves, which is a prerequisite for them to reconnect with their essential African selves.

This strictly demarcated view of race has specific consequences for approaching and understanding American history and culture, which John Oliver Killens articulates most clearly in his essay "The Black Writer vis-à-vis His Country" in Gayle's *The Black Aesthetic.* For blacks to flourish, they need to "build a literature of heroes, myths, and legends." To initiate the process, Killens refers to the "lives of Harriet Tubman, Frederick Douglass, Nat Turner, [and] Sojourner Truth," whose stories "are as formidable as George Washington's, and are based on a much more substantial reality."[63] Significantly, Killens tells his black readers that "slavemasters Washington and Jefferson do not belong to *our* children."[64]

Black integrationists reject the call for strictly demarcating American history and culture along racial lines because they consider the project untenable and incoherent. A 1970 article in *Time* magazine was Ellison's first attempt after the Haverford Group's initial meeting to challenge in print the black separatist position and to articulate the black integrationist philosophy. The subtle brilliance of this article is that Ellison addresses two audiences simultaneously. Separatists, black and white, have adopted an approach to American history and culture that is based on nothing more than an irrational fantasy, because it is impossible to understand America without taking into account the presence of blacks. For the black separatist agenda to work, its supporters have to demonstrate that America is primarily and perhaps exclusively a white country, which forces them to say that blacks were never allowed to and never did contribute anything of significance to the making of the nation. But for black integrationists, the black separatist position is historically uninformed and ultimately false. As Ellison claims, "Materially, psychologically, and culturally, part of the nation's heritage is Negro American, and whatever it becomes will be shaped in part by the Negro's presence." For Ellison, black separatists are wrong to suggest that the United States is a white country, because black people have played "a complex and confounding role in the creation

63. Killens, "The Black Writer vis-à-vis His Country," in *The Black Aesthetic,* 390, 390–91.

64. Killens, "The Black Writer vis-à-vis His Country," 391; Killens's emphasis.

of American history and culture," while white separatists are equally wrong, because they fail to understand or acknowledge the degree to which blacks have significantly contributed to the making of America's cultural and political identity. Given how much blacks have contributed to the making of the United States, Ellison draws the surprising but inescapable conclusion "that most American whites are culturally part Negro American without even realizing it." The problem in the United States is not that blacks, in becoming American, have lost their blackness or become white, as the black separatists assert. Rather, the problem is that American whites do not "know who and what they really are"[65] because they have failed to realize or acknowledge the degree to which blacks have contributed to the making of the United States and its people's identity.

Given Ellison's racially blended, integrationist approach to American history, culture, and identity, he would reject Killens's position, which suggests that blacks must embrace Douglass and Tubman and disown Washington and Jefferson as part of their history. What Ellison would say is that Douglass and Tubman are as central to the realization of America's national identity and democratic ideals as were Washington and Jefferson. Therefore, instead of urging blacks to disavow racist white Americans as part of their cultural-national heritage, Ellison challenges whites to fully acknowledge and own their actual American heritage, which includes Douglass and Tubman, and he issues this challenge not because it is something that whites should do, but because it is a sociological, political, cultural, and historical fact of being American. Ellison's racially integrated approach is brilliant, because it effectively exposes the incoherence of the separatist positions of both whites and blacks.

Understanding the nuanced position of the Haverford Group on the topic of race effectively overturns the frequent charge leveled against its members, which is that they were conservatives. Again, it is important to note that black integrationists and black separatists use words in radically different ways. For instance, in a 1967 issue of the *Negro Digest*, C. E. Wilson articulated the view of the black establishment that dominated by the late sixties: "The very style of the Negro

65. Ellison, "What America Would Be Like without Blacks," in *Going to the Territory*, 111, 107, 108, 108.

Establishment (the unofficial name for the traditional groups) exerts a tremendous pressure towards conformity and uniformity and, therefore, active conservatism. The pronouncement of these groups have been militant but their behaviour has been conservative."[66] Wilson expanded on this view considerably in an essay in *Black Fire* titled "The Screens." Members of the Haverford Group, however, considered the militant black separatists to be conservative, as Gates notes when he says that Redding "saw the urge to segregate anything black, as well as the urge among black nationalists to codify and celebrate our cultural difference, as politically conservative, at best, and as politically retrograde and irresponsible, at worst."[67] Gates is certainly right to suggest that Redding considered black separatists conservative, but his characterization fails to capture the nuance in Redding's critique. Redding certainly did not object to a codification or a celebration of black cultural difference, as Gates implies. He only objected to such codifications or celebrations when they were premised on or used to justify a metaphysical conception of race. When black separatists fault members of the black establishment for being conservative, they mean that black integrationists are not militant political activists. But when black integrationists fault black separatists for being conservative, they mean that black separatists have adopted a scientifically debunked theory of race.

That the Haverford Discussions did not get published immediately after the initial meeting is unfortunate for many reasons, but perhaps the most important is that we did not get to see prominent black separatists and black integrationists stage a formal and extended debate in print on the topic of America's identity papers: the Declaration of Independence, the Constitution, and the Bill of Rights. What occasioned contradictory approaches to these documents was a newly emerging theory of knowledge and a concomitant approach to history. In the late eighteenth and early nineteenth centuries, Immanuel Kant and G. W. F. Hegel initiated a revolution in epistemology, which was taken to its logical end in the writings of Friedrich Nietzsche, Karl Mannheim, Martin Heidegger, and Jean-Paul Sartre. The traditional view, that Truth is a mind-independent conceptual reality that humans

66. C. E. Wilson, "Can the Civil Rights Movement Overcome Defeat?" *Negro Digest,* January 1967, 19.

67. Gates, "'. . . and bid him sing,'" x.

could pluck out of some neutral and objective Heaven of Ideas, was replaced by the phenomenological view that "truths" are the logical product of an embedded human consciousness, and as such they carry traces of their makers' biases and ideologies. In *The Crisis of the Negro Intellectual,* Cruse uses this phenomenological approach to demonstrate that the Constitution is implicitly a pro-white and antiblack document, which is why he suggests that "there is something conceptually or legally deficient about the scope of the Constitution itself." More specifically, "the American Constitution was written, conceived, defended and glorified for the implied social benefits of a group—the white Protestant, Anglo-Saxon, North European American. Thus the Constitutional celebration of the sanctity of the Individual really means that some individuals are more equal than others."[68] For Cruse, it is no longer possible to treat the democratic ideals implicit in the Constitution as sacred and inviolable, because the phenomenological approach to knowledge exposes the degree to which a racial (racist) ideology underwrites the seemingly noble ideals of the founding documents, thus irredeemably compromising the integrity of the political misnomer known as American democracy.

Many Haverford members rejected this view, because they were committed to "the sacred principles of the Constitution and the Bill of Rights."[69] For the members of the Haverford Group, the sacred precept that all people are created equal is an inviolable truth, a Platonic ideal of sorts, and it is an idea on which American democracy is premised. If the United States has not lived up to this sublime principle, the problem is not with the ideal but with the people, which is why Ellison holds that all great American novels attempt to expose and clarify the contradiction between America's sacred ideals and its unjust behavior.[70] But Cruse would say to Ellison: you have a naive view of America's founding documents as well as of the way knowledge is constructed, because America's sacred papers were written not just for the benefit of whites but also to the detriment of nonwhites: "If you, as an individual, de-

68. Cruse, *The Crisis of the Negro Intellectual,* 7, 394.

69. Ellison, "Brave Words for a Startling Occasion," in *Shadow and Act,* 104.

70. Ellison develops the idea in a number of essays. See the following in *Shadow and Act:* "Beating that Boy," 99; "Brave Words for a Startling Occasion," 104; "Hidden Name and Complex Fate," 164. He also makes this claim in "Society, Morality, and the Novel," in *Going to the Territory,* 250.

rive from the WASP-North European ethnic heritage, you have more Constitutional rights than other lesser breeds."[71] For Cruse, there is no contradiction between the democratic "ideals" of the Constitution and the racism in the United States, because the founding documents were written by the (white, Anglo-Saxon, land-owning, male) people for the (white, Anglo-Saxon, landowning, male) people. Moreover, they were not intended to apply to the "lesser breeds without the law."[72]

Cruse's claim resonates all the more forcefully today because of Charles W. Mills's brilliant study *The Racial Contract,* which convincingly demonstrates how in the West a racial contract tacitly underwrites the social contract, thus determining the nature and agenda of the modern polity. What plagues the West is a certain type of epistemological blindness, which effectively renders the racial contract an "unacknowledged system." As a philosopher, Mills identifies the principles of abstractness and universality as the bases of the problem. White supremacist theories of knowledge have been premised on an "abstractness [that] typically elides, rather than genuinely includes, the experience of racial minorities." Consequently, Western political theory has advanced a social contract philosophy that seemingly applies to all people. But in reality, as Mills argues and demonstrates, social contracts in the West were not "between everybody ('we the people'), but between just the people who count, the people who really are people ('we the white people')."[73]

Applying Mills's work on the racial contract to America's founding texts sheds new and important light on Cruse's scathing remarks about the Constitution. For someone like Cruse, all concepts, no matter how noble, no matter how compelling, are human constructed. As such, they reflect their makers' biases and agendas. Therefore, to think, as many of the Haverford Group members do, that America's identity papers have avoided the taint of white supremacy or an antiblack ideology is more adolescent fantasy than naive idealism. The biggest

71. Cruse, *The Crisis of the Negro Intellectual,* 394.

72. Cruse's reference to the "lesser breeds" is an allusion to Rudyard Kipling's poem "Recessional"; see *Rudyard Kipling: The Complete Verse* (London: Kyle Cathie Limited, 2002), 261–62. Black writers were particularly sensitive to and incensed by this characterization. For an extensive analysis of black critiques of Kipling's "lesser breeds" characterization, see my essay "Moses, Man of Oppression."

73. Mills, *The Racial Contract,* 3, 2, 3.

problem here is the belief in the existence of nonideological knowledge. In fact, it is this belief that blinds some members of the Haverford Group.[74] At one point in the Haverford Discussions, Franklin argues that the Haverford members need "to take an affirmative position," which they need to communicate to the young black separatists. Their objective is primarily to cultivate "the life of the mind," which they consider a nonideological position. As Franklin says, "We don't have an ideology."

My objective here is not to say that Cruse is right or that the Haverford Group is wrong. Rather, it is simply to say that had the Haverford Discussions been published in 1969 or 1970, this would have prompted extremely useful follow-up debates that would have forced some of America's greatest intellectuals (separatists and integrationists) to refine their thinking about their theories of knowledge, the nature of America's founding texts, the degree to which racism taints the ideals in the Constitution and the Declaration, the most effective way of exposing subsurface forms of racism, the best method for realizing racial justice, and a vast array of other issues. And yet, it is not too late. The Haverford Discussions bring into sharp focus some of the most perplexing and uncomfortable questions regarding race and racism in the United States. Moreover, they are valuable not just because they shed new light on the thinking of some of America's greatest intellectuals, but also because they resonate with many of the yet-to-be-formulated ideas that would help us chart a more viable path toward racial justice. Much excavation work still needs to be done in order to clarify the strengths

74. Edward Said insightfully exposes the idea on which this view of knowledge as nonideological is based. The assumption in the West has been that " 'true' knowledge is fundamentally nonpolitical (and conversely, that overtly political knowledge is not 'true' knowledge)" (*Orientalism,* 10). Central to the work of those in the phenomenological tradition is, as Karl Mannheim claims, a distinction between "how men actually think" and the way "thinking appears in textbooks on logic." Mannheim, Cruse, and Mills examine how thinking "really functions in public life and in politics as an instrument of collective action." See Mannheim, *Ideology and Utopia,* 1. Based on this approach to knowledge, Mills and Cruse conclude that Western-constructed knowledge is inescapably ideological, that it is biased in favor of whites and against nonwhites. The solution to the problem is not to find a new way to access or construct nonideological knowledge—this is a naively unrealistic project that is no longer possible after the phenomenological turn in epistemology. The solution is to construct new ideological models, ones that are acknowledged to be ideological and are premised on a pluralistic model of social justice.

and weaknesses in the writings and thought of the black separatists and black integrationists. But the Haverford Discussions will help us to better understand the thought of some of America's greatest thinkers, and they will also enable us to define more clearly some unresolved questions that still need to be articulated and answered.

The Haverford Documents

In what follows are the Haverford Discussions as well as supplementary documents included in order to enhance the reader's understanding of the Discussions. The main section consists of the Haverford Discussions. There are three appendices. Appendix 1 contains brief biographical sketches of the participants from the first meeting of the group. Appendix 2 provides a list of Haverford/Hastie Group meetings, indicating when and where the four meetings were held and the names of the participants at each meeting. Appendix 3 comprises three letters written by Kenneth Clark. At the second 1969 meeting, when the group was planning and strategizing the publication of the Haverford Discussions, Clark said that he wanted to include some letters that he thought would illuminate the document. Clark's letters, which were all written before the first meeting, clarify some references in the Haverford Discussions and give readers a sense of the ideas and mood that gave birth to the Haverford Group.[75] To make the material accessible and engaging for a wide variety of readers, I have annotated the manuscript.

To conclude, let me emphatically state that this volume is merely a beginning. Much more work needs to be done. My objective has not been to make a final or decisive statement about the Haverford Group. Rather, this book has been an attempt to set the stage for future studies about an important group of African American intellectuals, a complicated part of American history, and the ever-perplexing question of race.

75. When imagining what the Haverford Discussions would look like as a published document, Clark suggests "a book of somewhere between a hundred and fifty to two hundred pages, that would draw from the proceedings of our discussions, and the statements which we all sent in. And I'd like to throw into the hopper for those who have the responsibility of preparing this manuscript, other relevant articles or speeches which, even if we have to get reprint rights on them—and I have some letters which I'd like to throw to the person." Kenneth Clark Papers, Box 320, Folder 2 (Hastie Group Meetings, 8–9 October 1969, Jamaica, N.Y.), 20.

A Note on the Text

There have been minor alterations to the text in order to correct typographical and grammatical errors. For all unusual errors I have included a footnote to clarify the correction I made and to indicate how the original manuscript reads. I have also reformatted the manuscript for the sake of consistency. The text is based on the manuscript found in the John Hay Library at Brown University. There are also copies of the manuscript at the New York Public Library, the Haverford College Library, and the Library of Congress (Manuscript Division).

The Haverford Discussions

Table of Contents

Friday Afternoon Session MAY 30, 1969

KENNETH B. CLARK: I'd like to ask Anne Reid to give us a brief statement of how the idea for this meeting developed; and after that, we will just throw on the table the one item on the agenda.

ANNE COOKE REID: First I'd like to say it is wonderful to have so many friends come together at once in our home.

I was interested in the kinds of people who were excluded from a great international meeting of intellectuals;[1] and it struck me that I know people whom I would describe as intellectuals. Then I began to wonder how those intellectuals—whose average age is close to half a century—saw themselves in the world today: How they saw themselves in relationship to their disciplines, their commitments and the domestic questionings of today. Where are these people who in many ways, I think, epitomize having had the best of two possible worlds however harsh the tone of the world.

Then I read a book that had to do with black Intellectuals[2] and I said, it's time to get some of these people together without organizations, without politics, without institutional representation and have a small quiet conversation.

I went to Ken Clark. Clark is a very impatient person with ideas; they have to grab him—and then he delegates the work to somebody else.

1. In December of 1968 the Institute for Advanced Study held a conference in Princeton, New Jersey, to discuss the issues facing the next president (Richard Nixon) of the United States. The institute, founded in 1930, is an informal community that provides a place for notable scholars to conduct theoretical research and interact with one another. The Haverford Group members will discuss this meeting in more detail below.

2. This is most likely a reference to Harold Cruse's 1967 book *The Crisis of the Negro Intellectual,* which I discuss in my introduction.

K. CLARK: Anne came to MARC[3] and talked with Hylan[4] and with me a number of times. She came at a time when Hylan and I were sort of going around in circles—the circles surrounding Brooklyn College and City College—while saying to each other, what, if anything, can we do, and from that point on not being too specific about what.

We were just aware of the ideas and clarity of Ira Reid,[5] Charlie Johnson,[6] Frank Frazier;[7] we kept saying, "Gee, you know, these guys stood for something." We keep hearing our people saying, "history"; and John Hope, as we said in North Carolina, one of the things that seemed to us to be among the first casualties of the present stage of the struggle is a sense of history, immediate and long range history. The names Ira Reid and Frank Frazier and Charlie Houston[8] and Charles Johnson and Abe Harris[9] and others—we need these guys and they're

3. MARC is the Metropolitan Applied Research Center, a solutions- and action-oriented research center based in New York City with the mission of improving the living conditions of the urban poor. Kenneth Clark was the founder and president. MARC was important to the Haverford Group because it funded the first meeting and provided the secretarial staff to produce the edited transcription of the Discussions.

4. This is a reference to Hylan Lewis. See the brief biographical sketches in appendix 1 for a description of him.

5. Ira de Augustine Reid (1901–1968) was a prominent sociologist who published many books about black immigrants, black youth, and black workers in the United States, including *The Negro Immigrant, His Background, Characteristics, and Social Adjustment, 1899–1937* (1939) and *In a Minor Key: Negro Youth in Story and Fact* (1940). His wife, Anne Cooke Reid, was a professor of drama and the coordinator of the first Haverford meeting.

6. Charles Spurgeon Johnson (1893–1956) was a renowned sociologist who specialized in interracial relationships. He published numerous books, including *Shadow of the Plantation* (1934), *Growing up in the Black South* (1940), and *Into the Main Stream, a Survey of Best Practices in Race Relations in the South* (1947). In 1946 he was named president of Fisk University.

7. E. Franklin Frazier (1894–1962), an educator, antiracism activist, and sociologist, received his Ph.D. in sociology from the University of Chicago in 1931. He became the president of the American Sociological Association in 1948. He wrote numerous pioneering books, including *The Negro Family in the United States* (1939), *Black Bourgeoisie* (1957), and *The Negro Church in America* (1964).

8. Charles Hamilton Houston (1895–1950) received his doctor of law degree in 1923 from Harvard Law School. He was a lead strategist in the NAACP's efforts to desegregate schools and a mentor to Supreme Court Justice Thurgood Marshall.

9. Abram Lincoln Harris (1899–1963), an economist, received his Ph.D. from Columbia University in 1930. In 1931 Harris coauthored with Sterling Spero *The Black Worker: The Negro and the Labor Movement*, a study of the African Ameri-

not here. Others who have worked with them and whose perspectives and methods they shared are here; but for some reason we have remained silent.

Then came Anne; she said, "What do you think of the idea of our looking at what we now think and having others, whom we have known and respected—and who have been part of the tortuous and difficult struggle to bring this nation into a twentieth century level of decency—what do you think of trying to get them together to look at the present climate, to re-examine our own thoughts in the light of what appears to be a popular shift in ideology." I remember, Anne, that even in our first conversation we put a great deal of emphasis on the importance of the young Negro in colleges today, and on our own anxiety about some of the things we hear from them. The dominant thing being publicized about the young Negro in college is his repudiation of what we consider some important values and goals; that he is considering integration a dirty word. In spite of the fact that what available survey data we have consistently show that no more than ten or fifteen percent of the general Negro population is moving toward or accepting the separatist position, the available evidence from the colleges seems to suggest that the young Negro in college felt a much higher percentage of separatism. We felt that this was some cause for concern; it certainly is the basis of the desire to have a preliminary meeting of this sort.

The format here is very simple. We have no papers. We deliberately decided against having position papers or any formal presentations. We decided that we would just invite a group of people whom we know and with whom we felt comfortable to do just one thing; talk with each other, to be as open-minded as we can in looking at and sharing experiences about the contemporary stage of discussion, confrontation, ideology, particularly in regard to the intelligent—college trained or not—young Negro. We have no preconceived goals. We thought if we arrive at anything, we will arrive at it through the discussion. We needn't feel frustrated if we don't arrive at anything.

ADELAIDE HILL: Ken, may I put a footnote to what Anne said before we start talking? I wrote a letter to Carl Kaysen[10] on the Princeton

---

can's role in the labor market. He also published *The Negro as Capitalist* (1936) and *Economics and Social Reform* (1958).

10. Carl Kaysen (1920–2010) received his Ph.D. in economics from Harvard in 1954, and served as the director of Princeton's Institute for Advanced Study from 1966 to 1976.

meeting, not knowing Carl terribly well and not wanting him to think I wanted to be included, but feeling that he had been derelict. I said, you know, how can you call intellectuals together and not have some of the names one could suggest. If you'd like names, I'd be glad to supply them for you. And he wrote back and said thank you, graciously, and said that Charles Hamilton[11] was going to be there—his name had not appeared in the *Times*—and that he was doing some consultation with the students on other names.[12]

JOHN HOPE FRANKLIN: Let me add another footnote to that, if I may, Ken. When I saw, Adelaide, that article in the *New York Times,* I also wrote. I wrote Shep Stone[13] in Paris; after all he's the President of the International Association for Cultural Freedom.[14] I pointed out to him that if they were going to discuss the problems of the world as intellectuals saw them, I thought perhaps they might enlarge their resources. I said I'd take particular exception to your designating as the one Negro intellectual listed the President of CORE.[15] I said I have nothing against him except that you don't have the other activists or

11. Charles V. Hamilton (1929–) received his Ph.D. in political science from the University of Chicago in 1964. In 1967 Hamilton coauthored with Stokely Carmichael *Black Power: The Politics of Liberation,* a landmark book suggesting a possible framework for social reform. For a brief discussion of this book's importance, see my introduction.

12. There were two *New York Times* articles about this meeting. The first one, published on October 28, 1968, was titled "80 World Intellectuals to Hold Seminar on Problems of U.S." This article announced that "leading intellectuals from throughout the world will gather at the Institute for Advanced Studies in Princeton, N.J., from Dec. 1 to 5 to assess many of the problems that will confront the next American President." The article lists the names of many participants, but it does not include Hamilton's name. The second article, which was published on December 1, 1968, and titled "Intellectuals Gather to Discuss Nixon's Problems," does name Hamilton as one of the participants.

13. Shepard Stone (1908–1990) was a writer for the *New York Times* who received his Ph.D. in history from the University of Berlin in 1933. Stone became the president of the International Association for Cultural Freedom in 1967.

14. The International Association for Cultural Freedom, originally the Congress for Cultural Freedom, was founded in 1950 as an anticommunism group. The association united prominent writers, scholars, and world leaders in defending freedom of expression, and received funding from both the Ford Foundation and the CIA.

15. The Congress of Racial Equality, a nonviolent civil rights group, was founded in 1942 by James Farmer. Roy Innis became CORE's national director in 1968.

even the heads of white activist organizations there; perhaps you might like to re-examine your list. I perhaps do not have enough finesse to indicate a personal disinterest. So when Shep Stone wrote me back, he said that they had invited Charlie Hamilton and they had invited Harold Cruse;[16] and he said, we considered inviting you, but you had participated in one of our conferences so recently . . . (*Laughter*)

And he said, I want you to know that we do plan to invite you to one of our conferences later.

I wrote him back and said you missed the point entirely. If I had been so interested myself in going to the conference, I would not have been so gauche as to have written you in the first place.

ROBERT C. WEAVER: In addition to what Ken said, and I think it's explicit in this discussion, it seems to me that not only do we have a problem of the position of the very articulate, very vocal young people who are divorced from society, but the attitude of the white intellectual community towards this situation, which is somewhat reflected in the stance of blacks and has an independence of its own. Many liberal whites are completely confused. They're either scared to death or else, in a guilt reaction, they're going to be so helpful and going to be so liberal that they're going to give us everything "we" want and we're going to end up with nothing.

K. CLARK: A la Antioch College.[17]

WILLIAM H. HASTIE: Ken, I suppose chronologically I'm the oldest here—I'll be sixty-five before 1969 ends—so I perhaps have seen longer this process that we're talking about and am tremendously disturbed by what is happening to the young black undergraduate today. I suppose we are concerned with two things. There seems to be a consensus around this room that the move toward separatism, the glorification of separatism as a desirable way of life for the indefinite future is not just

16. Harold Cruse (1916–2005) was the author of *The Crisis of the Negro Intellectual* (1967) and the cofounder with LeRoi Jones (Amiri Baraka) of the Black Arts Theater and School in Harlem. He was invited to the first Haverford meeting, but he declined. For a discussion of his importance for the Haverford Group, see my introduction.

17. Antioch College, in Yellow Springs, Ohio, is known for being progressive, and in the late 1960s it heeded African American students' wishes to live in segregated housing and built Unity House, an all-black dormitory. For Clark's critique of the college's decision, see his letter to Theodore M. Newcomb, reprinted in appendix 3 of this volume.

a negation of what many have tried to do, but is a dead end and a long range evil. I assume that is the consensus on which we can build—if we establish that consensus. If we don't, then of course, we have to discuss it. But if we can establish that consensus, the two groups of greatest concern, I would agree, are the young Negro and the general white community, who for one reason or another are being persuaded that separatism is something that the Negro wants.

I've seen this because I happen to be on the Board of Trustees of two colleges, Amherst College and Temple University in Philadelphia—one a small New England college, the other a big urban university. I'm also on something called a Visiting Committee at Harvard Law School. I mention those three because within the last year or two, I have seen and talked to a lot of the black students in all three of those environments; and certainly I would agree on the basis of my experience with what Ken says, that within the last two years—I think it's that suddenly or quickly—what may have been prior to that a minority attitude among black students has become the dominant attitude.

My son graduated from college last year. When he first went to college—that would be five years ago—there was no real clash among the black students.

WEAVER: And we might say, believe it or not, he, as his father, went to Amherst. I think this is important.

HASTIE: Yes. That is important. There were those black students who sought to share fully and in a completely relaxed way the life of the campus—and by the way, had an opportunity to do so which was vastly different from what was true in my undergraduate days. And there were those who wanted to maintain a black enclave within the college community. By the time he had graduated, there was a clash between the two groups. There was a resentment on the part of perhaps half, maybe more than half of the black students of their fellow black students who shared in a relaxed, personal and natural way the life of the general community, the friendships of persons of various races and nationalities and so on.

As late as this spring, I get the impression that the black freshmen and sophomores at Amherst—and there are many more of them than there ever were before—are dominantly separatists.

At the Harvard Law School, black students were assembling at lunch when I was up there and they asked me if I would meet with them; so I had a chance to meet with a large number of them as a group. Their—I may be overstating it, of course, but I think this is the trend—their interest in the law and the ordering of society is subordinated to their interest in immediate, almost full-time participation in the projects of the ghetto; so much so that they almost feel a sense of guilt about the time that they devote to the development of the basic professional skills.

One of them came to me afterwards as a result of something I said and said to me, almost begging me, "Do you really mean what you say? Do you really think that the time I waste in the three years of law school will be made up by what I can contribute afterwards?"

At Temple the black students want many more black students in the university, but they don't want the university to build any more buildings—see it's right in the midst of the ghetto—because this will have the effect of destroying some of the housing in the ghetto.

All that is to say I think you're completely right that, at least from our view, the present black college generation has lost its moorings or gotten, I think, some really dreadful notions. If anyone can redirect them or help redirect them, he'll be doing a very good service.

On what Bob was saying, as far as influencing the white community and people who can, who have determined the direction of the white community, I think that the danger of their accepting the separatist view as the fundamental black view and therefore not only salving their consciences but making their common cause with the separatists is an equally great danger.

I'll say only one other thing. It's preliminary in nature. I do think that the time has come when there has to be boldness and outspokenness on the part of people who think they have something to say that makes sense on the side of integration. I had one experience about a year ago talking to a group of law students at Howard. It was Law Day—just law students, not the rest of the university—and I took the obvious, I think, elementary line that once a person decides to study law, he has undertaken to become a professional in a discipline, and that means in its essence and very nature is committed to a legal order rather than to a destruction, by extra-legal means, of legal order. First of all, I sensed that they were shocked that anyone would take that line in addressing them, and I said that after talking to them I would welcome free give and take.

Well, they were so taken aback that anyone would confront them rather than them confronting somebody else that they were a little slow in getting going, but they did get going after a little while. And I remember one student who said, "The trouble with you judges is that you are nothing but lackies of the establishment." And I said to him, "Now, young man, you just stop right there. Let me get you straight. I am not a lackey of the establishment. I am the establishment." (*Laughter*) Well, he never recovered from that. I explained later what I meant, but I just use that example to say I do think that some impression will be made by bold and forthright statements of a point of view different from those which they, with a great deal of emotion and not too much reasoning, committed themselves.

That's much too much by way of introduction but let me say this too. I am worried. I said they've emotionally committed themselves. I don't think any of us here are in the advertising business; but maybe I'm worried as to whether our problem is a problem of selling in the advertising sense, or a problem of intellectual persuasion. I don't know. It probably is something of both. To the extent that reactions and attitudes are emotional, the product of both disappointing and bitter experience and of demagoguery, I don't know how far they can be countered by rational argumentation and discussion. To the extent that people are trying to be rational and reach conclusions rationally, of course it's important and valuable that they hear a different point of view. But I do think it's important that we talk about whether these are things that can be dealt with by rational or intellectual procedures or whether there has to be something that is a different type of selling. I don't know, but that worries me.

K. CLARK: One thing that Bill said that seemed to me to be, if we were going to try to have a systematic agenda, very high on the agenda, is to determine among ourselves whether there is or is not consensus on the meaning of this present black student confrontation. Or to determine how much similarity or difference of opinion is in this room on an evaluation of this, including evaluation of whether it is as separatist as indicated by the newspapers and the media. I must confess that I myself sometimes wonder whether a lot of this has not been generated, sustained and fanned by the media.

WEAVER: Good question.

SAUNDERS REDDING: And by some college and university administrations.

K. CLARK: I must say that for myself I personally would be a little happier if individuals whom I respect could give me the basis for feeling less concerned about the separatism—its extent and its implications and the consequences of it.

WEAVER: Just one footnote to that. I think there is a notion about separatism that worries me a great deal because I think they're intellectually either naive or dishonest or both. The notion is that you have separatism for a little bit, just like being a little bit pregnant, you know; and then all of a sudden you get your forces aligned and you stop having it. Well if that's sound ideology for the in-group, it's damned bad ideology for the out-group because you set up the society to react to the temporary condition only. I have a feeling that there is a lot of fuzzy thinking about this on both sides of the color line. I think separatism, although it may be inevitable in the sense of short-run developments, should not be justified by being called temporary. This is a rationalization on both sides; it's absolutely a myth. Maybe I'm wrong, but I get this feeling as I talk to the students and talk to others.

REDDING: I get the feeling that there is no fuzziness in regard to this in the present administration.

K. CLARK: Are you talking about the national administration?

REDDING: Yes, the national administration.

WEAVER: I would not concede that there was any situation other than fuzziness on racial matters in the present political administration.

REDDING: But I also get the very distinct feeling—and I will name the institution—that at Northwestern,[18] for instance, there is a deliberate intent on the part of the administration to bring in to that institution students who, by their standard criteria, cannot make it; so that they can say in two or three years, well, we tried it; and we tried it on their terms, under their own stipulated conditions; and it doesn't work.

And I think that this is not only true at Northwestern. I think that it is true in other institutions. There is an effort, I believe, on the part of some of these institutions to encourage this kind of separatism and to establish a level of accomplishment with these black kids which will justify keeping them separate. Now I may be completely wrong, but I don't think this is a knee jerk reaction. I've talked to several people

18. In 1966 Northwestern University, in Evanston, Illinois, formed the Northwestern University Chicago Action Program (NUCAP) in order to "'expose talented students from Chicago's inner-city schools to the predominantly white institution.'" By 1968 there were approximately 180 black students enrolled. For a brief discussion of the university's attempt to recruit black students, see Myers, "Shades of Black."

about this and I think that there is something to this and I think it should be examined.

HILL: Don't we want to separate the thinking around separatism that emanates from the black community and the thinking around separatism that has to do with black studies? I know they're related, but I think they have a little bit different historical roots, or at least we might speak more pointedly about one than about the other.

By the way, just want to say in parentheses that I understand from *Ramparts* that Saunders is the leader of them all.[19]

REDDING: I haven't seen *Ramparts* lately. I thought it had folded.

FRANKLIN: You didn't read the last issue. All three of us should be climbing in a hole because we're all supposed to be CIA agents.

I'm perfectly willing to relinquish that distinction. (*Laughter*)

ST. CLAIR DRAKE: I had come to this conference really with a vow . . .

K. CLARK: St. Clair, do you mind if I say that we're not really a conference? We're trying desperately not to be a conference.

DRAKE: —to keep my mouth shut until the end, partly because I'm always accused of acting like a Baptist preacher's son, with this starting to talk and never stopping; secondly because I was wondering where I really stood on this whole issue that brings us here. But I think I want to say something because the question of consensus came up, a question of where people do stand, and I was trying to think about this

19. *Ramparts* magazine, founded in 1962 by wealthy Catholic convert Edward Keating, began as a Catholic literary journal but became a New Left publication frequently attacked by the Catholic Church. A June 1969 issue argued that the American Society for African Culture (AMSAC) was a CIA-sponsored organization that used prominent African American intellectuals to monitor and control black liberation movements at home and abroad. When Hill says that "Saunders is the leader of them all," she is referring to the following passage from the article: "The organization also sponsored visits to Africa by American Negro scholars, writers, lawyers and intellectuals. AMSAC's representatives included scholar Saunders Redding, the man whom Harold Cruse describes as the chief of intellectual spokesmen for the American Negro establishment." See "The CIA as an Equal Opportunity Employer," *Ramparts* 7, no. 13 (June 1969): 26. Faith Berry notes that Redding eventually learned that the AMSAC was funded and controlled by the CIA, and this angered and frustrated him. See Berry's introduction to Redding's *A Scholar's Conscience*, 7. Redding is the only Haverford Group member who was mentioned by name in the article, but John Hope Franklin was also a member of the AMSAC, which is why he suggests that they have been characterized as CIA agents.

for a minute or two. It's probable that I am "the odd man out" in the conference because I suspect that, as we move along, I will probably be taking the position that in some situations it would seem to me that the demands for separation explode out of certain experiences which black students have had.

I was rather interested in the comment on Northwestern because this poses a really knotty problem, which is that the administration of the institution may have its deliberate intent to try to make a point; and students may feel that they have a justifiable reason for "separating."

When the affair broke out at Northwestern, I was very upset because I happened to be in Chicago at the time and a number of friends of mine came to me and said, "After all that fighting we did up there to try to desegregate those fraternities, to get that campus desegregated, here come black students almost unanimously—about 105—all of whom took the position, when they took that computer center over, they were sticking together; we want separate dormitories."[20] And I was very confused about this and followed the discussions of it on TV rather carefully. Then one night when the head of the alumni association was on Kup's program[21] and was discussing this matter, he said that he had been opposed to acceding to the black students' demands until he came out and made an investigation on the campus. Certain facts began to emerge that made him say he would go straight down the line with the black students. These facts turned out to be this sort of thing: that the superintendent of buildings and grounds, for instance, had stated that he knew that as black students moved across the campus the fraternity boys sometimes threw loaded beer cans at them, not even opened, and harassed them; and that at least on one occasion, a black student had almost been run down by white students with an automobile, deliberately attacking him; and he had never reported this to the

20. In "Shades of Black," Myers describes the event to which Drake alludes. On April 22, 1968, the black students presented a list of demands to the university. "A massive sit-in was held on May 3, 1968. Receiving no response to their demands, 150 Black students took over the Bursar's office. They posted a sign that read, 'Closed until racism at NU is ended.' Negotiations between Black student leaders and university representatives began immediately and 38 hours later an agreement was reached and the sit-in was ended."

21. Kup's program is a reference to *The Irv Kupcinet Show,* a popular television talk show that ran from 1953 to 1980.

administration because he felt they probably weren't interested! This was the superintendent of building and grounds.

I then got out and did a little more probing and found out that what you had essentially on that campus was a situation which I've been using as a hypothesis as I move around now. I've visited about ten campuses in the last year, specifically trying to look at what the heck is going on on these campuses—the University of Washington, three in California, and several others. Northwestern was one of the first institutions to bring on the campus a group of ghetto students picked from "the very bottom," that is, they started a ghetto tutorial program very early. And the irony of this is that the group of students that they had shepherded along and brought on campus became the group, eventually, who grabbed the computer room and said, "If you don't give us the separatism, we'll hit you."

Now, what emerged, as I probed into this, was that group of black students who were on the campus were not just reacting to the white community. You had taken here a group of Chicago ghetto kids who had been given tutorial programs, who had, on the intellectual side, been able to come up, but whose speech and general behavior and the rest of it, set them apart from the older middle-class type of Negro student who had traditionally been at Northwestern. (I'm falling into the Allison Davis-Warner-Drake-Cayton[22] lingo on this.) What you had was suddenly the lower-lower-class confronting both the white status-conscious community at Northwestern, and the upper-[23] and middle-class Negro community which also looked down on those kids because their speech was not the kind of speech that was considered proper, respectable. Their dress wasn't, their general behavior wasn't. And these students were suddenly aware of the fact that they were on completely alien territory, and I think the response then was to tend to group together.

Now you had this very able man from New York, Turner, who is

22. The social anthropologists Allison Davis (1902–1983), William Lloyd Warner (1898–1970), and Drake (1911–1990), along with the sociologist Horace Cayton Jr. (1903–1970), all studied class issues experienced by African Americans. Davis in particular focused on the effects of social status on education.

23. The original reads: "upper-upper- and middle-class Negro community." This strikes me as a typographical error, especially given that Drake mentions "the Negro middle-class and upper-class group" in the next paragraph. Therefore, I have changed "upper-upper-" to "upper-."

the head of the black students association.[24] But what he was really meeting was this, that, to a great extent, this was a group of ghetto Chicago kids who reacted against being on a campus where they were "hit" by both the general white status conscious group and the Negro middle-class and upper-class group and they simply withdrew. They felt that for their physical protection, as well as for what they call now "getting themselves together," they wanted to be separate and to protect both their egos and their bodies.

I think this shook me up a bit because I then was led to ask myself the question, "If I was one of them in that situation, would I not have exhibited this same sort of behavior? If I'm confronting this kind of world, you know, what do *I* do?" And my mind went back to 1947 and '48. I happened to have been in England during those years gathering data for my doctoral dissertation on race relations in the British Isles. One thing that interested me was that the first Labor government was in and had demanded that places be reserved at Eton and Harrow for kids of the working class. The press was commenting on the "beatings"[25] which Cockney kids were taking when, for the first time, they went into Harrow and Eton. In fact the press stated that the suicide rate at these schools went up because these Cockney boys were confronting that middle-class British situation. The similarities are very obvious to me.

Now, as I've moved around, I've just seen this situation out West on campus after campus, the San Francisco State case and, to some extent, the Santa Barbara case, for instance. I don't know about the East. (I'm living part of the year in the West, the other part in the mid-West.) We're bringing on these campuses first generation really lower-class kids—this is one of the things that happens when the Office of Economic Opportunity and the others get some money available to set up tutoring programs, they bring the youngsters on who have lower-class behavioral patterns, and this accounts, to some extent, for the reactions to things that happen to them. These kids belong there, of course; but problems are inevitable. I mean, coming out of the middle-class, if something goes wrong, you go into a discussion. If you come out

24. This is a reference to James Turner, the founder of the Africana Studies and Research Center at Cornell University. Today he is a professor of African and African American politics and social policy at Cornell.

25. I have inserted a closing quotation mark after the word "beatings." The original looks like this: "beatings?

of the lower-class and something goes wrong, as the guys in Mississippi phrase it, you "crawl the man," you know, you go after him with your hands or something else. The greatest tragedy of all, of course, is UCLA. When that discussion ended about who was going to be head of the black studies association, there were two dead Panthers lying on the floor[26] rubbed out by two members of Ron Karenga's US.[27] Well, I don't want to get into that, because we've got a whole ideological problem on the campuses now—the split between the so-called cultural nationalists who are for the dashikis and getting your "African roots," and the Panther group which is for the Marxist oriented type of revolution. When those two groups get on a campus and confront each other, you've really got a set of problems, some of which we've been experiencing at Roosevelt University recently.

But back to my first point: All I was trying to say was that I think that, over the last year, I have rather reluctantly come to the position that in certain situations, I can see where you've got a rough choice between insisting on no separatism at all or "sliding the point" and saying that, temporarily, it may be for the benefit of a specific type of student now on campus, that some degree of separatism might be admitted. And then the question is, "How can you control it and make sure it doesn't become permanent?"

I'm leaving Roosevelt to go to Stanford[28] and this is a very interesting case in and of itself because the most prominent black student

26. On January 17, 1969, a meeting was held at the University of California, Los Angeles, to discuss forming a committee to select a director for the university's new black studies program. A confrontation between a Black Panther Party member and an Organization US member at the meeting's close led to the shooting death of two Panthers, Alprentice Carter and John Huggins. The Black Panther Party was founded in 1966 as a militant group that accepted violence as a necessary means of attaining equality for African American citizens.

27. Ron Maulana Karenga (1941–) received his Ph.D. in leadership and human behavior from the United States International University, San Diego, in 1976 and his Ph.D. in political science from the University of Southern California in 1996. Karenga founded the cultural nationalist group US in 1965 to encourage African Americans to start a cultural revolution and to remain in touch with their African heritage.

28. I have deleted the word "must." The original reads: "I'm must leaving Roosevelt to go to Stanford." Alternatively, "must" might have been a typo for "just": "I'm just leaving Roosevelt. . . ."

on the Stanford campus at the moment, I suppose, is Johnny Scott,[29] whom Budd Schulberg[30] met in Watts[31] and discovered he had talent—he's writing poetry and playing with drama production. Johnny leads the "black studies" thrust.

By the way, the semantics of all this is very interesting. Stanford doesn't have a "black studies" Program. Stanford has an "African and Afro-American Studies" program. There is strong feeling—an undercurrent—they don't want the word "black studies." A neighboring institution, San Jose, has a *black studies* program. Afro-American today means the kind of in-between program. I think Harvard has this kind.

HILL: Harvard hasn't done anything as yet.

DRAKE: What do you call yours?

HILL: Harvard hasn't got anything yet. We call ours (Boston University) Afro-American.

DRAKE: Yes.

Now, I have a son who is a senior at Stanford and I got a phone call from him the other night and he pointed out to me that—let me just be personal about this for a couple of minutes because I think some of the personal data highlights what's going on. I've been teaching at Stanford off and on. I live out there half the year and have been a visiting professor twice. In January I was asked if I'd accept an appointment—a joint appointment in the anthropology and sociology departments, and become chairman of this African and Afro-American studies program, which at the moment has thirteen majors in an interdisciplinary program. They don't want a department of "black studies." Even I, now as the black person, or Negro, or an Afro-American . . .

K. CLARK: Or colored?

DRAKE: Yes, or colored—didn't think to say to the dean and the

29. Johnie Scott is currently a faculty member at California State University, Northridge, where he teaches in the Department of Pan African Studies.

30. Budd Schulberg (1914–2009), a writer of novels and screenplays, founded the Douglass House Watts Writers Workshop after the Watts riots in Los Angeles in 1965. The workshop targeted the area's youth, and produced several published authors and poets.

31. Watts is a residential area of Los Angeles that was the site of a six-day riot in 1965. The riot began on August 11 when a white police officer clubbed an African American man who was resisting arrest, and ended after the National Guard was called in. During the riots, stores were looted and burned, and thirty-four people were killed.

heads of departments who were talking with me—have you consulted the black students. I was rushing to get away and they had these talks with me, so I was given my appointment.

I got a phone call from my boy, who happens to be a member of the black studies association, saying that the fellows had told him to call me and tell me that if a statement appears in the press that they're fighting me that there's nothing personal about it. (*Laughter*)

K. CLARK: It pays to have a son.

DRAKE: Stanford had not consulted them about my appointment and the black students were mad. A few days later, the *New York Times* announced that I had been *jointly* appointed by students and administration. The black pressure had worked. The article went on to say, in effect, "We've made 'a great catch' and we think this is going to sort of quiet things" and so forth. At least, this was the import of the article.

The point is that these students went in and stated, "You aren't going to appoint any black person on this campus unless we okay it." So they hastily put together a committee and my appointment was announced in these terms.

Now, I also want to say that on that campus, there is a very real split at the moment between a group of students of predominantly middle-class background—for instance, my son, and a boy in the med school who is the son of a friend of mine from Chicago, and who incidentally managed to get a resolution through that if at any point black students "go into action" out there, they will never disrupt the educational process because they came out there to get an education. One of the boys in med school said, "How can I be a doctor and help the ghetto if I don't ever finish school? Therefore, anything we do will stop short of disrupting the educational process."

On the other hand, I have been told there's going to be on the table in the fall a demand for an autonomous black studies program and for an institute of black studies run by Johnny Scott similar to the Antioch one.[32] I suppose I'll be in the midst of that battle.

The point simply is that I think on some campuses, you get the split between middle-class black students and what I would call the

32. Antioch College created its Afro-American Studies Institute in 1968. The institute was made up entirely of African American students, and the director of the institute had the right to turn applicants of non-African descent away on the grounds that their background was not relevant to the courses offered.

upward mobile kid from the bottom, who sees their problem quite differently. I mean, one position is that we want a black studies program and we want it right away. The other position is we want something that's a little bit more, that takes account of the fact that we really came here to get an education. You'll get compromises.

Let me give my final example from Stanford. Another thing that happens is that some black students associations—Illinois and Stanford are good cases in point—do not just include students. The Stanford group includes all the black cafeteria staff, all the black people who work on the grounds, plus some people from East Palo Alto. My son tells me that this has been healthy in this sense—he also belongs to SDS[33]—that the black students meetings are the most orderly ones, the most restrained, primarily because these community people are in there sitting with the students and exercise a certain amount of moderation. This probably wouldn't be true for Ocean Hill–Brownsville maybe, but these Palo Alto groups become a brake on the students. Yet you'll get this kind of situation. About two months ago the cafeteria workers had asked for a raise and they weren't getting it. So the black students association decided to take the cafeteria over one day at noon and to give free food to the whole Stanford community on behalf of the cafeteria staff, who incidentally got their raise. At this point, some of the rougher students went over to the bookstore and simply pulled every book they could get off the shelf and almost demolished the bookstore. Now, this was an operation that was not sanctioned by the black students association, but you have this group of ghetto kids who are used to the rough stuff and they went in there and tore the bookshop up.

So, just looking at this one situation you see a very complicated problem. I think my own position—I ought to get it out in front—is that there are certain situations, I'd say on campuses like Northwestern—and I'm not sure about Cornell where they claim a cross was being burned in front of the black "sorority house"[34]—where the question comes up as to whether the separatism is not related to the fact that black kids are confronted by what they consider the hostile upper

33. Students for a Democratic Society, founded in 1960, advocated participatory democracy and frequently held protests against the Vietnam War.

34. On April 18, 1969, a burning cross was placed outside Cornell University's Wari House Cooperative, the home of the Wanawake Wa Wari cooperative. A group of black women founded the cooperative in 1968 in order to promote self-awareness and personal confidence.

middle-class white and Negro world, and they feel so alienated that this clumping together occurs. I think in other cases where this has happened, it's ideological. That's all I wanted to say. I think in some cases it flows out of reality situations; in other cases, it's ideological.

And I might conclude my remarks by saying, since we're going to be here for a few hours and I said I thought I was "odd man out," that my perspective on this comes from a set of rather peculiar experiences. I was just commenting to Weaver when we came here that I'm "back where it all began" for me because I finished Hampton[35] in 1931 and spent the first year of my life outside of college as a field agent for the Joint Committee on Race Relations of the Society of Friends[36]—what I call being Exhibit A. Part of my job was to go around to Haverford. When I first came to this place, I arrived here and some of the white students said, "Let's go swimming," and I was told no Negroes could go in the swimming pool at Haverford and the Quakers were having real conscience qualms about this. My "beat" also included speaking to Quaker meetings all through this area as a sort of "plant" to say a word about race relations. I visited George School and Westtown and many similar spots.[37] So I started off in a sort of "integrationist" tradition, not to mention the fact that I got fully integrated a few years later by marrying a Caucasian.[38] So I see all this also through the perspective of a person who is intermarried. Great ironies come in here. Until two years ago I took my "beatings" from the white community. I'm now taking them from black students who say "You talk black and sleep white." I always hit back on the grounds that what I do I do openly and not under cover of darkness.

REID: Tell them that you're white passing for black. I heard that three weeks ago.

DRAKE: As the years rolled on, Charlie Hamilton and Horace

35. A historically black college in Hampton, Virginia, Hampton Institute, which became Hampton University in 1984, is the alma mater of Booker T. Washington.

36. The Religious Society of Friends, more commonly referred to as Quakers, initially had two committees dedicated to bettering the living conditions of African American citizens and relationships between races. The two committees joined to form the Joint Committee on Race Relations in 1929, which lasted until 1955.

37. The George School, in Newtown, Pennsylvania, and Westtown, in West Chester, Pennsylvania, are Quaker day and boarding schools.

38. In 1942 St. Clair Drake married Elizabeth Johns, a Caucasian sociology major who attended the University of Chicago with him in 1942.

Mann Bond[39] and I became the three nationally known Negro academics who were very close to SNCC.[40] We were deeply involved during '65, the year before the Black Power "thing" was thrown out as a slogan. I had moving experiences during '65 when I went to meetings in the South. I was at a meeting in Atlanta that year in which, time after time, Negro girls would get up and talk about the summer of '64, when all the white kids came down South. I remember a girl saying, "We were running that office down there and it wasn't being run very efficiently and a group of Oberlin girls came in there and within two days they had letters going out regular, and things were really moving and we just all withdrew in our shell and decided the whites can do it so much better. It broke our spirit. So we feel it would be better to keep the whites out of here and let us do it ourselves." And it was a very poignant situation as these girls pointed it out—how inefficient they felt when they had to confront the white competition, and then saying they felt they'd better do it themselves. And so that on the southern front, I began to see why the southern kids came on with that "Black Power stuff." Then it took root here. Well, anyhow, what I was going to say was that I've seen since '66 this general shift over and you get "rocked" all the time. You aren't so sure "integration" is always best.

Ken, recently, some of your young people from Antioch met with me from this—what do they call it? The Institute of . . .

K. CLARK: Afro-American Studies.

DRAKE: —Afro-American Studies. I sat for several hours with a group of them recently. They came to Chicago, you know, trying to recruit people from the University of Chicago to teach in the project. They were trying to state their point of view. The whole impact of this and my other experiences, I think, is to say that I feel that probably you can't make a general rule on this matter of separation on campus. That's really what I'm trying to say. I think probably ultimately you've got to

39. Horace Mann Bond (1904–1972) received his Ph.D. in education from the University of Chicago in 1936 and was an administrator at several historically black colleges. He authored many books, including *The Education of the Negro in the American Social Order* (1934) and *Black American Scholars: A Study of Their Beginnings* (1972). Bond became the first African American president of Lincoln University in 1945.

40. The Student Nonviolent Coordinating Committee, a community-based organization of young people fighting against colonialism and racism, was founded in 1960. SNCC members were known for their Freedom Rides and sit-ins.

get down to cases and probably make a statement. For instance, I'll just throw out one hypothetical case: the Antioch situation—no need for this kind of withdrawal and pulling in; Northwestern, on the other hand, may be justifiable temporarily until the white guys stop throwing beer cans at your head.

So I wonder as we move into this if we cannot think of it as a question of whether some of the separatism doesn't flow out of concrete situations in which—like in the southern 1964 situation, or like the one at Northwestern, the students feel that survival—psychological or physical—depends on being separate for a while; or others where it's purely an ideological thing and perhaps cannot be justified. Then we still have got the problem as to whether we'd even want to make a concession for kids saying they want to do it temporarily because the long term implication of that might be that if you do it you can't be a little bit pregnant, as somebody said.

I hope I can keep my mouth shut for the next three hours.

M. CARL HOLMAN: I don't wish this to look like either a retreat under fire or one more of those walkouts that we've all seen. I would suggest, however, this is a peculiar way for intellectuals to begin. I can say this as a non-intellectual by posing first of all, the problem of the straight jacket of consensus in a meeting which is supposed to last for a day or something like that. This is the same position I took with some members of one of the black groups who said, now, we're all here together and all of us know that we believe in the gospel according to Malcolm. I'm afraid that it's very poor practice for intellectuals to form their opinions, as someone said, on the basis of the same newspapers that Ken has had problems with in the past. I'm more inclined to believe that others who were there are right when they tell me that no one has ever interpreted correctly what really did happen at Cornell. Am I to believe the reporter who floated around there and wrote the story about it? I think that what I had sort of hoped you would get into at some point or other is something having to do with the real meaning of these class conflicts and generational conflicts. I see, read, hear about some of you fellows; it seems to me that you represent a particular class; you are, as the gentleman says, the establishment, or a part of it. The establishment has been very seriously called in question, not just by the black students, but by a great number of other people and forces in this country at this time. I suppose I'm saying that it may be a mistake to base the discussion on what clearly is something many people don't know very intimately and firsthand, that is, the whole question of what's going on among the students.

Like Mr. Drake, I have a son who's in college, he's one of the black students in the Afro house at Wesleyan.[41] I, therefore, had a real problem when Roy Wilkins[42] announced that he was thinking of suing to have such places declared illegal under Title VI.[43]

The kind of thing intellectuals ought to be interested in—the class conflicts, the generational conflicts—I'm disturbed always to see white intellectuals writing about. I would like to see some of the black intellectuals, who can and should be writing about it, dealing with these matters.

But I'd like to go back again just touching on the SNCC days and some of us lower case academics who were involved down there in the south with SNCC, and look at a couple of things which I think black intellectuals, Negro intellectuals, Afro-American, colored, any kind of intellectuals who are in there, haven't looked at very sharply, and that is how what happened to SNCC took place and why it happened.

Now what is happening, it seems to me, in this country is that a number of black intellectuals are having to make their peace with this kind of question. They're in the truth-telling business, therefore what they believe, they tell the truth about. And so for that reason, I've always said that the black intellectuals who see things in a certain way ought to say this, and ought to say it clearly, whether people call them Uncle Toms for doing it or not. At the same time I think they have to be careful to know what it is they're saying and how it impinges on the minds of young people and of the older people involved.

I see among the black kids now in college something which I've not seen in college generations that I have taught before; it raises the question that goes back to what you're saying, Saunders. Should ghetto kids ever go to college? If so, when? If so, what kind of colleges and who first began pushing to get the ghetto kids into college? Now, a very non-radical gentleman said to me many years ago on the bridge at

41. The Afro-American Society of Wesleyan University requested that a house be reserved exclusively for African American students in 1968. The Afro-American house could accommodate six people.

42. Roy Wilkins (1901–1981) served as the executive director of the NAACP from 1955 to 1977.

43. Title VI of the Civil Rights Act of 1964 declares that it is illegal for programs that receive federal funds to discriminate on the basis of race.

Hampton, "You know, the problem with the NAACP is that it's bound to become irrelevant sooner or later because it is basically a middle class organization;[44] it showed it by beginning its interest in education at the point where the fewest black people were, that is, in terms of graduate and college education rather than down there where most of them were." Now, I . . .

RALPH ELLISON: It started where I came from.

HOLMAN: Yes. I know that, but what I'm trying to say is that the statement made by him, however unfair, if made in the average gathering of young black people would be taken as gospel truth, and it has already been. Now, the record-straightening that needs to be done in this country ought to be done by black intellectuals; it's not being done.

One final thing, it seems to me, is true. The black kids are being torn now, and I'm speaking about the middle class black kids. They're being torn because they do have a sense of community with the poor and they do realize that there are a lot more poor black people than there are middle class black people; they think that they ought to be in some way relating to that community. I can just tick off three issues in which the Panthers and all the militants with very poor notions of strategy, very poor understanding of the total situation, are very actively involved; and very few of the other people who ought to be are actively involved. Like it or not, the question of police, for instance, is a very serious question for poor people and especially for the poor black people in this country.

The whole question of criminal justice is something which is very important. This is an area which has been preempted by people who really, in many cases, ought not be there. They're there because there's a vacuum. I was out in San Francisco when the Oakland branch of the Panthers first started their patrols[45]—following the police around in an effort, as they said, to keep the police from harassing black people in the ghetto.

There's a battle going on right now in the administration, but it's not so well seen; it's half hidden. The battle on this question of income

44. The National Association for the Advancement of Colored People was founded in 1909 by white liberals who hoped to put an end to prejudice and lynching. Of the original eight leaders of the NAACP, only one was an African American: W. E. B. Du Bois.

45. The Black Panther Party was founded by Huey Newton and Bobby Seale in Oakland, California, in 1966.

maintenance, income security, the whole question of welfare. But the whole battle is a battle in which, as far as I have been able to see, the voices of the black intellectuals have not been heard, the black social scientists just simply have not been heard.

And, finally, I would say something about this whole question of the defense budget and the war. I can recall when Martin King first decided that he was going to come out against the Vietnam war. He said that when it meant taking his own board on; so finally he had to say I do this personally as a minister of the gospel, and so forth. He immediately was dropped several rungs in the civil rights hierarchy.

I've seen, as some of you have seen, the projections for the post-Vietnam budget—that budget is still going to be a budget in which black people, Mexican-Americans, poor whites, are going to be at the low, low, low end of the totem pole. All that nonsense about when the war is over, then everything is going to happen, it's just not true, because the projection is for a defense establishment that is going to be what it has been for some time.

You've got here the kind of brain power and the kind of talent and the kind of insights which are needed. As I keep telling my young revolutionary friends, I have never heard of a successful revolution that was not kicked off by the intellectuals, because if you don't have the intellectuals, you basically cannot have, even if by revolution you mean only the restructuring of the institutions, you can't even have the kind of revolution that's going to mean anything.

K. CLARK: Carl, may I ask, who are the intellectual leaders of the present black separatist thrust?

HILL: Ken, may I make a comment. I said some time ago that I thought that we ought to distinguish between the thrust coming out of the college and that coming out of the community. I think that coming out of the colleges, there are two kinds of problems; one that has to do with black studies, which you just discussed; the other has to do with the selection and survival or treatment of the students and I, if it seems useful, would like to talk about these.

HOLMAN: But some of my good friends and yours have gotten publicity for saying what is resented by these black kids. By saying that you bring these black kids in and you've got to give them remedial training because you know they can't cope. What has been very disturbing to some of the kids I've talked to from Brown and from Williams and from Wesleyan and Yale is that they feel that here you have a black man tarring with this brush every black kid who's in school, and this is something else. The demand for black studies, black teachers is not limited to those students who can't cope with traditional college work. There are exceptions to all these broad characterizations.

Now, for example, the Board at Federal City[46] kept insisting there must not be a black studies program which excluded whites, either as teachers or as students. The interesting thing is that the people working with this program came back with a statement that the Board was racist because the Board raised a question they don't even want to deal with. They said the Board was being racist because it talked about blacks and whites and they can't deal with that because they have a Japanese and a Chinese girl in the program.

WEAVER: Let me point out the New York City situation, some of the elements I found also in some of the campuses in the deep south, strangely enough the University of Alabama, where I spoke. The students in the City University are asking for the following things. First, they want to get enlarged enrollment, the two track enrollment, etc. Secondly, they want to have a separate orientation for all black students, whether the black student wants it or not. And thirdly, some of them want to have remedial work, if a student makes an A or B—in order to get enough English to get into college—counted as a college credit. Now, this leads to something that worries me. These are proposals for dilution of the educational process, coming from many of the black students. So what's going to happen to these students? What happened at Illinois? Well, the state institutions of higher education took all high school graduates and fifty per cent flunked out the freshman year—the first semester of the freshman year. If you have a double standard and no adequate program for remedial work, then many of those admitted are going to flunk out after they get out of college. You're talking about disillusionment now, you haven't seen anything if this comes to pass.

ELLISON: I'd like to swing this thing around to something that Carl Holman was saying about the ideological direction that the students are taking. I get around to a lot of colleges lecturing and I do talk to students, white and black, a few Negroes . . .

46. In 1977 Federal City College, the District of Columbia Teachers College, and the Washington Technical Institute were consolidated into the University of the District of Columbia.

K. CLARK: And no colored?

ELLISON: No colored at all. I had an instance out at Ohio Wesleyan, when in referring to myself as a Negro American a little fellow—you couldn't tell whether he was a high yellow Negro, or a Mexican or a Puerto Rican or what, but he did have a slight accent. And he said to me, "Hey, man, why do you call yourself a Negro?" I said, "Well, my mother and father were Negroes."

DRAKE: You haven't got yourself unbrainwashed yet.

ELLISON: Wait a minute. So he said, "Well, look, man, you shouldn't call yourself that." I said, "What should I call myself?" He said, "You should call yourself black." I said, "What do you call yourself?" He said, "I'm a white man." I said, "Well, you don't look white to me. Come on. You've asked me." He said, "I'm from Iran." He was showing his solidarity with the black man.

But there is something which I think we as intellectuals might well address ourselves to. It worries me, but I'll be slightly personal. When I came up from the south to New York and began to spend a lot of time in the library, I was struck by two things—well, by one thing. That is, in reading back-issues of *The Crisis*,[47] *Opportunity*,[48] *Topaz*,[49] and all of those publications which came out of the ferment of the twenties, you had a forum wherein there were discussions as to how our group of people related to the larger American society and to some of its intellectual currents. The first prizes given to our poets and writers came not from the outside, but from *Opportunity* and *The Crisis*. These magazines retained a kind of vitality, although I was terribly critical of them, up until about 1939, roughly, when the great emphasis given

47. *The Crisis*, the official magazine of the NAACP, was founded in 1910 by Du Bois. Its intent was to show readers the negative effect racism has on society and to record general news.

48. Published between 1923 and 1949, *Opportunity: Journal of Negro Life* was the National Urban League's magazine, which was instrumental in making the art and literature of the Harlem Renaissance possible. Its focus was on African American cultural and intellectual life.

49. I have not been able to locate a journal with the title *Topaz*. However, in 1927 the journal *Opportunity* published *Ebony and Topaz: A Collectanea*, edited by Charles Johnson, which contains work from such luminaries as Jessie Fauset, Georgia Douglas Brown, Sterling Brown, Langston Hughes, Zora Neal Hurston, Anne Spencer, Arna Bontemps, Alaine Locke, Abram Harris, Helene Johnson, and Countee Cullen, just to name a few.

to the Negro thing—self determination in the Black Belt that you got from the Communists—made it quite plain that this was an ideological matter.

I don't know just why these magazines were withdrawn (one completely and the other reduced to the role of a house organ), the point I wish to make is that the loss of these magazines resulted in the creation of an intellectual vacuum. Those of us who wished to think seriously about the relationship between the Negro American community, traditions, political and social interests, music, art and literature, and the larger American culture were forced to carry on our discussions catch-as-catch-can and were left with such explorations as were to be had in the pages of the Communist *New Masses,*[50] *Science & Society*[51] and *Politics*[52] and in the various socialist magazines. For it was here that the discussion continued—though not on a very high level.

In fact, it seems to me that it was not until Malcolm X came along with his great rhetorical gift for disseminating barbershop ideas—and I say "barbershop" ideas because there was nothing that I ever heard him say that I hadn't heard in pool halls, barbershops and shoeshine parlors all my life; but it wasn't until Malcolm that we had a vigorous attempt to define American reality from our Negro American point of view. Unfortunately, Malcolm X was not an intellectual and yet today it is his ideas, his formulations which you get from large numbers of black students on the campuses of our great universities. Even at Amherst—I was there for a lecture only a few weeks ago. And you're getting these ideas parroted by kids who obviously have very bright minds but who have nothing else to work with. They are ignorant of much of the work that exists and they have no intellectual grasp of the complex experience out of which they've come. But in the fervor of their militancy they're trying to create an ideology . . .

K. CLARK: With the clichés.

50. Published between 1926 and 1948, the *New Masses* was an anticapitalist journal that offered a comprehensive critique of American culture and society from a communist perspective.

51. The scholarly Marxist journal *Science and Society* was founded in 1936 and continues to be published today.

52. *New Politics,* a socialist magazine founded by Julius Jacobson and Phyllis Jacobson in 1961, is still in print today. The journal supports progressive agendas such as feminism, anti-intervention movements, and labor unions.

ELLISON: —out of these clichés. This is a pathetic thing. You find it over and over again. And I . . .

K. CLARK: It really is tragic and pathetic when you talk with these kids, bright kids . . .

WEAVER: They're so damned smart. This is what disturbs you—and it disturbs me when I face up to the fact that they address themselves to real issues and come forth with proposals which are often superficial.

ELLISON: So we are remiss.

DRAKE: Of course. This is one of the arguments for some kind of black studies stuff, in the sense that as I move around, I find the kids of this generation never heard of *Crisis*, never heard of *Opportunity*, think that all the protest began when Rosa Parks sat down. Those are the ones who have a long time stance and the others think it all began with Malcolm.

REID: Well, St. Clair, this doesn't bother me—the fact that they haven't heard of these things doesn't bother me as much as what was suggested which I bit my tongue on . . .

HASTIE: When you tell them, they then reject it.

REID: Sure, I just learned that this year. But there is an intellectual community—and I won't use now the word I used the first week in December, which I didn't think was fair to say—I felt that there was an intellectual community which had rather abrogated its rights and privileges.

K. CLARK: We're intimidated into silence.

REID: Some of us, all of us haven't had the same years of opportunity to do something, I grant you, but have abrogated a kind of responsibility nonetheless. The kids today don't want to hear history, but that's another story.

HASTIE: May I interrupt just to say this. When Carl Rowan[53] spoke at Amherst, I'm told—I wasn't there, unfortunately—he had the biggest audience any speaker has had at a lecture in many years. The chapel was crowded with standees. I mean that stands out.

K. CLARK: Ralph, you haven't finished, have you?

53. Carl Rowan (1925–2000) was a prominent journalist during the civil rights movement. He later became deputy assistant secretary of state during the Kennedy administration, and was an ambassador to Finland. In 1987 he founded Project Excellence, a college scholarship program for African American high school students.

ELLISON: Well, no. There's another side to it—and I had this to say to the Amherst community: We've all—speaking of Americans generally—we've all been victimized by the inadequacies and hypocrisies of American studies and especially by the history textbooks. They've been restricted, they've left out far too much of American reality, and because of it students, former students, and teachers have been consigned to a dangerous state of ignorance. So it seems to me that we're only going half way if we stop at criticizing people like Moynihan for attempting to define social reality for Negro Americans;[54] for they are only a small number of a large group of people whose responsibility as *intellectuals* is to make some adequate sense of this complex American situation. Much of what is lacking does revolve around the presence, treatment, and interpretation of Negro life, but on the level of which I'm speaking it isn't simply a black problem, it's an *American* problem. Therefore I say that we've got to go to work on them, on American intellectuals generally. And not simply on those who play politics with their interpretations of Negro American life. We must give our attention to all those who make claims to intellectual integrity while ignoring our complex presence within this society.

WEAVER: Of course, there's the other aspect, too, when we look at these things from the point of view of black studies as contrasted, say, to studies of Africa. You can't talk about what's happened to the black man in America without talking about what's happened to America while the black man was happening to it and while it was happening to him. This is what disturbs me about the isolationism in so much of this.

MAMIE PHIPPS CLARK: This is on the issue of separatism, and I think it goes back to some remarks that Bill Hastie made. I'm not an intellectual, I guess I'm a statistician; but I'm trying to solve a problem. He wondered whether the basic issue for the approach to this problem with the black students was a question of salesmanship or selling or whether it was a question of intellectual persuasion. But I thought that his remarks implied a different kind of strategy than those two, and that was the strategy of some kind of surprise confrontation which was well timed. And it seemed to me that we could think of this concept

54. Daniel P. Moynihan (1927–2003), a U.S. senator from 1977 to 2001, received his Ph.D. from Tufts University in 1961 and began working in the Department of Labor the same year. Moynihan is controversial for his 1965 report *The Negro Family: The Case for National Action,* which attributed African American poverty to matriarchal families.

on a mass basis, a surprise confrontation which is well timed, which is massive, and which is directed at not only the black students but at that white population that Bob Weaver is talking about. Well, maybe we would come out with something. I can't conceptualize what this would be at this time.

K. CLARK: Mamie, you're probably taking our agenda for this evening, tomorrow, next week, next month, next year or something. It's true that if we decide after these preliminary discussions that there is a role which we can take without being ludicrous, you know, or if there is something beyond just a preliminary looking for where there is or is not consensus, a preliminary diagnosis, and if we feel stable and confident enough about the nature of our diagnosis, then we really would have to come to strategy or just put our tails between our legs and slink away. But I think that comes after . . .

M. CLARK: Too early.

K. CLARK: I think so. I may be wrong, and it's up to you.

PHYLLIS A. WALLACE: I wanted to ask one question, whether the black intellectual community is not invisible to the students?

K. CLARK: Invisible or rejected. Let me say rejected.

HOLMAN: Much more largely invisible than rejected.

K. CLARK: Well, may I give you a little evidence to the contrary. These are confrontations starting with Howard and going to Columbia, then Antioch and Brandeis in which I have been. The fact is that while I am—I do sense, you know, the kind of pathos, being caught with the clichés, I do sense that the youngsters are terrified. I do sense that they have not done even the reading which they purport to have done, such as *The Wretched of the Earth,*[55] or Malcolm. If they have read it, they certainly have not read with depth and understanding. But they do know that a Bob Weaver and a Ralph Bunche[56] and John Hope Franklin have made it in ways in which they are ambivalent about. They want

55. *The Wretched of the Earth,* a book about Algeria's struggle toward decolonization in the 1960s, was written by the Algerian psychiatrist Frantz Fanon and published in 1963. Fanon argues that colonized people come to believe that violence is necessary for their mental, social, and political well-being.

56. Ralph Bunche (1904–1971) was a political scientist who received his Ph.D. from Harvard in 1934. He won the Nobel Peace Prize in 1950 for his work as principal secretary of the UN Palestine Commission. Bunche was a member of the Haverford Group, though he never attended any of its meetings. Clark sent him information about the meetings.

to and they don't want to, and they're guilty and they have the tendency to react to those whom they think have made it not only by name calling, the name calling is general; but if they're in a specific situation with you, they seek—not just the dozens[57]—a testing of how much bullying they can get away with and how much—the person who stands out is the leader of that UCLA-USC experience that I had about six weeks ago. The leader has to take the leadership in rejecting the black bourgeois, the black intellectual, and asserting this and doing it as ungrammatically as possible and with the profanity. You either take that or say you're not just totally invisible. In fact, you are part of his problem.

DRAKE: One place to look at this if you want to ask about the invisibility is to look at what kind of reading lists black studies associations lay on the line when they're coming up with their own proposals for programs. We're not invisible then, because you see the first thing the "brothers" do is say we want books by black scholars; and then, you see everybody's name coming up. I've just seen a list very recently . . .

FRANKLIN: It's very interesting on that thing. I just got a list from Santa Barbara. We've got to have some black scholars. My name happened to have been on it, also Basil Davidson's name.[58]

But they will tell you that they can tell on the first page who is a black scholar from what he says, but then they come up with this mumble jumble.

DRAKE: But they do want to use the names, you see, of the black guys who made it in the previous generation. At Roosevelt, I was looking over one list and they had it headed "Black Books by Black Scholars"; so I sent it back and called attention to the names of Basil Davidson and Christopher Fyfe[59] and I said, "Either you ought to take them off or change the title." So they finally left the white names on but *didn't*

57. Originating in the African American community, the dozens is a potentially dangerous game of witty and insulting rhetorical exchanges. The goal is to use escalating rhetoric until one person dominates the other or the exchange erupts in violence.

58. Basil Davidson (1914–2010) changed the course of African studies with the 1959 publication of his book *Old Africa Rediscovered*. The book was unique in that it detailed the history of African cultures instead of merely covering their interactions with Europeans.

59. Christopher Fyfe (1920–2008) was the author of *The History of Sierra Leone*, an immense textbook for African studies published in 1962.

change the title! Then, I said, "Why didn't you change the title?" They said, "Just forget that." They kept the white names on, you know.

FRANKLIN: They're black. Honorary blacks.

DRAKE: But I just want to make a point. I do think when they need the black prestige figures, they use them. For the courses they give, they're running as fast as they can to get Franklin and Frazier.

WEAVER: But most of them aren't reading Franklin and Frazier. They're putting them on the list but they aren't reading them.

Let me put one footnote to that. I don't want to cut you off, but I just want to add one thing because this is a point and I don't want us to lose it. I refer to our discussion of a lack of visibility. There is the fact that these students, although they are being very chauvinistic in their talk, are not totally chauvinistic; they're part of their generation. And it's the thing Bill talked about, the establishment that they're against, too. This gets all mixed in, so you can't ever leave that out.

HOLMAN: That's right. And the whites—the whites feel that they're responsible . . .

ELLISON: They're getting things so mixed up that at a girls' school in February, the question—well, during a session with these girls, I talked of two young women that I knew who had had a chance to go to a higher job category in private business and one girl was offered the opportunity of being the publicity director in a very large publishing house—one of the largest American publishing houses. She had worked in the office and knew it. She had been tapped for this not as a showpiece but because she could deliver. But she rejected the job because *she* was afraid that she would be rejected, would be bruised too much.

The other instance had to do with a young woman who was working with a fund raising organization, had been assigned to a group to work in its office and ended up being proposed as executive director. And this sparked antagonism on the part of a very important trustee of the organization. She fought, she got the job and the trustee had to get out. So I asked the girls, I said, "Well, what do you think of this," I mean, "these two attitudes?" And they told me that the girl who had stuck and fought had collaborated with the establishment and had finked out and that the proper conduct was that of the young woman who rejected the job.

REDDING: This was a white college?

ELLISON: This is a white college, but I'm talking of black girls.

WEAVER: This is the generation gap, in part.

HASTIE: May I say one thing? I really think—and maybe I'm pushing my point of view, but I think on the first point that we have a consensus—at least of those of us who spoke—that it is desirable, perhaps even desperately urgent, that an effort be made to communicate a point of view and a body of ideas, not only to blacks, particularly young blacks, but even for the benefit of your second class, weak-kneed, subconsciously prejudiced white educators who need a push the other way. I don't think any of us disagree with St. Clair about the reality of the problem and the difficulty that you were speaking of at Illinois and Northwestern.

DRAKE: Really short term, long term.

HASTIE: Well, I don't even agree with you on that. I would say even short term—I would like to . . .

K. CLARK: We'd like to keep those beer bottles from being thrown.

HASTIE: But I don't think that there's any disagreement being expressed and when we come back we can go on from the point that . . .

K. CLARK: —anyone who disagrees with it, that this is the consensus that has emerged.

HILL: The consensus is we should respond.

K. CLARK: Respond, and I think the other thing, something that Bill is saying, not only respond, but respond in terms of asserting our opposition to any form of separatism.

WEAVER: I think we have—if we take any position on separatism, it has to be preceded by an analysis of understanding of why this thing has occurred. I mean, this, in my mind, is the essence of the matter. You may not agree with it, but you've got to understand it . . .

FRANKLIN: I have several things to say, but I just want to put in here that I think what we probably might do later on is we do not subscribe to a kind of separatist ideology that seeks an endowment of special racial talents, that are very frequently being bandied about now. We all get that. I mean, I've been fighting for forty—thirty years or so, the notion that anybody has some kind of special angle on something. I mean, I've been fighting Dr. Josiah Nunn and Cartwright[60] and all the others and I'm not going to stop that fight, even for the sake of my

60. I have been unable to identify Franklin's reference to Josiah Nunn and Cartwright.

students who come up to me at Hampton and this, they say, "You know we're more emotional."

WEAVER: Particularly around exam time.

FRANKLIN: And I think this is where we really can stand, or that we've got some special body of knowledge that can be shared only with somebody else. I think it's very important as intellectuals or as academics that we say that what we have to say we have to say to the whole world and not to this little jim crow bunch of Negro kids.

WEAVER: I see, to use the current vernacular, "you ain't got no soul." I can see that.

FRANKLIN: And I want to talk about soul. (*Laughter*)

REID: We thought that if we could bring it to a peak of thoughtfulness that that would be a good time to cut it off and let the thing simmer.

| END OF SESSION

Friday Dinner Discussion MAY 30, 1969

(*Beginning of tape inaudible*)

WEAVER: Wait a minute, now. I want to get something straight. You mean that the kids in our colleges have to relate to the blues by sort of a course or something?

K. CLARK: By a course?

WEAVER: You said they were trying to relate to it.

HOLMAN: Not by a course. The New School for Afro-American Thought, and they bring films, you know, the sort of thing that would be great if it were done at the Institute of Modern Art, you see, it's acceptable . . .

ELLISON: I understand what you're saying, but I can't accept it.

REDDING: My own feeling is that there have been certain people in "predominantly Negro academic settings" who were not scholars, but they've been important people. You know, George Washington Carver ain't left a paper.[61]

61. George Washington Carver (1864–1943), an agricultural scientist and humanitarian born a slave, dedicated his life to improving farming techniques—and, in turn, the lives of poor farmers—in the South. Carver is most well known today

K. CLARK: That's right. Nor a formula.

REDDING: No. No paper, no formula.

WEAVER: But peanuts.

REDDING: But he was a great teacher.

HYLAN LEWIS: What you suggest to me is the question, what is the most important thing that the intellectual can do at this point. What is the most important intellectual role? Is it teaching, interpreting . . .

REDDING: No. I think one of our troubles is—I think that the good teacher is an interpreter. I think this is what the scholar is. I think that we have had at this point enough of the rah, rah, us blacks.

Gobineau—just go back to the end of the 19th Century. You've got Gobineau,[62] you've got Houston Chamberlain.[63] You've got all these people who are saying rah, rah, us whites, you see. So I don't think we can counteract that with rah, rah, us blacks. I don't think we can, but I think that kids should feel that they're in a position to say rah, rah, us blacks. Do you see what I mean? And I think . . .

ELLISON: I've been saying it all my life.

HASTIE: May I say something, Ken? There's been repeated reference to us intellectuals, a phrase I don't use. I think what we're saying is that we are all serious minded, thoughtful human beings who have some sense of, interest in and awareness of what happened yesterday and have some real concern for what is going to happen tomorrow or the next day. And we are trying to evaluate what is happening today, both in the sense of historic perspective and in the sense of the promise of tomorrow. Now, if that makes a person an intellectual, okay. In any event, that's our common ground. I think we have the feeling that lots of the young people are not soberly and as objectively as is humanly possible going through that process; and that we want to try to go through that process, and if possible, to help them in going through

---

for his interest in the way legumes, such as peanuts, could replenish nutrients in overused soil.

62. The French diplomat and Nordic supremacist Joseph Arthur comte de Gobineau (1816–1882) published a four-volume treatise *Essai sur l'inégalité des races humaines* (*The Inequality of Human Races*, 1853–55).

63. Houston Stewart Chamberlain (1855–1927), a British political philosopher who later became a German citizen, was the author of *Die Grundlagen des neunzehnten Jahrhunderts* (*The Foundations of the Nineteenth Century*), a history of Europe that glorified the Teutonic peoples and demonized Jews. Chamberlain is generally considered the founding father of the Nazi Party's anti-Semitic platform.

that process. That to me is what we're here for and what we have in common.

LEWIS: Could I add a footnote to that? Part of our problem is the intellectual as a political animal. We can deal with the intellectual function in terms of the handling of symbols, creativity and so on. But I think we really are here concerned about what effect . . .

K. CLARK: Can we effect this present process?

HASTIE: In terms of what it's going to mean for the future of our society and the black man in our society.

LEWIS: That's a value question and it's a political question too.

ELLISON: Politically, you see, we are boxed in by numbers. You're not going to change that. You can use violence; you can use threats; you can be Jack be limber, Jack be quick, Jack jump over the candlestick, but be sure it doesn't singe you. I mean, this is going on now. This is part of the technique of confrontation, black and white. But as intellectuals, there is something else. We are thrown right back to that moment when young colonials, most of them white, or passing for white—Bob Weaver's here, so they must have been passing for white—were taking the best ideas and concepts, political science, political philosophy, and applying them on what for Europeans was a new land mass, and by God, making them work. What we're talking about now, really is intellectual power. How do we make real political, sociological, artistic, you name it, insights actually work in a situation where we are by definition outnumbered?

K. CLARK: Hy, may I make a point here because I think that Ralph has just put his finger on something. After we get through the whole moral, ideological thing, at the base, I suppose, certainly at the base of my thinking is a very practical problem of what does an oppressed minority do in a situation where certain kinds of techniques and methods that appear to have worked for oppressed majorities throughout the world are now being offered as if they can work equally for an oppressed minority? And one of the things that fascinated me whenever these kids mentioned Fanon's *The Wretched of the Earth* is that they never ask themselves the basic question of how relevant is Fanon to American Negroes when Fanon was talking about oppressed people who were in the majority?

LEWIS: They haven't read Fanon.

K. CLARK: Clearly.

This is a practical problem that if it isn't addressed, it can only lead to sort of a romantic—a romantic sort of suicidal rhetoric. And the danger, of course, is the possibility that it could be actually suicidal. But if you say this, the stock response up to the point when I was being responded to is that this is another manifestation of being white brainwashed, you see; that you're really giving a sophisticated form of Uncle Tomism if you ask to look just at arithmetic. What are tactics and strategies given the fact that you're outnumbered ten—nine or ten to one. We don't like to talk about this.

ELLISON: Well, I ask the kids, "Do you know how to shoot a gun?" And most of them don't. I was brought up shooting guns. In the winter of 1937 I supported myself by killing game.

DRAKE: I just have a couple of brief comments to make. I think we have brought the problem around to this locus, and it's probably going to revolve around "power" for a few minutes. I think it's rather interesting, it seems to me, that the only thing that I've read recently where somebody has made a stab at trying to make a statement of the power relations and where it led you is this piece by Arthur Lewis.[64] It's interesting to me that it was an outsider who did it. This happens so often. I think one of the most effective things said about the upsurge of the Black Power trend was said by a Nigerian, Essien Udom*,[65] you see. C. Eric Lincoln had something to say about the Black Muslims, but he didn't put his finger on what the African scholar did.[66] The Nigerian looking at this thing says to us, "What these middle-class Negroes are thinking about really isn't what these blacks out there are thinking." And he said that ever since Marcus Garvey, this has been so.[67] He was right, too.

64. The British economist and professor Sir Arthur Lewis (1915–1991) received his Ph.D. in industrial economics from the London School of Economics in 1940. He won the Nobel Memorial Prize in Economic Sciences with Theodore W. Schultz in 1979.

65. *Black Nationalism.* This reference to the title of Essien-Udom's book is in the original. In 1962 E. U. Essien-Udom published *Black Nationalism: The Search for an Identity,* a work that examines the role the Nation of Islam played in the formation of ethnic consciousness, black empowerment, and a national identity.

66. C. Eric Lincoln (1924–2000) received his Ph.D. in social ethics in 1960 from Boston University. Lincoln was the author of *The Black Muslims in America* (1961) and a coauthor with Lawrence H. Mamiya of *The Black Church in the African-American Experience* (1990).

67. Marcus Garvey (1887–1940), a black nationalist, founded the Universal Negro Improvement Association in 1914, an organization that sought to engender

Now, I think Sir Arthur Lewis of Princeton, as a West Indian looking at all this from the outside, at least gave us a model to use and it seems to me that what Arthur Lewis said in this article was, "Look, down in the West Indies we know where we're going."[68] I think he said this explicitly, "We're going to take an island over and we're going to make it a nation, but you're not a majority in the U.S. and therefore you've got a problem that functions in two separate dimensions. One of your problems is the problem of how do you consolidate your local communities and get maximum control of local institutions in your local communities?" And then he said, "There you've got parallels." If I paraphrase him correctly, he said, "In the Polish community, most of the businessmen, most of the professional men, and so forth, are Poles. This is true in the Italian communities, too. This is an American pattern. It ought to be true in black communities."

This becomes a problem of community control. This requires a certain kind of training for a certain kind of leadership. He felt it ought to be given at the high school level or the junior college level. Therefore, he was for even the conventional Black Power kind of studies at those levels on the grounds that here we are dealing with those particular kinds of problems. Well, let's take the term of the people out in the street, "You've got to get yourself together." That was the Bustamante position in Jamaica.[69] There, we've got ourselves together, see. These Black Stone Rangers in Chicago were out shooting each other up.[70] They haven't got themselves together in any sense other than to shoot a Disciple. Somebody's got to deal with this problem, and at the moment,

---

unity and pride in the black community. Garvey believed that those of African descent needed to relocate to Africa and form their own state to truly escape oppression.

68. Lewis's article, "The Road to the Top Is through Higher Education—Not Black Studies," was published on May 11, 1969, in the *New York Times*.

69. Sir Alexander Bustamante (1884–1977), a leader of the Jamaican trade union movement, combined several unions to form the Bustamante Industrial Trade Union in an effort to unite workers of all classes, jobs, and races. He formed the Jamaican Labour Party in 1943 and was the prime minister of Jamaica from 1962 to 1967.

70. The Blackstone Rangers, also known as the Almighty Black P Stone Nation, is a Chicago street gang that was formed between 1961 and 1963 by Eugene "Bull" Hairston and Jeff "Angel" Fort. At the time of the Haverford Discussions, the Rangers allegedly had up to 8,000 members, largely made up of the smaller gangs they acquired over the years.

only the Panthers are trying to deal with it. How do you politicalize Chicago gangs, if possible, and divert them toward constructive activity? Arthur Lewis would say that's a real problem, it is a local kind of problem.

Also, it's realistic to think you're going to be segregated a long time. One of the things he thinks you've got to do is get the nonsense out of your head that you're going to be desegregated spatially within any foreseeable point of time. Just take the logistics of Chicago—how could you desegregate Chicago?

ELLISON: I don't even know whether that is desirable.

DRAKE: It may not be desirable, see.

The second thing he moved on to is that you've got the problem of "separation." That's a separate, distinct problem from introducing segregation on a college campus. In the community you've got the segregation there spatially already. This poses a problem for you. How do you make the most of this in terms of mobilizing power? Not so on a campus.

Arthur Lewis moved on and said, "You're only one-ninth of the U.S.A."—and I like the neat way in which he phrased it. He said you ought to set your other objective as getting eleven per cent of every single kind of power position in the U. S. This was a *New York Times* article and he included eleven per cent of the *Times* editorial room.

K. CLARK: And General Motors.

DRAKE: Yes, eleven per cent of General Motors' board room, too. You could take this as a kind of model, "How are you going to learn how to do that?" So then he argued this—"You aren't going to learn how to do that by taking," as Bayard Rustin would call them "soul courses."[71] Then his argument was, "Why not, when you're thinking about your thirty top institutions in the U. S."—he being at Princeton, of course, he had Princeton in there—"think of those as the places where you go to get that engineering, where you go to get that medicine; this is where you learn to 'beat that man at his game' and to go ahead and get your eleven per cent of these posts that are scattered through this society."

71. Bayard Rustin (1910–1987), a major proponent of nonviolent protest, served as a political adviser to Martin Luther King Jr. from 1955 to 1960, and organized the 1963 March on Washington. Conscious of the way his homosexuality might affect the perception others had of the civil rights movement, Bayard often chose (or was forced) to work behind the scenes.

Then he goes beyond that. "You're not going to prepare yourself to sit in the General Motors board room if you're going to be demanding your separate black clubs, because, how are you going to size that man up? You've got to learn how to deal with him and you learn how to deal with him when you go off to Harvard or Princeton and associate with him. You go there not to get your soul courses, but to learn how to be efficient." Now, we may not agree with Arthur, but I would say that in a sense he was doing the kind of thinking which I think we need to do.

My final point is simply this: Ken raised the point about how we can talk to people. It would be interesting to see what would happen if you went to a bunch of black students on the campus or in the community with this sort of Arthur Lewis perspective and say, "Now what kind of quarrel have you got with this one?" Well, of course, some will say, "Who wants to train people for The Establishment? We don't want those posts."

But I think a more serious problem, as I move around, is another one. You'd never quantify it, so I don't know what proportion of people we're dealing with have these particular ideas. But I learn an awful lot about the U.S.A. by weaving backwards and forwards between here and Africa. I spent from October '58 to February of '61 as head of the sociology department at the University of Ghana. Is Franklin Williams coming along?[72]

K. CLARK: I doubt it.

LEWIS: He's not coming.

DRAKE: When I said Ghana, I got to thinking about him. I was pre–Franklin Williams' era.

ELLISON: He went over there and learned how to be a black man. I heard him say that.

DRAKE: And that was a very crucial two years in Africa—in the history of Africa. In those days, as you know, Accra was sort of the center of the whole "getting themselves together" for the liberation movements in Africa.[73] As early as '61, I was detecting an attitude among South Africans and Tanzanians which duplicated itself here five years later; you could have almost predicted it would happen.

72. Franklin Williams (1928–1990) was a member of the Haverford Group, but he could not attend the first meeting. He did attend the second and fourth meetings. He was a lawyer and civil rights activist who assisted Thurgood Marshall. Under President Johnson, he was appointed ambassador to Ghana.

73. Accra is the capital of Ghana.

The first one was this. They had had interracial action groups. The boys were gradually beginning to say, when you take in a group of white people in your action group, your masses are always raising the question, "Who's making up our leaders' minds?"—The same question Malcolm X raised later about the NAACP. I talked to those African National Conference[74] fellows who split out and started PAC in South Africa.[75] They said, "Look, we realize white people have something to say to us, but we can't maintain any kind of leadership position with the white man always being in our inner circles because your masses say, how do we know the white man isn't making up your mind." Julius Nyerere[76] founded his political party, TANU, with the rule that no Indian or white man could be in this party.[77] But it wasn't racist. He said, "Any white man or any Indian can run on our ticket." I remember after the first election, Julius Nyerere had his picture taken holding up one white woman's hand and one Indian's hand because they had won on TANU's ticket, but he isn't going to let any Indian or any white person get in TANU. Stokely comes along a little later with the phrase, "Define yourself for yourself, then make your coalition."[78] Well, this kind of thing one could see in Africa before Stokely came along.

But what was most disquieting was something very different; what I call a Rap Brown syndrome.[79] I used to call it the Samson complex. You may recall that after Samson's hair grew back out, when he got his strength back, the Philistines brought him to make sport of him . . .

ELLISON: You neglected to say that he was blinded.

74. The National Conference is held every five years by the African National Congress (ANC), a civil rights and political organization founded in 1912. At the National Conference, the president is elected, committees are formed, and the ANC's program for the upcoming years is determined.

75. A South African liberation movement, the Pan Africanist Congress (PAC) broke away from the ANC in 1959.

76. Julius Kambarage Nyerere (1922–1999) was the first president of Tanzania (1964–1985). He was the creator of African socialism, an ideology based on the communal agricultural lifestyle practiced by African peoples before being colonized. In the original manuscript, the name was misspelled as Nyere, and I have corrected the spelling.

77. The Tanganyika African National Union was founded by Nyerere in 1954.

78. Stokely Carmichael (1941–1998), a social activist for racial equality and, later, separatism, coauthored *Black Power: The Politics of Liberation* with Charles V. Hamilton in 1967. Carmichael was involved in both CORE and SNCC.

79. H. Rap Brown, now known as Jami Abdullah Al-Amin, published *Die Nigger Die!* in 1969. For a brief discussion of Brown's work, see my introduction.

DRAKE: He was blinded. And as Milton said, "Samson Agonistes, eyeless in Gaza, grinding at the mill with slaves." He has to know his place. They brought him to the hall and he said: "Where are the pillars?" And when he got to them, he pulled them down, see, and Samson died. But while he was dying, he was probably saying, "Man, look at all those Philistines dying! Just look at them, see!" I call this the Samson complex, or the Rap Brown complex.

An awful lot of boys in the ghetto have this position. And among the South Africans, it's all over the place. Their position is, "We may not enjoy it, so we'll destroy it. We don't care." You tell them—you say—"Well, look, you're going to blow the place up. What'll you have?" They answer, "We won't have anything but those damned Dutchmen won't have anything either, see?" I do detect this attitude—one doesn't know the proportions who share it. I don't know whether you get this feeling or not that it's there.

ELLISON: I "read" about it. I "read" about the guys burning that Harlem tenement.

DRAKE: They went and got the buckets, put the kerosene around. He said, come on, "Let's burn the . . .

ELLISON: Ed Charles said they had that feeling in 1921.[80] This is not new.

DRAKE: I think we just have to write off that proportion of these people who feel that way. Isn't any use trying to talk to these fellows.

LEWIS: Just write them off?

DRAKE: I don't think you can deal with the boys who . . .

FRANKLIN: May I make a point? That isn't a problem for the intellectuals.

DRAKE: If a guy feels that there is no hope, we aren't going to be able to get anywhere with him. I have found no way of talking to those guys because their position is . . .

LEWIS: What do you do about it?

K. CLARK: Have we shifted our focus from the students . . .

DRAKE: Not many students have this Samson Complex.

WEAVER: Without knowing how we got into it, we've shifted from talking about philosophy and about objectives and about overall diagnosis of where we want to go, where we should go, into tactics. And it's been my experience that once you get tactics and philosophy mixed up,

80. I have been unable to identify Ellison's reference to Ed Charles.

you end up with lousy philosophy and horrible tactics. And I think that we ought to talk about where it is we feel we ought to go and what our objectives are.

Then I think we can turn to the tactics. Once you start talking about the tactics without knowing what the tactics are being used for, then I think you're in great difficulty, and I'm afraid that's where we are now. We're talking about tactics without having really talked about where it is we feel this society in which we as black people are going to be a part, is going to go.

ELLISON: May I make a stab at some of the things which I think we should *not* do. And since I believe that we are basically involved in a discussion of rhetoric I'll make it a negative statement: I think that for many, many years one of the basic problems of Negro leaders has had to do with how—given our numerical position in this society and our relative political powerlessness after 1879—they can actually win a following. They have been up against the proposition of what is the true source of power in the black communities, and of how to release that power and give it effective direction. How do we "get ourselves together," to use a phrase which comes up over and over again; and to what does a Negro leader appeal when he seeks to gain a following? What rhetoric does he use?

Now, one of the appeals was directed to our yearning for education. The other was toward our desire for education and our desire for equality of political participation. The DuBois-Washington argument.[81] Both were to an extent effective. But the problem remains and all during the intervening years our leaders have searched for rhetorical levers which would allow them to move the black masses in the direction of achieving their political will. In trying to find a lever our leaders have subjected us to a lot of sloppy rhetoric, and most of it fixed upon the single factor of race. They've been concerned with the appearance of

81. Ellison is referring to the famous debate between Booker T. Washington, who endorsed vocational education for blacks and opposed political agitation for "social equality" in his famous "Atlanta Exposition Address" in 1895. See chap. 14 of his *Up from Slavery*. W. E. B. Du Bois criticized Washington's approach in his 1903 book *The Souls of Black Folk*, because he believed that "Mr. Washington's programme practically accepts the alleged inferiority of the Negro races." Du Bois insisted on agitating for social and political equality, and he made the case for a traditional form of higher education for a certain segment of the black population. See chap. 3 of *The Souls of Black Folk*.

things, the surface of things, and upon the most obvious physical differences between the appearance of whites and blacks. Currently, much of the rhetoric appeals to our aesthetic sense and I hear men, very smart men, who are long on charisma and short on analytical ability telling us that we must have black pride, that we must believe in ourselves and that we must "do our own thing." But from where I stand this type of exhortation simply takes off from the negative definitions which hostile whites—or miseducated whites—have thrust upon us and attempts to convert these definitions into positive values. And it does this while failing to examine the living realities of Negro American life upon which these misguided and vicious definitions have been based. "Black is Beautiful" we are told but I see little indication that this facile attempt to politicalize aesthetic matters is based upon anything more profound than the desire to refute the contention of many whites that black is ugly, grotesque and evil. And yet there is a service to be performed in evaluating Negro American aesthetic preferences, taste and style.

I doubt however that it is possible to build a viable vision of the Negro American predicament by basing a rhetoric upon the simple inversion of white racism into a black racism. Our situation cries out for new definitions—or at least for conscious intellectual restatement of those abiding attitudes and values which have been acted out, if not stated explicitly, by our people as they have repudiated theories of white superiority. It is our task to define who and what we are with as much intellectual precision as is possible. And since we are an inseparable part of the American nation and its culture, let us accept the obligation of defining it from the perspective of our own backgrounds and insist that its values be brought in line with our own group's aspirations and needs.

Getting back to aesthetics and rhetoric, it seems obvious to me that almost everything Negro Americans do in the way of self expression and group expression is so eloquent of an implicit pride of being that it is an affront for our leaders to exhort us to "black pride." Our pride is expressed in our sense of style, which is so expressive of what life should be and of what men should make it be that the entire American culture has been strongly influenced by it. In fact, it has been so strongly influenced by our particular stylization of the national experience that culturally every American is, to an extent, Negro American. So it's a waste of time and a negative approach to exhort our people to pride. Better, let us examine the inner shape and the sources of our pride. Nor do you tell them that straightening the hair is an expression of self-hatred. Taken out of the context of "white superiority," straightening the hair is an aesthetic dimension; it grows out of the human impulse to take the given and modify it as an expression of one's own will and taste. And if a guy wants to bleach his face, let him bleach his face. But don't politicalize it because if you do you dehumanize him, you deprive him of a basic human freedom, the freedom to make art of his own features. And when you politicalize this impulse you instill that self hate and that self disparagement which whites ascribe to us.

I've watched the results of this politicalizing of aesthetic impulses very closely. Our leaders set out to accent the positive without stopping to discover what the positive really is and now what do you have? You have absolutely handsome little black girls going around looking like minstrel men and gollywogs, with their lips painted white and their eyes done up in grotesque eye shadow. Look, listen to me. Maybe I'm being absolutely foolish but I believe this politicalizing of matters which should have been left to the realm of aesthetics has unleashed a lot of chaos, ideological as well as visual. It is the black leaders' sense of frustration growing out of a failure to analyze our situation creatively that causes them to fall back upon this dangerous rhetoric. They fail to recognize that they're reducing aesthetic matters to a matter of pathology. You even had Martin Luther King joining in the chorus 'They say Black is Beautiful.' Hell, I always knew that black was beautiful, with all the black kids that were born around me. Someone must have thought that black women were beautiful. Someone loved them because certainly they weren't always abandoned.

K. CLARK: Available . . .

ELLISON: Available but not as easily available on a moral level. But we've found ourselves repeating this cliché, trying to make political capital out of it and it turns into dragon teeth every time we do it. The kids are absolutely confused. You see a little blue-eyed kid at Michigan State who is doing all he can, probably teasing his hair to make it bushy, and you can't have a conversation with him because he's saying again and again—repeating Malcolm X—"I hate that white rapist so-and-so who raped my mother." And finally you say, "Well, look, man, maybe you should go out and put some flowers on his grave, because if he hadn't given you the complexion that you have, you wouldn't have a goddamned thing to say."

I'm trying to separate this political cluster and I'm saying: Let's put aesthetic things in their proper perspective. Aesthetically we are very, very powerful people. No one has had as much to do with shaping the cultural forms of the United States as Negro Americans. True this comes partially out of Africa but the mixture of elements and the specific conditions which gave form to our style of expression was and is American. But to fall into the morass of defining complex meaning in terms of aesthetics of skin color, in terms of lack of pride, this is an absolute mistake. We have got to just say, yes, we love one another, we like our group style, or we quarrel with certain aspects of Negro style, we don't like those niggers over there, they don't like me over here, but we are all together, and when we get out on the dance floor and we like the music, things work well. But we have various political objectives, we have a variety of origins, we have a variety of class backgrounds, we have a variety of values and personal traditions and scholarly traditions, regional and religious. This is all true. I'm sorry.

K. CLARK: Ralph. All right. I just would like to make a comment before I ask Saunders. But you started out by saying that you would start negative, but as I listened to you, you were really saying something affirmative, that actually the problem, the job of the Negro is to affirm—and affirm what he is, but . . .

ELLISON: Yes, but you don't affirm anything by telling our kids that they have to have black pride. Those little bastards are as proud as hell. And always have been. It's a waste of time, it's a disservice. Just as it is a disservice when we concentrate on the problem of race and civil rights to the neglect of motivating our kids to go and take on the world in *all* its dimensions and with *all* of the many disciplines evolved by men as a means of humanizing reality.

HOLMAN: You'll put all the psychologists out of work.

ELLISON: I would put them out of this particular business.

WEAVER: How much impact will any one of us here—individually or collectively, have in playing a leadership role and deciding tactics? I think we're kidding ourselves. And I think what we ought to be sitting about here talking about is where do we think we ought to go in the situation of 1969.

K. CLARK: All right.

ELLISON: Just let me answer this. I wasn't speaking to us as leaders. I'm not a leader. I'm a guy who spends most of his time in a room by himself, not even with my dog.

K. CLARK: One should.

REDDING: I simply want to say this, not in response to Ralph, but that I think it's relevant. Ralph, I think that you're probably right in saying that we have tended to politicalize . . .

ELLISON: Terrible word.

REDDING: —this whole business. When you say to these black kids that, look, this business of wearing your hair in a bush, etc., etc., is aesthetic, you know, and that it has nothing at all to do with race; they're going to come—and that blue-eyed kid is just as beautiful as the black skinned kid—they're going to come back at you with this question: But whose standards are we going by? You see.

ELLISON: Yes.

REDDING: And this is the political thing. St. Clair mentioned—and then I'll be through. St. Clair mentioned Ghana from '59 to '61. I was in Kenya in '62 where I attended a black writers conference—African writers conference. And at that meeting, there were representatives of American, white American, publishing houses and white British publishing houses, who offered these writers a prize. Oh, it was quite a big prize, you know, for the best book by an African. And after they had offered this, there was a big discussion which Langston[82] and I and Robie Macauley could not join in;[83] Robie, of course, because he was white, and Langston and I because we were Americans.

ELLISON: Y'all were white, too.

K. CLARK: Yes, to the Africans, they were white.

REDDING: Here's what the Africans said. They said, "Look, who will be judging this contest? You white Europeans, Europeans?" And the publishers had assumed that yes, they would be doing it. And on the basis of that assumption, these African writers said, "Oh, no, we don't want it. Who are you to judge us? Your standards are not our standards."

Now, it seems to me that the difference is that actually our standards, the standards of the American Negro have, until recently been western, European, Anglo Saxon standards.

ELLISON: Just as your language is.

REDDING: That's right. Just as our language is. And that the only

82. Redding is referring to Langston Hughes (1902–1967), one of the most prolific and famous writers to emerge from the Harlem Renaissance.

83. Robie Macauley (1941–1995) was the author of numerous short stories and novels and an editor for the *Kenyon Review* (1959–66), *Playboy* (1966–77), and the Houghton Mifflin publishing company (1977–88).

way we can change this is—if it's desirable to change it, which is a question—is by the kind of infiltration that we have done with our music, with our language—you know, with our perversion, if you will, corruption, or whatever modification.

K. CLARK: Which is how a culture grows anyway.

REDDING: All right. Fine. We cannot do this—we cannot make a program of this because the moment you make a program of it, you are going to be met by all kinds of walls rising steadily above you. I mean, you know.

Now this these kids will not understand unless they're told, unless they're taught to understand what the opposition is and how it comes about.

K. CLARK: Adelaide.

HILL: I want to say I think that we have one important role to play. I think the young people who are coming into colleges and who don't want to go along with this rhetoric have no place to go. That is, take any college campus in America, this September, when a whole lot of black kids will be coming on, some will be kids who want leadership that we could give; others are going to be caught into whatever happens to be the thing on their campus. And I think what we've all seen in the last one or two years is the youngster who wants to think independently has no leadership. He doesn't know where to go. He may or may not know Frazier or Allison Davis or Sterling.[84] He may have found out by himself, but he has nothing to hang to. He's an isolated, lost and sometimes frightened youngster; and that kid, by and large, I think, is going to be the one on whom all of them are going to have to depend ten years from now. And I think that we, a little bit out of date and old perhaps, have responsibilities to him and we might, at some time, want to discuss how we can institutionalize our responsibilities or systematize them.

K. CLARK: Let me give a specific illustration of that, Adelaide. When George and I were at Columbia during the last confrontation,

84. The professor and poet Sterling Brown (1901–1989), along with Arthur P. Davis and Ulysses Lee, compiled in 1941 *The Negro Caravan,* a comprehensive anthology of African American literature. Brown was known for his criticism of the way white authors stereotyped black characters, and, by contrast, for the way he himself created realistic, heroic black characters in his poetry. He began teaching at Howard University in 1929, and remained there for almost sixty years. For a brief discussion of the Haverford Group's view of Brown, see my introduction.

the one that lasted three days, as we were sitting in the office of a dean, he said one of the most poignant things that I had heard since being involved in this. He said that about two weeks before the Negro students sat in the Admissions Office a delegation of Negro students came to his office and said to him, "Look, we are Negro students at Columbia and Barnard, too, and we are concerned about the fact that we are ignored. Nobody is paying any attention to us because we have not been a part of the confrontation. We want to be at Columbia on the same terms as any other student at Columbia, take our same chances." And I asked him, "Well, what happened?" He said, "Well, all I did was to say I'm glad to hear that. Will you say this publicly?" And I think that he said that they promised to say it publicly.

REID: One did.

K. CLARK: One did? But apparently—the group didn't? There were no supports, apparently. They were almost asking the administration to help them find some way of asserting their individuality.

ELLISON: Well, we've got to give them that support. That's all.

FRANKLIN: That was the point I was trying to make earlier.

K. CLARK: There are two or three even at Antioch, by the way, I understand.

REDDING: Most of them at George Washington now . . .

K. CLARK: I'm sorry. John Hope.

FRANKLIN: They fall in the same category, in a sense, intellectually and otherwise, that most of the college and university students do today; they have their work, they want to do it. They are not politicized. They find themselves under enormous pressures to move in one direction or another and they look around for some kind of sustenance or support and they feel dependent. They feel dependent even in the area of encouragement to remain independent. It's not that they want to be persuaded to go in one direction or another. It's that they want to have some justification for doing what they're doing. And I think people don't give them that. But now, as I was saying before we came over here, it seems to me that what we have to do as individuals and as a group, if we can get to the point of being a group, is to take an affirmative position, if I may say so, Ralph, with respect to what we think the life of the mind is all about, what we think people who are interested primarily in the development of their own intellectual position are all about. We don't have an ideology. I hope we don't.

K. CLARK: Except an ideology in favor of freedom.

FRANKLIN: Yes. We ought to say that they don't have to have one either and we ought to begin to move against what I would call the false ideologies that really feed on a specious kind of racism; that because they're black, they have to be moving along a certain line. Because they're black they have to feel that they have certain qualities that are inherent to their blackness. Because they're black they feel that they have to adopt a certain course of action, and they have to act in a certain way. There's nothing that is inherently good in their being black. I think we have to say that. I think that we have to say that there's something that's terribly inherently good about their being human beings, about their being people; that as people and as human beings, they can move in the direction that they see fit. I'm not interested, frankly, in creating a society in which everybody is goose stepping, and if they don't they are ostracized, they're among those who are not elect. I think that these young people who are, I won't say uncommitted, but who have a commitment to themselves must be made to feel that this is a worthy commitment and that they don't have to eat turnip greens if they don't want to. They don't have to dance a jig, as a white man in Tulsa thought—in 1925, Ralph—that I ought to do because I was black. Now Negroes say they can, you know, they can dance a jig better than those people. I don't believe it. And I think that they must be supported in their feeling that they don't have to believe this. The important thing, it seems to me, is to give strength and support to the independence of the individual who works out his own way . . .

K. CLARK: Wasn't this what we were fighting before when we were fighting the white segregationists, the white racists? He was trying to deny us our right to be individuals, to be seen and evaluated and to live and to struggle as individuals. We have as a part of our group someone who has been literally on the firing line in this with sort of administrative responsibility. Ed Williams went from the State Department into the clover of academia just in time to get it at the University of Chicago with the actualities of what we're talking about, primarily in terms of words.

Ed, does anything that you've heard this afternoon and dinner make any sense to you as public affairs Vice President of the University of Chicago, with a white and black student rebellion . . .

LEWIS: He's got a white and black constituency.

K. CLARK: Is that, by the way, an integrated rebellion at Chicago or is that split?

EDDIE N. WILLIAMS: The part of the iceberg that has been showing these past few months is not very much integrated. The disruptive students have been white; there are black students who have concerns. However, I suspect, because white students have been doing their thing, the black part of the iceberg has not really manifested itself.

One comment I would make is that having dealt with black students and fitting somewhere perhaps between the students who are in college now and some of you here, I'm not convinced how all this will work. I'm not sure that they are prepared to respond at this time to any kind of intellectual approach. I think they've committed themselves to a course. What seems to me to be very important is what they're saying—although in many ways they are not articulating it very specifically—they're raising a question, and I think some people touched on this, about certain values in American society.

HOLMAN: Precisely.

WILLIAMS: I think it's a waste of the intellectual's time—those intellectually qualified by all of the qualifications that have been enunciated today—to talk about the immediacy of the situation in terms of black protest, or black studies, or Afro-American studies. As Dr. Clark said a few years ago about black power, that that was the Watusi of the civil rights movement, i.e., fad, I think that much of what we're seeing today will pass.[85] It perhaps will move into some of the more bureaucratic, more institutional, more disciplinary aspects of the academic community; and I think this is very good. That's what we'd like. When we're studying American literature, we'd like to have the black heroes as an integral part of that. To get the pendulum to swing in the right direction, sometimes you have to go way out of the way in order to start it swinging in the opposite direction. And I have a feeling that this may be what we're seeing now. So it's kind of an aberration. I'm not sure we need to be too much worried about it. Personally, I'm not awfully—I'm not very much concerned about the kids who learn about fire by playing with it and getting burned. As someone said earlier, when kids play near the precipice, somebody falls off. I think that's unfortunate. I think that's tough. But that's reality.

WEAVER: Are you saying that we are now in the situation where obviously we have these political factors in something that should be a

85. The watusi, like the twist, was a dance craze in the 1960s.

matter of scholarship and intellectual pursuit, but that we do nothing about it and that this is a fact of life that we have to live with?

WILLIAMS: No. I'm not saying you do nothing about it. What I'm saying is that I think that what you do about it principally is to address yourselves to what I think are the fundamental questions they're raising. Do we accept the basic precepts and values, as we now know them—and you can talk about the whole examination complex or you can talk about employment or you can talk about college entrance. Is this valid? And I think they're raising that question.

HASTIE: Suppose we say, no, they're not valid—how does that change the . . .

WEAVER: Bill, before you get to that.

WILLIAMS: Do something about it.

WEAVER: Let's assume that we accept the fact that there's a lot wrong with what we now have in all of these areas. Are we saying that because there's a lot wrong, that when a group of students, white or black—it makes no difference as far as I'm concerned—say that this is wrong and therefore we're going to tell you what you do about it, do we accept this? I think that's the sixty-four dollar question. That's what I'm facing right now.

WILLIAMS: Well, my position is I think it's just as bad to accept black students' demands or insistence that A, B, or C is the answer as much as it is to accept the white definition or solution that A, B, or C is the answer.

K. CLARK: Ralph.

ELLISON: Yes. I want to suggest that very often we ascribe initiatives, responsibilities and motives to whites which are focused in an unstated devil theory. We assume that white people are omniscient and they are far from it. *All* Americans have been harmed by the racial divisions in this society, even down to the nuances of grammar and symbolism. So this goes back to what you just said. We have the responsibility for arriving at basic truths. And if we don't grasp the ironic fact that we are in the position, not of dominating the society numerically or even politically, but of being able through the urgency of our position to keep perspectives clear, we've missed an opportunity. We are called upon to name things with a precision which, up to now, the other group has had the luxury of ignoring. What is unclear to them had better be clear to us because we are far more vulnerable to the stresses and strains of reality than they ever were. We must not assume that every dereliction of insight is a product of maliciousness. Often it arises from sheer ignorance. And I'm saying that we are going to have to do, in our own terms as intellectuals, for the quality of American life what the black baseball players have done, what the musicians have done, what certain cooks, lawyers and physicians have done. We're going to have to take the full responsibility for the health, direction and values of this society on our own shoulders. Because, as ironic as it sounds, it is our designated role. It is a role designated for us by history, by the urgency of our group needs, by the multiplicity and complexity of Negro American experience and so on. Therefore we get off the track when we start talking about the cynicism of governmental and educational institutions; for while cynicism often exists we cannot afford to move on that assumption. These are times of social disruption and transition, and like our own leaders these administrators are often playing it by ear. They don't know what the hell they're doing.

K. CLARK: Most of them.

ELLISON: As I attempt to perform my civic responsibilities I come in contact with members of the so-called "Establishment" and often, like the rest of you, I am the only Negro, Black, Afro—what have you—in the bunch and I talk with these people and I listen carefully, as novelists are obliged to do. Well, I've found that many of them are both sincere and knowledgeable, while others are sincere but naïve. Others are absolutely devious and concerned with their special interests, and I get the impression that some just want a black face around and don't want to be told the truth. But in terms of philosophical perspective, in terms of grasping the far-reaching implications of American democracy, *many* of them, regardless of motivation, simply don't know where they are! Very often I get the impression that they are listening and hoping that someone, even a Negro, will come along and say something helpful and intelligent—or what *they* might consider intelligent. You know that this is true.

K. CLARK: Ralph, what you say is such an awesome responsibility, but . . .

ELLISON: Well, it's our responsibility. It's *ours*. Goddamit, it's ours. This man right here knows that when he's on the court he is responsible for the law. He is a vessel of the law. And as a Negro American he knows that he can see certain things that other people can't see because they suffer from the trained incapacity which prevents them from seeing. He's been disciplined by his background and his education in the law to grasp matters which might escape even the white judge of high integrity and goodwill.

HASTIE: We're not sensitive, true enough.

HOLMAN: Let me go on here and talk about what I see as some of the issues that have to be addressed. One of them—someone said that here are problems which have to do with what is truly the life of the mind, you see. If you are a black student today, are you going to go do your own thing, you see, in terms of the life of the mind, be an individual, concern yourself with what you as an individual can be and not get bothered because people are trying to pull you off the track and get you involved in one communal thing or not. This is a very, very difficult problem for kids now and we have to understand why it is. I mentioned Vietnam. It's very interesting that all of you, including those of you from campuses, have at no point addressed this. I think in part the reason is that when I was in school and it was a problem for some of us that we really might go to war, you see, we noticed the great disparity between what we were sensitive to and concerned about and what they were sensitive to and concerned about; and in large part, it was because we were vulnerable and they were not in that particular . . .

K. CLARK: Who were the "they"?

HOLMAN: They—the faculty. The faculty were not.

Now, the question of power is a question which has been raised by students and by people outside.

FRANKLIN: Before you go on, let me say that I used the term "the life of the mind" and I wasn't concerned with myself. I was concerned about what the students—how they look at their problems. Do they look at them with their guts or with their head or what—or their heart or what?

K. CLARK: John, I don't think we need apologize for that.

FRANKLIN: But we have to at some point revive this as important, you see.

HOLMAN: It is important.

FRANKLIN: I'm not going to make the concession that some other kind of reaction is a solution. We are here talking about how you solve your problems. You solve them with your noggin, you see. This is all I was saying about the life of the mind.

M. CLARK: I thought it would be helpful if at this point you would kind of summarize what we've accomplished so far and indicate some kind of—not precise direction, but some goal that we want to accomplish for this meeting.

K. CLARK: Well, let me try. I think we took this afternoon and arrived at general—I don't want to use the word "consensus," but general understanding among us that we share concern about developments in the civil rights struggle in general, but specifically, the developments on campuses as far as the Negro, black students are concerned.

We shared our concern about the implications of the separatist thrust as indicated by black studies demands, the facilities for Negroes. We gave examples of this. We sought also to try to get some understanding of what this was reflecting. We—some of us felt that it would be important for us to understand that some of these demands and some of the situations had more immediate and specific reality in a particular place than others; and I think certainly St. Clair Drake was the chief exponent of the position that it may be that it's important for us not to be too general in our thinking in any possible statement about black separatism, blanketing it.

We also felt that, after we got back to discussion at dinner, as I understood what was being said, we got more into the diagnostic part of this, and as we flirted with that, it is clear that we were moving toward possible tactics. And Bob talked—I think it was Bob—warned us against confusing understanding and perspective with premature preoccupation with tactics.

WEAVER: That was my point.

K. CLARK: And that we now seem to be at a point where we are on the verge of being more specific or see whether we can be specific about where we stand and what we suggest about what can be done about this. This is my sense of what has happened in the afternoon and the evening. At the end of the last session, in response to questioning from Bill, I said that I would hope that this evening, at the end of this evening, we would be preparing ourselves for being able to devote tomorrow to suggesting where we go from here and why and how.

WEAVER: Well, Ken, since I won't be here tomorrow morning—unfortunately, I have to give a commencement address. And that *is* unfortunate! Any college president who makes a commencement address is a fool. In fact, I often feel that any college president is a fool. (*Laughter*)

FRANKLIN: I think that college presidents should quit while they're behind. (*Laughter*)

WEAVER: I think there were two points that were raised which were not properly given as much consideration as they might. And one was so obvious that sometimes you ignore the obvious. This is the thing that Carl was talking about and that is the fact that what we're discussing is not only a black problem, but it's a problem of a whole generation of very sophisticated youngsters who are completely disillusioned with the society of which they are a part. They're challenging its values. They are assuming that the university should become the center where you make social change. Obviously, it can't avoid this, but I don't think it can be the spearhead, but that isn't important.

And the second one was the matter of choice, and this is something that disturbs me as a practical administrator because in my college the problem is that the coterie of black students which—I don't know if it's a majority although it may well be—have decided that they are going to decide what all the black students do. This I find very difficult to accept as an administrator and even more difficult to accept as a human being. I think these are two issues that we have to face up to, whether it's tactics or philosophy. With all that's happened, it has not necessarily been the majority of the black students who did it. There have been those who were intimidated so that they would not express any position, and rightfully, from their point of view, they shouldn't. And this disturbs me a great deal.

K. CLARK: Well, certainly there were many specific, disturbing components of this which we all experienced; part of it we didn't put on the table, but it certainly is true that the coercion, the impetus of this thing to create a climate within which Negro students lose individuality and lose personal identity if they are categorized . . .

At my own college, for example, I am sharing the fact that we will not be able to have any Negro students who will dare to major in psychology. You know, I wonder what's going to happen to the Negro student who might be interested in biology or . . .

ELLISON: They will say that it has no bearing on the community.

K. CLARK: That's right.

ELLISON: Which is a lot of foolishness.

DRAKE: At this point, Ken . . .

FRANKLIN: Let me—I just wanted to say that with regard to Bob's first point and on that point that you were making, Ken, I think that we really ought to, while it is true that the Negro students are a part of the disillusioned generation, I think they look at the world and they look at their problems somewhat differently from what some of the other students do. And we ought to recognize this—this difference so far as their perception of what their problems are and what their role is. I think there is a substantive difference. It is to be seen, perhaps, best of all in the general reaction of Negro students to the programs and strategies and efforts of the other reformist elements in the college and university communities. And I think that this indicates that they're doing some independent thinking, that is, that they're not being swept up in the general swirl and to the extent I think we ought to recognize the fact that they do have some capacity to perceive their problems as being different and they will not go along with that other crowd.

The other point is in connection with this group on that point, is that they almost invariably have specific programs or objectives, however muddle-headed they might be or however much we might not think too well of them, but they're quite specific in what they want. And I think that as we think about them, we ought to be thinking about addressing ourselves to their program. They have more of a program than the other kids have.

WEAVER: John, can I put a footnote to that? One thing that's impressed me, coming out of the relatively relaxed situation in Washington—(*laughter*)—to the relatively relaxed academic situation—is the fact that however muddle-headed they may be, the Negro students, or the black students, are so much superior in their presentations and in their dedication than the white students who are clamoring. In the first place, most of the white students are coming out *against* something. The Negro students are coming out *for* something. They're coming up with a program. Sometimes it's horrible. But dammit, it's a positive thing and they are very articulate; the guys who speak for them are just unbelievably good in speaking for it.

FRANKLIN: I wasn't meaning to suggest at all that what they stand for is either well presented or indeed praiseworthy, but they have some stand that they take. And the other point is that within their group, once they separate themselves off from the non-black group . . .

WEAVER: Which they do very quickly.

FRANKLIN: Yes, which they do very quickly. They then have a problem of internal organization and strategy and this is what I think is rather unfortunate, but understandably so. They feel that if you're going to have any clout or any effect, then you've all got to be one. This is a part also of the large ideology, too. After all, this is a participatory democracy and everybody goes down the line with what everybody wants. And while this might be praiseworthy from the point of view of the society at large, I think it goes counter to what do you try to do when you take a student in any discipline and you try to move him from where he is to where he ought to be in terms of his intellect, namely if you try to develop some independence, you see, and the enormous pressure, as Ralph says, under which these students who have not committed themselves to a particular program, under the pressure which they're placed it makes it almost impossible for some of them to function. And the result is that you've got tremendous loss of direction and energy and everything else, because they're squares and they need this large group of people who are seeking to find their own way in their own terms—need to be told that this is a worthy pursuit. It is a worthy pursuit when anyone decides to try to develop himself and tries to arrive at a way of looking at life and its problems that come out of his own experience as well as out of some . . .

The point is the tactics they employ involve the destruction of your position and of your right to have a position. Then it becomes substantive and I think this is very . . .

K. CLARK: Ralph.

ELLISON: Well, I think that we're going to have to fight on two levels. We've got to assert the reality of those conditions and those values which made us what we are and which continue to motivate us. We've got to do that.

The only man in the room who has made us the beneficiaries of his experience, his growing up, of the conditions which formed his taste, his values, his mind—is Saunders Redding.[86] Oh, I'm not going to judge, I'm speaking generally. Now Bob Weaver has had one of the most complex of all American experiences, and Drake (who didn't even remember that during the war he tried to teach me to play chess or that when I was a seeker he instructed me in certain knowledge which I needed) hasn't either. So these kids do not have the benefit of what you've lived and learned, and seemingly the general American discontinuity between the generations and between the regions and between

86. Ellison is referring to Redding's books *No Day of Triumph* (1942) and *On Being Negro in America* (1951), in which Redding poignantly documents some of his struggles to define himself independently of the coercive forces in both the white and black communities.

the classes has hit us Negro Americans with an impact that has left us staggering. So the kids are suffering from a basic disorientation. No one had to tell me who my grandfather was or what values he stood for, or what my father and mother, or what any number of old black Oklahomans stood for. They passed their traditions along to the young . . .

WEAVER: Same with a lot of middle-class Negroes.

ELLISON: No. No. I'm saying something else. I'm saying that we are people who don't write, that we . . .

REDDING: You mean don't write about our experience.

ELLISON: Yes. Where is there a black Education of Henry Adams?[87] Who has tried to project so much of American experience through his own consciousness? Bob, who other than yourself knows what it means to start from where you started and become a cabinet member? Who knows what it really means, its implications for the coming generation of our youth? I know something about John Hope's father and knew about John Hope as a legend. He was a legendary character and was known and admired for his mind even when he was a kid in Oklahoma. And I'm not trying to flatter him, I'm trying to get at something else. I'm trying to say that we must not allow this very rich experience which we all share to be lost. And it *is* being lost over and over again. You talk about diversity. The kids don't understand the concept within unity or unity within diversity. That is why "separatism" is so important to them. They feel that the only way to hold on to that which they find meaningful and rich in the Negro American experience is to move out of American society. They haven't been taught how the process has worked for other American groups. They don't understand that we can have group unity without becoming "white," just as whites have become culturally part black without losing their identity. This is even true of crackers.

I get awfully annoyed when some little kid comes up to me and says, "Well, you believe in integration because you've been brainwashed." And I say, "No, but my brain has been cultivated so that I can see beyond black and white and I know where Coleman Hawkins learned to play that saxophone and I know that it wasn't a matter of

87. Henry Adams (1838–1918) was a historian, professor, and writer who penned *The Education of Henry Adams* (1918), a book detailing his attempts to reconcile himself with the rapid developments of his day. He was President John Quincy Adam's grandson.

cultural purity or cultural racism.[88] He learned it at racially integrated Washburn College, out in Kansas. He was a conscious musician who was trained in Western musical techniques and tradition and he took what he learned and extended it and created something startlingly new and uniquely his own and uniquely Negro-American. He integrated his knowledge with his inherited Negro American musical tradition and, like it or not, whites were involved in the process."

K. CLARK: This would be helpful to these kids if we could come up . . .

ELLISON: To these kids and to *all* American kids. It's precisely what happens in this dark, unexplored area of American life which is so mysterious and troublesome. Where do we find elements of our spirit, our values, our traditions, our style in the larger American culture? What metamorphoses have our contributions undergone? These are some of the unstated questions which are implicit in the position of the kids. And some of the answers have been around for a long time but have been ignored. Mark Twain wrote the classical novel *The Adventures of Huckleberry Finn* in which he discovered a way of giving colloquial American speech a literary dimension, and in the preface to that work he paid his respect to the Negro idiom as a creative factor in the American language. In 1824, Walt Whitman was looking at the cultural sources at hand and writing about the Negro American idiom as a source of American poetry and the basis for an American grand opera.[89] So when the kids and those leaders start talking about separatism and integration and the non-melting of the pot we should remind them that on the level of language we have been integrating since before there was an American nation. And the blindness that the white scholars are suffering is the same that many blacks are suffering—except that we have the effects of the pluralism of American culture as a more active force in our lives and thus, and often in a negative way, we are more conscious of its pluralistic nature.

We have it through received-tradition, if you will, but as American

88. Coleman Hawkins (1904–1969) was a famous African American saxophone player known for his ever-changing style and impressive skill in improvisation. For a brief discussion of Hawkins, see my introduction.

89. Walt Whitman (1819–1892) was an American poet known for his emphasis on individualism, his patriotic poetry, and his use of free verse, as seen in the collection *Leaves of Grass,* first published in 1855. The year Ralph Ellison mentions, 1824, is incorrect—Whitman would have only been five at the time.

intellectuals we must tell the young, both black and white where we and they come from.

Kenneth had a wonderful grandmother whom I met only a few times, but she certainly was a living refutation of some of the easy nonsense one reads about our matriarchs. But I've never read anything that he wrote about her.

K. CLARK: I just keep talking about her.

WEAVER: You're a little on sinking ground when you talk about Mark Twain because Mark Twain's characters—Nigger Jim is not something that you would talk about with these young black militants.

ELLISON: Well, I do talk about it and they talk with me about it. They seek me out, perhaps because I've written about it.

DRAKE: Just a brief thought. You've got a double problem here. One is this problem—you see, we're dealing with the problem of availability of materials, the rich experiences that Negroes have—are available. One of the ironies of this, as I would think, and I might be corrected on this, but I'm getting this flood of stuff coming over my desk every day. This whole thrust toward black studies has got everybody, from *The New York Times* and Arno Press, writing out reprints of material.[90] I'm talking about junk. Some is junk and some isn't. Anybody who wanted to write his autobiography now, he'd probably get somebody to give him an advance on it. But what I want to point out is that the irony of it is that this is only happening because all these kids started raising hell.

ELLISON: But we're really talking about being American, the complexity of the American experience as seen from our point of view.

DRAKE: All right. Okay. The problem which we may want to address ourselves to, and maybe it's premature to do it now, is how can anything that we come up with here be communicated, given the general set of attitudes which black students have at the moment. I think it's a double problem. It isn't so much that material isn't available or that even the point of view you express isn't available.

ELLISON: Well, anyway, now these kids are calling my home and coming by. It's always been available to them; but I haven't been fashionable. Now they are seeking me out and I warn them right off that I stand for certain unfashionable attitudes. They say, "We know that, but we want to discuss certain ideas with you." There are groups from sev-

90. Arno Press, founded in 1963 and located in Manhattan, was known for reprinting old reference materials and scholarly works.

eral universities and some of the angry poets, disciples of Leroi Jones.[91] They're coming out to talk with me and I talk with them.

DRAKE: So you feel that we've reached the point now you can get a hearing.

ELLISON: Yes, wait a minute, Kenneth. Let me say this. I think we—I'll use the metaphor of the difference between shooting with a rifle and shooting with a shotgun.

WEAVER: Be careful. He's from California.

ELLISON: All right, I'll be careful . . . Intellectually, we cannot spend too much time concentrating on small targets. In our situation we must shoot with a shotgun, not with a rifle. Our targets are many and are scattered and we must make a variety of ideas available as quickly as possible—and here's where the conflict between matters of tactics and the necessity to work out a conscious philosophy arises. I am absolutely with those who feel that this is not the occasion for working out a strategy because I feel that we should first discuss why our kids are as they are and why we are in our present predicament. What did we do wrong? What did we do right? And let us set about making the materials of our experience and our thought available to the young. Far too much of Negro American experience is intellectually uncodified and unwritten and we all would benefit if a start were made in that direction. I would like to have such materials for my own instruction . . . I met Ken years ago and from a certain distance I've watched him develop, but I want to know what he makes of it philosophically. Obviously, Ken, you've found a place in the society and I don't mean in some mystical "Establishment," but a place where you can use your talents and mind creatively. But what are the moves in the game, the difficulties, the dangers, the satisfactions, the strains upon integrity? Black boxers and baseball players, football players and even waiters, pass their experience along. Most of you are, as far as our group is concerned, involved in pioneering activities. You are familiar with territory that was once forbidden. You've plunged through the stage sets of racism and encountered a measure of the complex reality which lies on the other side and it is you who are in the position, perhaps better than

91. Amiri Baraka (1934–), born LeRoi Jones, is a writer and political activist who wrote several violent, hard-hitting plays about racism in the 1960s that were performed Off-Broadway, such as *Dutchman* in 1964. For a brief discussion and analysis of Baraka and his importance, see my introduction.

most Americans, black or white, to pass on whether it is more valid to regard the American promise with an attitude of hope, faith and skepticism or whether to pronounce it unworkable and a fraud. I think that this is something of what the kids are demanding of us by their actions and by their stance of disenchantment. They are demanding this type of knowledge and they're not getting it, perhaps because it requires the most broadly critical and informed assessment of American society and its processes—and this is far beyond the narrow categories of race and civil rights. And so the kids are suffering from ignorance far more than from their all too fashionable stance of alienation. But we must remember that they are kids and that kids try to protect themselves from the unknown and from the pain of groundless hopes. And since ours are not only black kids but *American* kids we can expect them to try to put us on the defensive with charges of being brainwashed and with epithets of Uncle Tom and so on. They're testing to discover what is real and what is illusory. They're going to put you on and put you off, but if you believe, as I believe—and here is my testimony of faith in their basic sincerity—I believe that behind their masks and costumes and rhetoric the kids are in a state of profound despair and uncertainty. And I believe that this state has arisen, paradoxically, from a broadening of opportunity for Negro Americans. A hundred years of negative supports, guides to conduct and expectation have begun to crumble and the new opportunities reveal themselves as ambivalent. The kids are faced with the opportunity and necessity for competing for prizes which were seldom available to black Americans before, but we failed to prepare them adequately for the psychological stresses of competition. Many are kids out of strong backgrounds but because of the loss of a crucial continuity between their generation and ours they appear to be more victimized by racism than we ever were. For in spite of the reality of discrimination and the climate of contempt in which we grew up, our parents and grandparents and teachers inspired us and instilled a faith in our powers to define ourselves. They believed that we could find paths through a difficult, complex, and often malicious social reality.

But some of the kids appear to accept white racist definitions of Negro American life style and values as possessing an underlying reality and they betray that acceptance by the passion with which they scream "No" to racist accusations. Many look upon their parents with contempt and they reject their human complexity for an oversimplified pseudo-identity based upon a mystique of blackness. That is why I say, don't tell them that they have to have "black" pride, for to do so is to reaffirm the white racist charge that Negroes/Blacks *have* no pride. Being human they have pride and by exhorting them to some abstract pride only confuses them and gives them an excuse to goof off from the difficult but necessary task of basing their pride upon concrete accomplishments. They can call themselves what they will—Afros, Blacks or Martians—but if they are to compete they must compete as individuals and that's where the anguish and the loneliness of the human condition comes in. I doubt that the neo-tribalism which some of the kids are asserting offers any antidote for the agony of being some of the most complex of Americans. False pride certainly won't help them either.

WEAVER: Well, Ralph, I want to interrupt you because I think what you say, by and large, is true. But there's another situation that we are all facing and I think we ought to be honest about it, is that these are kids that have all these problems; they're also kids that are being manipulated like hell.

ELLISON: Yes.

WEAVER: We have kids in every one of the city colleges who have a diversity of points of views and I believe that they're being intimidated to take a particular point of view and I think if we don't face up to that—at least to the degree of ascertaining the facts—we're just being dishonest.

K. CLARK: We haven't any hard evidence. I remember when we were over there we were talking about cynicism and Ralph used the term sinister. We have no hard evidence of the role of the far right in supporting . . .

WEAVER: Or the far left.

But I was referring earlier not only to outside manipulation but manipulation and intimidation by segments of the black community.

HASTIE: Nothing could be more sensational or cause more attention than a documented story of the extent to which black separatism is being the dupe and tool of the extreme reactionary forces in the country. That would be tremendously sensational. It would arrest attention and it would be talked about widely by the young and old and cause a lot of attention.

I remember the American Bar Association meeting two years ago when there was a session—the room was full of people, standees—talking about legal problems for civil rights and a visiting lawyer from the Union of South Africa got up and said that this whole civil rights program is futile. It's just not achievable in the sort of society, in the biracial society that you have. The only program that will work is one of distinct self governed racial communities, and no black separatist could have more eloquently or clearly stated his program than this man did. So it may well be that one of the things that can be done is public presentation of the relationship, either advertent or inadvertent, between the black separatist programs and the programs of the white racists of various sorts.

WEAVER: This isn't an easy thing. And if you are going to make a commitment to it, you've got to make a commitment to the fact that you're going to be harassed and possibly endangered.

I think that there's one thing that we might agree to and I'm almost sure that I'm not wrong on this, but maybe—there should be a journal; the journal should have a very good group of editors and a remarkable editor. God knows who it would be. But after all, it happened the first time. Maybe it would be the second time—that he would appear.

But seriously, I'm saying that I think we need a journal where we get the whole spectrum. The reason I say this is many black students don't read extensively—as a matter of fact, they don't read much of anything, but if they can have their piece in there and a piece from John Hope Franklin and St. Clair Drake . . .

DRAKE: And the head of the Black Panthers . . .

WEAVER: And edited—it's going to have to be edited by a black man—a tough black man . . .

ELLISON: A very black Negro, if you will.

HILL: Well, I don't need one more journal. I'm sorry. I don't mean to disagree with you because I love you, but I think we ought to read the journals we've got. And I . . .

LEWIS: We don't got them.

HILL: Wait a minute. We've all lived long enough to see a number of journals go up and down in the larger society. Now it's the *New Yorker,* now it's *Commentary,* now it's the *Atlantic Monthly*—up and down they go. And we've got two or three journals out there now . . .

WEAVER: What are they?

ELLISON: Name them.

HILL: I'm going to name them. We have *Phylon.*[92] We have the Journal—okay, I don't . . .

K. CLARK: *Negro Digest.*[93]

HILL: —the *Journal of Negro History,*[94] and oddly, this is an old line with me. I just feel that it's so much easier to say you're going to start something else rather than it is to take what you've got and jazz it up a bit.

K. CLARK: We've apparently got to that point where everybody is talking at once, but before we get to that point—I'm sure we will and we ought to, in the informal after . . .

We have said this evening more clearly than we said earlier that the situation is grave. We tried to spell out some of the dimensions of the gravity of it and some of it we mentioned and pulled away from. We said also more clearly than we said before that our kids, our Negro students in colleges, no matter what their style, you know, no matter how they tried to obscure it—and the word despair was used, but they are in desperate straits. They're going to try to bluff it through if they can and from what I heard in a variety of statements, they needed help and we sort of stressed that their state of desperation was not isolated, but reflected larger problems. Some of us said that we could help them only to the extent that we try to help in the larger value and state of health of the society and the academic community. Some of us felt that we ought to try to help them as directly and specifically as possible. Aside from differences as to how to help, there were certainly no differences on the need to help.

Then Carl moved in and said, look, here are some of the possible ways of helping these kids and one way he automatically ruled out. He felt that it would not help them for us to come out with another con-

92. Established in 1940, *Phylon* was a journal committed to academic and social issues in relation to African Americans. In the middle of the twentieth century, *Phylon* was considered one of the most respected literary journals for black intellectuals and academics.

93. Established in 1942, the *Negro Digest* was an African American journal that sought to make vital social and political issues accessible to a wide audience. It was basically a black version of the *Reader's Digest.*

94. Founded in 1916, the *Journal of Negro History* was an academic journal committed to a scholarly and accurate representation of African American life and culture.

sensus statement in which we assert that we are against black separatism and that we assert that we are against their tactics because this has been tried and has led only to blockage in communication. It has fed into their paranoid reaction against anyone whom they think made it.

He suggested as a second possible way of helping that we find some way of periodic communication.

HOLMAN: You should have been in the State Department.

K. CLARK: And certainly Ralph zeroed in on that, even before it was specific by saying that part of their desperation is a void, you know, that there are substantive things about being a Negro in America which somehow or the other, we have defaulted in not communicating to these kids. As a result, others with simplistic, dogmatic things have moved into this void and here we are silent. And we agreed that we're going to look at this. We're going to look at how does one—the only question I have in my mind about this is that this clearly is a long range sort of thing, see. This does not meet the immediate desperation and its manifestations of the kids. And I for one don't know whether the gravity of the present crisis might not be such that it's an intellectual's optimism to think he has only long range roles.

FRANKLIN: I am informed that there will be this summer a concentrated effort on the part of certain groups to organize for the fall disruptive activities among dissident students and that blacks—the black students will be expected to be the focus of this business. My own personal feeling is that there ain't a hell of a lot of time and I don't know what—in the little time that's left, I don't know what we can do. I don't think that—certainly you can't get up a journal in the time we've got, but I do think that something—if this group is to play the role which I think it is probably smart enough to play and strategically placed enough to play, if it's going to play that role, it ought to start playing that role as soon as it can.

WILLIAMS: I saw Dr. Clark less pessimistic than some people about the possible liaison between the black students and SDS. I think SDS might make a pitch as they already have, but I just don't see it.

K. CLARK: You think the black students will resist this?

WILLIAMS: I think they will resist it. The point I really wanted to make was an addendum to something that Kenneth said about all that had been said here. And I think there is something else that has been said, although we have not been articulating it in so many ways.

One thing is I think there's a great assumption that this group has something to communicate to young people. I think your interests die aborning if you don't also assume that they've got something to communicate to you, and therefore, it's a two-way communication. And saying that, it leads me to the point that I had hoped to make earlier, hoping that playing the role of the devil's advocate to some extent—I know it's rather late to do that, but it seems to me that what really has to be done is to try to reestablish some form of communication of identification with young people. At lunch, Ralph raised a series of questions which may have seemed academic and somewhat rhetorical. Where did everybody come from—and we all know the answers. We've identified a lot of black folk heroes around. Now, what impresses me about all of this is that they all came out of black socio-economic and cultural environments. Are we not saying that we may be far closer to the students than we realize in terms of separatism? Now, it's a matter of degree and impetus and definition. And perhaps they go overboard, and I agree that they do. I don't agree with the extremist definitions that they put on separatism. But at the same time, I hear things spoken here that say something good has come out of this in terms of literature, in terms of music, in terms of ideas, in terms of creativity. And then we . . .

FRANKLIN: And in terms of opposition.

K. CLARK: Right. In terms of opposition—opposition to separatism and the rejection of separatism . . .

WILLIAMS: Yes. But see, Ken, I argue that. You cannot say that this was good for you and therefore it is not good for others. You may disagree on what separatism is. I think separatism is one of these vague terms like propaganda . . .

DRAKE: No. Not in the students' definition.

WILLIAMS: I don't assume that the students know what they are defining. And I go back—that this group has far more experience, much more maturity, can help them to define and articulate whatever it is that is bothering them when they talk in terms of separatism. You have implied a certain form of separatism. You came out of a separatist environment and you say that spawned something good.

K. CLARK: Excuse me one moment. Tomorrow we would like to start at 9:30 in order to be able to wind up by 12:30 the latest.

I would like to ask each of us between now and the time we start tomorrow to try to think of answers to the basic question of what do we do or what can we do as a group in terms of what we consider the most important aspect of this problem.

| END OF SESSION

Saturday Morning Session MAY 31, 1969

K. CLARK: Each person take a few minutes to state what he feels to be the major direction that we should take and why; and then we will come back and see if we can put them together in a collective plan of action.

Ralph, do you want to start and tell us what you think?

ELLISON: Kenneth, I think I talked so much that you should start with someone else.

K. CLARK: Do you want me to start with the ladies? All right. Phyllis, how would you summarize in terms of suggestions, next steps, our discussions?

WALLACE: Well, I felt that the suggestion I made earlier this morning that some time soon—within the next two weeks, all of the participants here write in two or three pages your views, thoughts, comments, recommendations and suggestions and that these then would be submitted to Dr. Clark and from that, we would get, I think, an overview of how the group felt and perhaps come up with general recommendations for action. We've had this exchange of ideas. I think each one needs to go back and think about it briefly and put something down on paper. That would be my first suggestion.

In many ways, I'm not on the firing line and I'm not presently at a university. However, I think that last night the urgency of the problem was stated and restated; and I do think that a priority would be what to do in the short run, and that would be what kinds of programs could we put together for the fall and winter school year. Now, I'd like to just ask a question. To what extent do you have some young people who are in the colleges who are not so militant, who could be saved, whom you could work with? Could you identify these youngsters who are more or less what we were like when we were in college? Identify them as a group—maybe five here, ten there, and then begin the process of talking to them because they will have to be the agents, they will have to be the ones who will really communicate with the more militant kids. So that it would seem to me you need a mechanism of communication from this group to the youngsters, because you do have the generational gap. If we think of what could be done with them, that would be a short range program.

On the other hand, I also believe that it's very important to try to communicate with whites, the administrators, social scientists, people who are concerned because they need to know that you have a group of what I would call black social scientists who are concerned and who are willing to do something as a group, because I think that individually, all of us work with people in our professions, we participate actively in the meetings, we exchange ideas with white social scientists. But I think that we need the kind of group action so that I would suggest for the short run perhaps what was suggested yesterday, a kind of Madison Avenue approach to the problem and then go on for the long range kind of emphasis on intellectual persuasion. How do you see people in the short run and pull them from one side of the street to the other side of the street.

K. CLARK: Mame.

M. CLARK: Well, I would still like to work on a little problem that I was trying to pose yesterday and that is some kind of dramatic confrontation of these militant students. And I don't know what form yet, but I like Phyllis's notion to go back and think about it and write it down, because I think you've got to have something which is dramatic and something which is public, actually, and use something which sets these kids back on their ears.

K. CLARK: You mean take the initiative, that we . . .

M. CLARK: Yes, and it has to be timed very well.

I also think there are two other paths we could take. First of all, I believe that the public statement is important. I know that Roy Wilkins has made one. Bayard has made one. You have made one. But it seems to me that everyone has to make one now because it has to be individual voices, you know, and these have to be timed perfectly so that they don't all come at one time, but they build up and make a kind of snowball in terms of public statements against separatism and in support of the group that Phyllis was talking about—the student who wants to learn.

I think there's another thing that members of this group can do, and that is lend support to the other members when they do get out there on limbs. How this can happen will depend on each person's individual style as to how he would support another individual who is out there in the street, so to speak, either making a statement or whatever.

Beyond this, I don't know what I have to contribute at this time.

K. CLARK: Adelaide?

HILL: Well, I agree with what has been said. I think I would emphasize the problem about black studies. I think that's because where I sit as opposed to the other possibilities. As I said yesterday, I'm really not awfully exercised about the separatism-nonseparatism, although I realize it's a part of the environment in which we're functioning. But I have a feeling that if you have a statement of principle, a statement of concept, about how black scholars who think of themselves as being scholars have been so regarded for a little while do in fact view this particular development. And so this is going to be a very crucial summer. The scholars like Vincent Harding[95]—and there are many others whom I don't even know—are busy hammering out manifestos or statements of philosophy; it would be dereliction on our part, as a group of scholars, not to deal with this thing, because somebody is going to—defined in some way and all these various institutions are going to react to it. I think that this in itself will help define that invisible student because I do believe—I agree with Phyllis and Mamie on this—that that student needs help. We need help. But I think the help can best be given myself around a statement of how we would regard the legitimacy of black studies. And we haven't really discussed that particularly—we talked around that, but I would say that if we wanted to write to you, it would be helpful to have at least a statement from each of us on that and to be compiled and then however it's projected, it would be all right. If it's in a joint article, whether it's in a letter to the *Times* or whether some other way, but I think it's got to have the instrument.

K. CLARK: Bill.

HASTIE: I've been thinking about the ways of effectively communicating with our people, whether it be about separatism overall or the evolving black studies programs or what. In addition to the ways that have already been mentioned, with the increasing demand both of the college authorities and of the black students all over the country for

95. Born in 1931, Vincent Harding was a civil rights activist who served as chairman of the Department of History and Sociology at Spelman College, director of the Martin Luther King Memorial Center, and director of the Institute of the Black World. He is best known for his work with and writings about Martin Luther King Jr.

blacks to come to the campus and lecture or lead discussions and so on, it seems to me that it might be worthwhile to mobilize or identify a rather substantial cadre of individuals, such as the individuals in this room, who could be identified—I'm not sure just how or who would do the identifying to university people—to the black students, as people with professional standing, with knowledge and interest in the problems of black students, who are willing and eager, time and circumstances permitting, to come and talk, provided those people have had the opportunity; we've all organized our thinking to some extent and I think all of us are aided in our thinking by this. But what comes out of this may be something that will also help to organize and direct the thinking of such a cadre of individuals who would fan out as requested into the college environment to talk to administrators, and faculty and students.

I think too that our college presidents and administrators—these policy making people, have both formal and informal groups and gatherings and I suspect that most of them would be rather eager—and startlingly—to have responsible black scholars to come and talk with them. Not exactly the way we're talking, but to give them the gospel according to our version anyhow.

I think those are methods of communication that probably could be developed between now and the fall. I also think—Adelaide said this—that more and more individuals who have access to the journals and publications must follow up so that the two or three things that have already been written in the last few months of the last year are supplemented by others which obviously would not be just repetition. Someone said yesterday—St. Clair, I think it was you—that it's important to describe and point out how the students got this way; and I suppose the understanding of how they got this way is a necessary base on which to build any argument that the way they're going is a misguided way.

Those are the only new things—things that haven't been discussed so far that I wanted to throw in the pot. I would say, just because a couple of people have used it today and also yesterday—I for one, in our thinking and acting, don't like it—directing our focus on militant students because that gets into—that suggests a critique of particular tactics rather than a . . .

K. CLARK: Principle . . .

HASTIE: —principle and direction of effort. I might regret some of the tactics that students use in working toward goals that I entirely approve of, but I would think that we dilute and weaken our effort if we combine our criticism of tactics—we got into a criticism of tactics—as distinguished from describing the philosophy and direction of struggle in the goals to be achieved. So at that point, I pass the ball to John.

K. CLARK: For those of you who just joined us, we are going around getting from each person his ideas on what we—where do we go next, some specific suggestions.

John Hope.

FRANKLIN: I think that you've probably both read that—those suggestions. I think those of us who are here read it through the next week or two, kind of make a clearer statement of a couple of pages on what we think about these problems and send them to Ken as a clearing house and maybe out of that will come some . . .

I think one of the things we ought to bear in mind is that we come here out of a wealth of experiences and activities, some of which are directly relevant to our discussions here and some of which are not. We deal with that student or this student in various ways.

I think that what we ought to focus on here is how we as a group of responsible thinkers in this area can contribute to clearing the air, keeping it clean and keeping as much in focus as possible. This has to do not so much with a criticism of tactics as it does with trying to provide a solid base for any kind of approach which of course means that we ought to be concerned very much with the building up of a body of myths and of lore that have little or no relationship with the truth. If we insist on all of us looking at the problem not through the eyes of those who might be wedded to witchcraft or lore or voodoo or something, then I think we have the responsibility of making certain that people are telling the truth. This is what I was suggesting yesterday when I spoke of the myths and which are a part of the new ideology. This is the bond of the new kind of racism that's springing up from my point of view, it's as bad as any other kind of racism.

And the thing that really disturbs me about the movement that is going on is that it does have these attributes of racism where Negroes now feel, some of them, that they have special qualities, special talents . . .

REDDING: Genetic endowment.

FRANKLIN: Special endowments, even perhaps superior endowments. Now, I don't believe that it's any better for them to have it than it was for the white racists who advocated it, and I think we need to say something about the new racism that is—I think can have no long range permanent good. People suggest that, well, you've got to instill pride and the rest of it. If there is no other basis for pride than a bunch of lies and a bunch of misrepresentations, then I'm not certain that pride itself has any virtue—it might, but then it could have another basis than that. And the terrible thing about it is that you see it at every level. I can understand how it can exist and flourish in some quarters. I cannot understand how among college and university students it can have any real validity or any real value. If that's what they're engaged in, then this is not the business of education anyway. We ought to say something about that. We ought to try to keep that before our young people.

And the other thing which I think someone has—maybe one or two have already mentioned, that is, that if our goals are sound, we ought to commend these goals to everyone including these college administrators who don't seem to have any set goals or they operate on the basis of expediency. They are diluting their own educational programs. They are bypassing certain principles of education which in no other case, in no instances would they bypass—at least, they haven't up to now. And so they're treating this as something special, a kind of aberration, a kind of temporary situation and I don't believe they should be permitted to do this. And this has to do, Adelaide, with the whole notion of what black studies is all about and if it has—I'm not here going to discuss or debate it—but if it has intellectual and educational integrity it must have it in terms of the total educational enterprise. And that can be argued, but this thing has gotten out of hand. If you look at some of these curriculums for black studies, you will see that it's just a lot of . . .

K. CLARK: Full of mockery.

FRANKLIN: Yes, and with all due respect to you and Mamie, you know, they're advocating—there are courses being introduced now called the psychology of black sports which is a case in point.

REDDING: Really?

HOLMAN: John Hope, you must be kidding. The psychology—what is it—the psychology of black sports?

FRANKLIN: One of the leading—I mean, this is at a leading university. I'm not talking about some place you never heard of. I'm talking about in a leading university.

HOLMAN: They're not using this in the old Negro sense of a sport is a guy who hung on the corner . . .

FRANKLIN: I haven't seen a description of the course, so I couldn't . . .

Who's going to tell these universities that this is a lot of foolishness? I refuse to be a party to this kind of thing and I think the sooner somebody says to the university dean or president or whatever it is that, you know, this has no validity, the better. I think along the same line, very frankly, that we ought not to permit this sort of thing to be spread and it certainly is incipient now and is being bandied about that this whole field has some mystique, this whole black can be a part of, you know.

Now, I would argue this—of course, I won't insist on it. I would argue that, you know, there's nothing special about a black teacher; there's nothing special about a black student. Surely, we can—I hope we can all agree on the fact that if there is a body of knowledge to be acquired that any student ought to be competent to acquire it. Otherwise we—it seems to me, we are saying that give Negroes an opportunity to become educated in all these spheres, but at the same time we're saying that only Negroes should be educated about black studies which is, you know—this is intellectually unsound in principle.

K. CLARK: Or this is the only education that's relevant for them.

FRANKLIN: Yes. Well, literally though, if we keep on with this and you know, everybody's got to be educated in something relevant in the black community which means, you know, history and sociology and psychology. Then I don't know who's going to feed them or who's going to take care of them medically and all the rest of it. And this is what I think we have to guard against too. If there is a viable area of intellectual academic knowledge, it's like all the rest of them, namely that some of—everybody doesn't go into it; that people who have special interests go into it and let it go at that.

Over the long run, I think that we ought to develop some systematic form of communication with the larger community. I'm not prepared to say there ought to be a journal that comes out monthly or quarterly or what have you; but I do think that there ought to be some form of systematic and regular communication. And this is—this should be a communication that holds true to the matter of what is valid and what is truth. Here maybe it can be a debating society that can do it; but if it's a debate, it has to do not with myth making but with truth telling.

Finally, I think that as we have things to say on this, I think we ought to search out as quickly as possible the ways in which we can say them. Now, I've been making talks around the country this spring called The Future of Afro-American History,[96] at which I've tried to do several things including pointing out that, you know, we had a little history before 1960. And which also addresses itself to the function of history generally and what role this ought to play. It's going to be published by the New School and I understand it's going to get wide circulation. I think there are others of us who have made statements and we ought to try to get them known, ought to publicize them or see to it that if somebody's going to tape it and publish it, we ought to tell them where to send it and that sort of thing. This is a sort of a short cut to the—in anticipation of some regular way of communicating with—if we've said anything—got anything to say within the next few weeks, I think we ought to try to be certain that as many people get a chance to see it as possible. It's very interesting, on this point which we've been talking about, whether students will listen or not listen. I gave this talk at Harvard and the New School and the University of Cincinnati and Irvine, California. And I must say it was well received in all quarters and by most of the Negro students if their response is an indication.

Well, I might have something to say later.

K. CLARK: Ralph.

M. CLARK: Kenneth, may I clarify something before you go ahead?

When I was talking about the concept of dramatic confrontation, it wasn't in any sense a criticism of the tactics of the students. But, for example, if we could have a compilation of the tell the truth statements which John Hope Franklin is talking about and present that in a dramatic fashion so that it reached a nationwide audience, this, to me, would be a dramatic confrontation.

K. CLARK: And certainly the television media seems to have been preempted by the myth makers, for the most part, and we have not exploited that as systematically and effectively as we should.

HASTIE: This is—may I say this has more immediate possibilities in effective communication than anything that's been said so far because

96. This lecture was published as "The Future of Negro American History," *The University of Chicago Magazine* 63 (February/March 1970): 15–21.

they're looking for programs in this area and there's no reason this couldn't be a weekly or twice monthly half hour and once it becomes dramatic and—in saying things that stir people up and irritate people, I can see that it could build up a real audience.

ELLISON: Well, I'm really just speaking to ideas which have been expressed. It's my experience that you do have kids on those campuses who need support, who are alert and who are not accepting the cliches which have become the going thing now. But they are badly educated and are being educated by badly educated teachers in great institutions. We must recognize that it is a fact that in many areas our educators are badly educated because the racist thing which has existed in the society has blocked off reality; it's blocked off a sense of history; it's played all kinds of hell with the brightest of people. Now, this is basic. This is Harvard, this is Yale, this is Columbia, this is everywhere. These kids, our kids, are coming up against militants. They're being intimidated and being kids, they don't like to stand alone. I guess we're all like that at some point of our lives. So they need other energies, they need reality projected for them. And we're the people who can do it. This is our obligation. We must not only tell the truth, but recognize that so much of what we operate out of, our basic assumptions about what this experience has been, we don't project. We don't write it down. We don't write it down—we have the experiences behind us. We have some sense of what our people have projected as value and have acted on all these years. Now it has to be spelled out. These things must be made manifest to the kids because we have created a vacuum and all this junk is in there. That's enough of that.

The other thing is about continuing some sort of discussion group. I think that a journal is necessary, of some kind. I won't insist upon how it's gotten together, but we need an organ; we need an organ so that we can really put guys like Vincent Harding and Ron Karenga—who's making a lot of noise about aesthetics[97] and other things which I don't know that any of us gripes about—we've got to put them in a perspective. We've got to have them where we can see what's going on because the kids are grabbing it. They're grabbing it and they're using it as an

97. This is most likely a reference to Karenga's "Black Cultural Nationalism," *Negro Digest*, January 1968, 5–9, which was reprinted in Gayle's *The Black Aesthetic*, 32–38.

excuse for not doing their homework. They're shucking. There's a lot of that going on, and I find the idea that anything they're not interested in is irrelevant disgusting. I've had kids denounce me for advising them to read Dostoevski on the ground that he had nothing to do with black experience![98] My reply was that they should read him before they pronounce him irrelevant, because in *The Possessed* he described their predicament long before they were born . . .

Now the other role which this group can perform—and the country is dying for some sort of format—all right, let's call it a "think tank," is to provide a forum through which American problems can be attacked from the perspective of our special group experience. Let's get ourselves a "think tank." Let's project and solve some of the nation's intellectual dilemmas. Let's anticipate crucial developments. Let's originate models which can be studied for solutions to problems which arise in areas which are apparently unrelated to Negro life. Let us do what the NAACP did when it got the civil rights movement on a productive track. Their achievement has always impressed me and I keep waiting for people who were involved to make its implications the conscious possession of any person who wants to learn how the climate of justice was improved in this country. I understand that Charles S. Houston of the Howard Law School had the brilliant idea of training cadres of constitutional lawyers who would make a frontal assault against segregation, and by using the regular device of the mock court in a creative manner they projected imaginatively the fight which later would change the country. They anticipated their opponents' arguments and were prepared for them. They studied the judges and they got the aid of the social sciences in preparing their arguments. I don't know how their projection, their dramatization actually worked in the classrooms but in reality . . .

K. CLARK: Very well.

ELLISON: Well, certainly it changed the face of the country and it gives us a model. Why can't we do this? They did what the think tanks do today. They were using drama, a kind of game theory and the techniques of creating scenarios long before people like Herman Kahn

98. Fyodor Dostoyevsky (1821–1881) was a renowned Russian author. His novella *Notes from Underground* significantly influenced Ellison's *Invisible Man* and Richard Wright's *The Man Who Lived Underground.*

began to make their presence felt.[99] Let's extend it to other areas. As the old saying goes, "We got brains we ain't never used!"

HASTIE: But the militants—the separatists are detractors from that effort—let's put it that way—deny that the face of the country has changed. They say nothing is significantly—no relevant differences exist today from what it did in the 1930's. That's one of the myths that has to be dealt with.

K. CLARK: That's a profoundly dangerous myth, too.

ELLISON: It really is. It boxes everybody in. As I told some critical kids, I said, "Look, you want to penalize me and attack my integrity because a few concerned people made sacrifices for me and inspired me, and because I have tried to do things for myself. Well, if that makes me a fink in your view of things—to hell with you." And as for separatism, I tell them, "Okay, you don't like it but right now I'm not for separatism. I know too much about Boley, Oklahoma and other such efforts to take the idea seriously.[100] But when the day comes that we not only have a black man on the Supreme Court but a black Chief Justice, and when there is a black Chief of State, a black head of the Securities Exchange Commission, a black Attorney General and a black President—*then* if you want to separate I might go along with you. Because by then we will have people in the group who will know how to govern a modern state. As of now the people who yell for separatism don't possess that kind of knowledge—and you're telling me that you don't have to learn."

Well, this is foolishness and the kids are just dying for someone to come along and say, "Look, this is foolish. You know that this isn't the way it is and you know this isn't the way it's going to go"—but who tells them so? Very few of us tell them. Instead we respond like white folks respond when they see Negroes acting the fool. They're often

99. In 1961 the military strategist Herman Kahn (1922–1983) founded the Hudson Institute, a national security research center. Kahn's research was focused on nuclear weapons and the future, and he wrote several controversial texts on these subjects, such as *On Thermonuclear War* (1961).

100. The town of Boley, Oklahoma, was founded in 1904 as one of several all–African American towns along the Fort Smith and Western Railroad. For a short time, the town was a success. Land was sold at extremely low prices, freed slaves were happy to live without prejudice, and some white Americans were pleased to be free of the "inferior" race. However, Boley's prosperity did not last long. By 1913 surrounding communities had conspired to prevent Boley's citizens from voting, and an African American woman and her son were lynched.

outrageous and they appear to have no relationship to their elders. It's said that they're a new breed.[101] Well, I'll be damned if they're any new breed. They're good American kids who have been led off on a willful break with the continuity of their experience—*even* as they cry out for the restoration of the black past—and they're trying us for all they're worth. They're throwing a tantrum before the complexity of our generation's vision of social reality and tolerating tantrums from our kids is not in the Negro American tradition. So somebody's got to start whipping heads, at least intellectually. We must not discourage their initiative and we must praise their courage, but when they're involved in foolishness it is our duty to tell them so. Now that's enough from me. I do think however that we should have such discussions as this on some sort of permanent basis. It has long been missing.

K. CLARK: Carl.

HOLMAN: Well, having talked enough yesterday, I'm going to try to go quickly through some notes. I'm in agreement with a great deal of what I got here in time to hear. I'd like to suggest that MARC might do some things immediately and that one of the things—you've probably already agreed to do this by the gist of what I heard earlier.

Maybe you have to arrive at a journal by coming at it the way the English did, you know, in the seventeenth century, you begin by doing small pieces. I'm not for the continual pamphleteering approach because I think that that gets you into such a fragmentary way of approaching what you're going to do it becomes sort of counterproductive in the long run.

What I'm thinking about is you ought to begin with this particular conversation and I think the notion of having people write down their afterthoughts and getting them in to you and if you were to publish as number one in this conversation series what came of this meeting, especially when, though you have a general kind of framework of consensus, you give each person a chance to put his own perspective into play there. I think if you'll publish that, the next step which isn't normally taken has to be taken; that is, somebody's got to see to it that in Chicago, that in New York, in Los Angeles—because many of us have contacts that we never use except for other people. But what I'm think-

101. Ellison is probably referring to Peter Labrie's essay "The New Breed," which was first published in the July 1966 issue of the *Negro Digest* (4–14) and then reprinted in Jones and Neal's anthology *Black Fire* (64–77).

ing about is that when this appears, it ought to be talked about; it ought to be written up in whatever happens to be the relevant section of your own local papers. I think that the . . .

K. CLARK: We have the model of the Kerner Commission Report.[102]

HOLMAN: I think you ought to set up some other conversations and one I would suggest that you do—that MARC sponsor two conversations on black studies; that one of these be a discussion in which you bring in administrators—some whites and some blacks—who have been through the mill.

And I think you need to have some black intellectuals there because these people have to be questioned by someone—it isn't a question of whether you can get them on a TV show, it's a question of whether the interviewers are competent to ask the right questions. And so I think that is one.

The second of the black studies conversations, I think you ought to publish that too in the same way, circulate the same way. It ought to be one in which you have students and faculty, a cross section of them. And I think in that case—I think St. Clair would be a very good person for this one because he would be, I think, able to bridge and at the same time probe and question.

WALLACE: Do you think that the—I know that the American Council on Education has a committee.[103] I know a vice president in charge of kind of being concerned about this problem and maybe they might be invited to participate in the first group.

HOLMAN: And then I'd like to return very quickly to the question of the mass media. I think there are some black guys around the country who got into this, you know, in a number of ways. The interesting thing to me, and I was thinking of this when John Hope Franklin was speaking, so much just simply bad black history is now—I'm not

102. To investigate the cause of the race riots of 1967, along with what could be done to prevent future riots, President Lyndon B. Johnson formed the National Advisory Commission on Civil Disorders. This group, often called simply the Kerner Commission after its chairman Otto Kerner, wrote the Kerner Report, released March 1, 1968. The report baldly states that the riots were a response to white racism and prescribes solutions to be implemented at the national level to improve living conditions in the inner cities.

103. The Academic Council on Education is an organization that brings together representatives from all types of U.S. accredited, degree-granting institutions to solve problems in the higher education system.

talking about what we've been discussing. I'm not talking about vicious and deliberate attempts to do a kind of indoctrination. I am talking about the fact that on these black radio stations, it is now the vogue, you see, to have little snippets of black history, you see.

HASTIE: J. A. Rogers.[104]

HOLMAN: First of all, a lot of it is irrelevant and then to complicate it, some of it is wrong. I heard a girl asked a question and they gave an answer, sorry, you were wrong, except she was right and yet, two days later they were still running this. Now, these black stations, as well as the white ones, are important because one of my basic disagreements with some of the young black kids on this is the whole notion that you've got something too good or special to be shared. Now, the white kids, and the popular music lovers listen to these black stations because that's where the message is coming from. And I think somebody needs to start. I'm thinking about somebody just cutting some simple tapes. Suppose you had a Hastie doing a short tape which they can flood throughout those black networks, which really put the whole business of what was done by that group coming out of the Howard Law School in terms of the legal revolution that they thought about. People are hungry for it, but what they're getting now is a smattering and very often a distortion of what's really there.

And then finally, I would say these three things, which are reiterations in part of what you said before. Ultimately, you need a journal, periodical of some kind because there has to be an expression of affirmative concern for the goals and issues that nonacademic blacks have and what I always object to is the notion again that the field is preempted. That nobody was concerned about poor people; nobody was concerned about the problems of blacks until whoever is currently featured on TV discovered it.

I think this very badly needs to be looked at. And once again, in every area of serious concern whether it is welfare and how that income security system is going to turn around, whatever it happens to be there should be the broadest range of involvement. These issues should not be either the exclusive domain of recently arrived white experts, or of the propagandists of the black left or the white left. And we've focused

104. Joel Augustus Rogers (1880–1966), Jamaican born and largely self-taught, was a journalist, author, and historian of race vindicationism. His writings, such as *From "Superman" to Man* (1917), strove to expose race as a mere social construct and prove that the supposed "inferiority" of people of African descent was a myth.

on our theme of the retrieval of our diverse history, which I think is something which badly needs to be done. Again a journal is a good continuing way of getting it done. And it also means people can go back to it and take it off the shelf. If we want these kids to have things that they can refer to and go back to, you have to have something which comes out in series.

Finally, I think some of us can begin to focus the use of the talents we have in the black community on a certain kind of investigative current research. I'll just take one example and then I'm through.

Phyllis and some of the other responsible black economists need to look at some of the schemes and proposals now being floated as a new kind of black entrepreneurship before once more people are disappointed and become alienated and further embittered. That kind of investigative research on current myths that are being perpetrated—this isn't being done and I think it ought to be done.

K. CLARK: Saunders.

REDDING: I simply want to endorse two of the proposals, two of the ideas that I've heard set forth. One is a continuation or—yes, a continuation with modifications, of course, of what has been described as a think tank.

And the other is the journal idea. I too feel that a journal is necessary, is needed and I think that it is—that this journal would reach a much larger audience than probably we envision. I base that on the fact that within the last four months, I have had—I myself, if you'll pardon the personal reference—have had to turn down roughly seven invitations to write on the black studies thing from journals of various kinds and various degrees of quality. So that there is an audience, and of course, we need to get that audience. I mean, you know, there—it's no good to be talking to ourselves. We've got to talk to everybody. We've got to talk to the whole community and unless we do that, there's no point in talking—because it is that other community or the large surrounding community that can refuse to do anything about the present situation, except what they're doing now and I think that this would be bad.

Well, that's all, this is . . .

K. CLARK: Okay. St. Clair.

DRAKE: We've had a wealth of not only very good suggestions, but suggestions that are also feasible and this always becomes important, you know—to define things that can be carried out. But anyhow, I just wanted to comment for a few minutes on my own general reaction to our conference. I think when I came yesterday, my first impulse was to think about how wide the gulf was between our group and a group I had just been with Wednesday night. Charles Hamilton and I are leaving Roosevelt University. I'm going to Stanford and Charles is going to Columbia. Now, the Black Students Association at Roosevelt has found us very difficult to deal with. Their general position has been one of having nothing much to do with either of us, with Hamilton being defined as "the guy who wrote the book with Stokely and then went over to The Establishment" and I being defined as "the black man with the white wife"; and so, you see, there's a problem for them: "How do you cope with these two persons?" Well, there was a great deal of ambivalence about us. But on the other hand, black professors in the so-called white institutions are also visualized as symbols who represent the black world, too. And so, you have a sort of code on this. Some of the kids told me privately, "We never attack you two when white people are around. If there's a public meeting where we think we're going to get in a fight with you, we convene a business meeting at that time so we won't be there."

Well, anyhow, now that we were both leaving I was very surprised Monday when a member of the Black Studies Association said he wanted me to come to a "rapping" session and to drink beer as a goodbye last Wednesday night. I went and stayed up nearly all night with about 40 or so black students from Roosevelt and some other Chicago colleges, and various other types who were sort of streaming through to pay their "last respects" to the black professor.

The whole meeting was so different from this. There we were sitting on the floor, "rapping"—a very wide variety of people, very, very different from us here today. The whole style was different. But as our sessions here have moved on, I suddenly realized that the gulf wasn't as wide as I thought at first. As I think back over this little "rapping" session as they called it—and those who weren't interested in anything serious went off in a couple of rooms by themselves and "rapped" some other way—the group that was serious sat around on the floor with people coming in and out, and most of that evening turned out to be an expression of thought around very serious questions, which I think gives a point of contact with us. A militant Chicago policeman broke open the question of "What kind of education you cats ought to be getting in college." And then the talk began to revolve around whether they ought to be taking things like engineering, medicine and other such things or ought to be taking straight black studies. There was quite a bit of diversity of opinion on this. But a dialogue was going on in that group! There weren't any other professors there, but they were very serious about this issue, with a split in opinion. The policeman, incidentally, stated that he thought the main thing black people need is the equivalent of a "think tank." You see, as a policeman, he said, "I know what *they're* doing. I know what *they're* thinking and some of you cats are talking instrumentally all the time. Sure, get your medicine and so forth and so on, but you've also got to have some people who *think.*" Then he started off talking about the older generation and began bringing up scholars from the past. He said, "At least they used their brains; I don't have any, but at least they used their brains."

What I'm trying to point out is that I was very surprised that in this session there was dialogue going on inside these circles. And in two or three other black student groups I've popped into recently, I felt this was true. So I think there's a basis within black student groups themselves for dialogue and that one of the problems for us is that of feeding the ammunition into circles like these so that people are strengthened who share our side of the dialogue when it goes on. There are these splits—that's the point. You get a range from the "true believers"—and I'm just noting down what we really have to cope with—at one end, the Republic of New Africa[105] and RAM,[106] the Panthers, and US—which are cults really, and sometimes cults of violence, who are in this exercise trying to win peoples' minds, as well as the spectrum of opinion that shades off from them. Now, ultimately, I suspect that all of these "cult" groups are ultimately police problems, but we don't want to get into that question.

105. At a conference on March 31, 1968, led by the brothers Milton and Richard Henry, militant black nationalists named and elected a government for the Republic of New Africa: a black nation inside the United States comprising land from Louisiana, Mississippi, Alabama, Georgia, and South Carolina. The RNA's goals included eliminating racial oppression, attaining reparation payments in both land and money from the U.S. government, and giving its citizens up-to-date medical care and education.

106. RAM stands for the Revolutionary Action Movement, and Robin D. G. Kelley argues that this "small group of black radical intellectuals and activists" could be "called the first black Maoist-influenced organization in history." The group formed in the spring of 1962, and its primary leaders were Donald Freeman, Max Stanford, and Wanda Marshall. See Kelley, "Stormy Weather: Reconstructing Black (Inter)Nationalism in the Cold War Era," in Glaude, *Is It Nation Time?*, 72, 73.

Ultimately, these groups are probably going to be "taken care of"—won't be there to debate. Somebody mentioned that they wouldn't be there probably because they'd kill each other off. But also there is a perspective that they won't be there to debate because they may get picked up and "put away," you know, by the larger society within the next few years. We shall have to take our individual stands one way or another if that happens—and I, personally, am against such repression. But, in the meanwhile, other groups along the continuum are active, too.

I think what we need to worry about, or think about, is how the dialogue that's already going on can be sustained. I don't like to see this in terms either of "saving" the kids from something or an attack on militancy. Rather I see it in terms of giving people a range of opinions—a range of material that they can use as their own dialogue goes on; and secondly, a point that hasn't been mentioned up to now; of how we do this; how you strengthen those students who don't want to be pulled into a totalitarian straightjacket. I think that really is the problem that came up last night, that there are an awful lot of youngsters who just want to get on with their work or want to be free to move ideologically in their own way without intimidation.

Let me quickly finish what I have to say. What I really was going to say at the outset was that I think fundamentally . . .

FRANKLIN: St. Clair, I just want to interrupt. You were saying that the dialogue would at least help to save these kids.

DRAKE: No. I don't like to use the term "save."

FRANKLIN: Well, then you said—you mentioned totalitarian straightjacket, I understand that you . . .

DRAKE: Did I use the term "save" for them?

FRANKLIN: No. No.

DRAKE: The question which we want to discuss is "How do you deal with that silent majority which is under great pressure," and maybe somebody else ought to talk about that a little bit, but I think that that is an important problem, on how you strengthen them.

Well, what I was going to say was that this summer is coming up. School is out and we've talked a bit about ways of getting through to these young people, and most of these suggestions I thought were very good ones. I have thought, also, that there might be some value in trying to get some kind of a formal statement together. If we got these conversations of ours set up and they were printed or mimeographed or xeroxed, and we tried to confront all the black student associations when school opens in the fall with these pieces of material along with a little covering letter saying, "You're getting ready to start your program. This is some thinking that has gone on among black professors that you might want to use in your own meetings during the year." We could tie this in with Bill's suggestion that we've got available a group of speakers who might be able to go out as these associations lay out programs for the year to carry on this dialogue with them, saying, "After you've discussed this in your group, if you feel you want to take issue with some of it or you want to discuss some of it, we can get somebody to come and 'rap' with you." If we could get a backlog of money from somewhere to make it possible for persons to fly to campuses for the weekend and get with the student groups, I think it could be done.

Two black organizations I know have been playing around with the idea of convening a conference of black student leaders. I hope really that it doesn't come off. I think this would be a disaster and fiasco, in a way, to put all those different kinds of black student leaders together and they start fighting each other. I think a much more healthy thing would be this kind of thing where we could confront people on their individual campuses and you'd get some kind of real discussion going.

So this was really the burden of my suggestion—that over the summer, if we could think out a program—and we've mentioned "dramatic confrontation"—of trying to set up a kind of dramatic confrontation with black student groups on their own campuses through the fall as their program develops, it would be a healthy thing.

Now a sideline to that would be the one of dealing with the white administrators, but I look at that as something separate. I do think that given the fact that debate is going on in these student groups—if something prepared by us fell into the hands of students saying that Ken Clark, for instance, was available to come and that this kind of discussion of ours had gone on, that some black students within the black studies associations would take the position that, "Man, we've got to have this meeting and get the cat out here so he can talk to us." Others will be glad to get you because they want to grapple with you intellectually, not because they agree with you.

So that's my only suggestion, that over the summer we can think about combining some of these ideas in terms either of a formal statement or some pamphlet material, and assemble a roster of available speakers and, then, as soon as school opens, to have all the black students associations receive the material. There's a job of getting master lists. I think really we do need this list—master list of the black students associations in the U.S.—who their officers are, etc., as well as a little information we can get fed in from here and there, a kind of "Who stands where?" We need our own "intelligence arm" for this—"Who stands where within specific black studies association groups?"—so we know who our friends are.

I want to point out, too, that something of a little dialogue has been going on in a journal which I think is read within the black community pretty widely, and I think the students are reading it too, *Negro Digest.* You see, Hoyt Fuller is very much interested in these problems.[107] He has his own point of view, but I don't think he bars the pages to others. He wants to sell that magazine. Vince Harding and the fellows at Atlanta have already had their piece, "Toward a Black University" presented.[108] So I would think it might be worth at some point approaching Hoyt Fuller about "Why don't you have an issue of the *Negro Digest* in which the people who don't agree with their general position are given space?"

Another thing that I've been thinking about is that probably we ought to make a clear statement of the kind of goal we're after which I would assume is that *ultimately* we want a single society without racism or any double standards of achievement. Really, this becomes the kind of long term thing we want. And a part of our dialogue might be structured in terms of what are the obstacles to reaching that kind of a goal, and the dangers as far as some of the current things that are going on are concerned, without saying we oppose in a blanket fashion all that the young people are doing. There are dangers as well as possibilities. And if we did that, there are certain areas that I think should be discussed quite specifically. One is black studies programs. There are questions. Should they be interdisciplinary? Should there be separate departments? Can whites teach black history? Should black students be off by themselves in courses? These are questions that in a dialogue can

107. Hoyt Fuller (1923–1981) was from 1961 to 1976 the editor of *Black World* magazine (originally *Negro Digest*), where he dedicated himself to publishing the work of African American writers who he thought deserved attention but were not receiving it from mainstream America. Fuller started his own journal, *First World,* after *Black World* ceased publishing, and taught African American literature at various universities.

108. For a discussion of the black university, see the March 1968 and March 1969 issues of the *Negro Digest.*

be raised with students in terms of "You just ought to be thinking about the problem here of dangers as well as possibilities." Recruitment of students, double admission standards—"Do we really want this?" Separate living facilities, separate recreational facilities, ties and coalitions with non-black groups—these vary from campus to campus—"what is the nature of them?" "What are the problems?" The problem of the new racism, which John Hope Franklin raised—"What things are proper on the campus, and what off?" I think I have students who would concede the point that we ought not to be myth making on the campus, but who would argue that they felt that when they were out on the South Side that they ought to have the leeway to espouse what I call, "Claim The World Negro History," on the grounds that they're inspiring the black kids. They would draw a distinction between history as propaganda and history as scholarly research. I think there is this whole question of whether some things aren't proper on campuses, that's all. Well, I would like to see this broached in terms of the statement of a goal and then the raising of the question—"What are the dangers as well as the possibilities in all the black 'stuff' that's going on on the campus," in relationship to some goal like this.

I'm sure we could get a dialogue going. You'll get fought, of course. There would be some of the Panthers and these other groups I mentioned who will say, "We don't want to discuss that stuff," but you know, they're the minority. I think we've always had this split in opinion where there are blacks, except in a few places. Incidentally, I have a daughter who's at San Francisco State and has been involved in the commotion out there. I'm pretty close to it all.

Okay, that's all I have to say.

K. CLARK: Eddie.

WILLIAMS: I suppose at this point I would like to say that I had something strong to say, but I don't. There were a couple of points that have already been made, Ken, that impressed me. I'd like to take a second or two to reiterate them. I like the idea of a so-called think tank, particularly if it leads to what Mamie referred to as some kind of dramatic confrontation in terms of a statement or a projection of some kind.[109] The idea of a publication also interests me. I'm not sure I

109. In a conversation, Williams told me that Kenneth Clark and the Haverford Group were in part the inspiration for the think tank the Joint Center for Political and Economic Studies. Williams is president emeritus of the center, which he headed from 1972 to 2004.

like all that is implied in the term "journal." I don't think anybody has related to that. Journals tend to be read by the people who write them and not by anyone else.

I think more attention needs to be given to the total medium which is television, because I think this is where we make the greatest impact; its impact is far greater you know, in terms of the immediate situation, than the printed matter can possibly be. And since we're moving toward a listening and viewing public rather than a reading public, I think this is particularly important.

St. Clair made the main point I was going to make, which was to—and I know MARC can do this and is doing it—to try to seek out and support some of the more responsible black student leadership around the country. Give them a platform for articulating their views, take them away from coercive influences, etc. And to some extent, these young people may be in a much better position to capture the imagination of their peers than those who are here and who are sort of, unfortunately, automatically suspect. And I think a lot of interest could be put into this. I will just reiterate the point that I made yesterday. At this particular time, it seems to me that throughout there is a questioning of many firmly held values, not just in terms of black students, but in terms of the white students, and not only in terms of the militants and the radicals. There are serious thinking responsible men who are raising key questions about certain values of American society, particularly certain values held within the academic community. What's of interest to me is that this questioning of values is far more radical, really radical than the questioning made by many students whose protests I consider to be more or less superficial. The demand for open admissions—that doesn't make sense to me. The demand that the University of Chicago move out of Woodlawn—that doesn't make sense to me. I really don't know where I come out personally in terms of compensatory programs. Bring in 500 black students without any reference to qualifications and put them in some kind of program and set up first class degrees and second class degrees? I have a lot of problems with this. This is perhaps a value question. Somebody needs to deal with it. I'm not sure that administrators, particularly on predominantly white campuses where they are feeling this kind of pressure, have any guidelines and they're reacting politically. When the squeak gets bad enough, they're going to put some oil on it. And it seems to me that's not the way to run a railroad, that there ought to be some systematic thinking and planning in this regard. Maybe we need to think about some other form of education, something that goes between a high school and, you know, a first class undergraduate experience. I don't know. It seems to me somebody has to be thinking down the pike in this regard. Where do we want to come out in 1979? I would just hate to see us locked in in a value system now which perhaps ought to be changed and which may very well be changed in time. I don't know what that change would be. But I think this kind of group has to bring to bear the kind of critical examination of where we want to come out with respect to this pluralistic integrated society that we are hoping for. And I think somewhere in here there is perhaps a contribution that young people can make. There's a hell of a lot that they can learn, but I think it also dramatizes to them and lets them know that there are others who are not satisfied, who are concerned with change and improvement, who are not just sitting on their duffs and that we do not, as they accuse us of doing, take the position we have made it in the white world and therefore that we're satisfied with our own comfort and the heck with anyone else.

FRANKLIN: I just want to add, if I may—but Eddie said something which I think is very important. He suggested something, namely, whatever we say and do, it should never be possibly interpreted as any—as giving aid and comfort to the present social and political economic system; and it will add authenticity and validity, and it will commend itself at least to the young people we're trying to reach if it's quite clear—and it ought to be quite clear that this is by no means any kind of endorsement of anything. We have to come down on the evils of our society as hard as they do.

K. CLARK: Hy.

LEWIS: Yes. I think it's been said, but I'd like two things. One, what the group might think about taking *Phylon* over for a special issue and have someone serve as guest editor and bring out the results of this session rather quickly. But I think that we need to move rather quickly to get these things circulated in as many different forms—rather quickly.

DRAKE: You think this might be a medium through which the report, for instance, of this conference might be stated?

LEWIS: Possibly, yes. It's one way of going—to move rather quickly.

HOLMAN: Well, I had petitioned the chairman for an opportunity to say something about timing the report—we were agreed when the wrap-up came . . .

LEWIS: Well, let's come back to that.

HOLMAN: Well, what I was going to say about timing has to do with that. And what I was hopeful of was that you have your speakers who are going to be available and if you had this material and if you're thinking of other things are going to start moving in the fall, that there are presidents, deans and other administrative faculty officials who might want to add as a portion of this college orientation this fall the speaker and the discussion pieces which you have done over the summer. This puts you under great pressure in terms of how fast you produce it.

LEWIS: I would also like to have put into the discussion some of the things that are going on. Other groups are talking in similar fashion and Adelaide, for example, the Black Academy.[110] Are these some things we might share here?

HILL: Well, I wanted to say two kinds of things. One, the Black Academy sort of brings it up. We get hung up, I think, as soon as we decide who we are—that is who is like us. Now, of course, inviting a small group of people here today is good because you can't have but so many people. But after you go beyond that first kind of group to get a definition of where you want to go, you get into pitfalls. And I don't know how one can get over it. I mean, it isn't a problem in all situations. I was thinking about the black power meetings, for example, where everybody was black was welcome and if you're black you can come, it's all right. No problem at all of eligibility. And in the old fashioned pre–Civil War conventions when you were free, you came; when you weren't free, you couldn't make it. Simple as that.

But in all kinds of situations, every time we have a new group, whether it's the Black Academy, or the various other groups that we all know about, there's something about the selectivity that seems to build into it the seeds of its own destruction. And maybe a journal—though I'm not for a journal myself for reasons that I tried to say yesterday—I'm for continued communication, but—maybe a journal would have a functional role and that those who wrote for the journal would meet as a group and those who didn't—who didn't contribute

110. The Black Academy of Arts and Letters, a nonprofit organization dedicated to supporting African Americans gifted in the arts, was founded in 1969 by fifty African American artists and academics, Adelaide M. Cromwell among them. The organization offered scholarships, held banquets and award ceremonies, and ran filmmaking festivals to encourage creativity and celebrate the accomplishments of the African American community.

and didn't try to be heard, wouldn't be identified with the group and it could be self-determined, not exclusive.

But I think I want to be sure that there is some mechanism for determining how we do not *exclude* but *include* the relevant people for there are a lot of black scholars or people who regard themselves as scholars who may find it difficult to communicate with us and we with them. We are talking just as though we are a group over here and out there are only those black students. Out there are a whole lot of other black people our age, a little older and a little younger who have some reputation in various quarters. And I think the question Hylan posed then with us is almost as important as reaching out to the students.

The other thing on which I really wanted to comment was this student business. And this is the kind of example that happened locally that I think is interesting. I know a small girls' college, and I think it's kind of typical for the kind of school this is. They have about ten or fifteen black girls there. And the kids have got the same problems that St. Clair talked about yesterday—not ideological problems, but problems of alienation. So they had a series of speakers and I was one of the speakers. And all the black kids sat together, of course. And then about two weeks later, no, the day that I came to speak, they had presented their petitions to the administration—their "non-negotiable" demands. Two weeks later a delegation from the black students came to see me. They said we wanted a black studies program. They said they had talked with the administration and the administration had said they could go out and get X thousands of dollars to study how it should be done; they would buy it. So they said, "Do you know how we can get this money?" So I looked at them. I said, "You know, the administration doesn't believe that and you shouldn't believe it and that's not the way to get it done." Well, we talked—they were very concerned about that. We talked about it a while. But then I said to them, "Look, don't you think it would be a good idea if we had a conference of groups like yours—if you can get together for me a list—" This is the same thing we're saying on a national level. "You get together for me a list of the black student groups whom you know exist on all of the campuses in your region—I'd like to have a conference with you. You could run it, but I would be the hostess for you." They liked that idea. Now, whether they're going to do anything about it—because that's what generally happens—the kids like the idea, but then someone else has got to do the work. And I think that what I would say in terms of what we talked about now, on the basis of that case history, that before this thing was done nationally, there might be some advantage to doing it regionally.

I would say that students should be reached—they should be reached before fall because this year is going to be a crucial one. But I think it should be done regionally rather than nationally. You could have a national meeting almost any time after three or four regional meetings.

HOLMAN: Well, at first I didn't understand. I didn't know we were talking about meetings . . .

DRAKE: I had projected the meeting idea.

HOLMAN: Yes, because the value of bringing somebody from—I think you have to for a colloquium of the conversational kind we're talking about—bring somebody from the west coast, somebody from a middle west school, but you wouldn't have more than four or five—not as many people or certainly no more than this. You wouldn't try to get, for the purpose of getting viewpoints expressed which you could publish, you wouldn't need, you know, to convene a full conference.

And on the journal, I think that again that the important thing in a magazine would be that it would have to be open to all kinds of . . .

REDDING: I would not conceive of such a journal as being a kind of house organ, as it were. It would be a journal of opinion and opinions of various shades—varying shades, you see.

LEWIS: Can we come again to the point that Carl was mentioning, that is the matter of timing and the different types of communication, different stages. The journal itself is a thing that may take some time to get mounted, but in the meantime, what do we do?

REDDING: Well, I think—Ralph, I don't know whether you would agree with me. I talked to Hiram—or Hiram talked to me last Saturday—Hiram Hayden.[111] But I'm almost certain that *The American Scholar,* for instance, would love to get a summary of this conversation.[112] And as a matter of fact . . .

111. Hiram Haydn (1907–1973), the editor of the *The American Scholar* from 1944 to 1973, received his Ph.D. in philosophy from Columbia University in 1942. Haydn was a founder of Atheneum Publishers and the editor of several renowned authors, including William Styron, William Faulkner, and Redding.

112. *The American Scholar,* the award-winning magazine of the Phi Beta Kappa Society, was first published in 1932, and was inspired by a speech of the same title delivered by Ralph Waldo Emerson to the Phi Beta Kappa Society of Harvard in 1837.

ELLISON: They're probably planning an issue.

REDDING: They're planning a discussion, yes.

ELLISON: He wrote me and asked me if I could do that. I couldn't. He even gave me a deadline.

REDDING: But I must say that I rather like the—if this has any value and I certainly believe it does, perhaps it shouldn't be one of these journals that has a particular clientele, like *The American Scholar.*

HASTIE: I thought Carl was thinking of—when he said—I think you used the term publication number one.

HOLMAN: Yes. Our own.

HASTIE: One of the things that the Center for the Study of Democratic Institutions gets out.[113] Have your own . . .

HILL: Occasional papers.

HASTIE: Occasional papers, yes. You could have your own . . .

K. CLARK: And widely publicized.

HASTIE: I think that this wants to reach the kind of people who really—no single journal that I can think of reaches at the present time.

DRAKE: Of course, individuals in the group might be encouraged to write for these special issue journals.

K. CLARK: Anne, do you want to . . .

REID: I think that we have put forward as many ideas as we can handle in the next three months. If we can deal with these sensitively and sanely, the motivation to go to New York last December and talk to you has certainly been met. I think we're told that we must do something and we can do is the result of having a conversation with people who can and must do. When do we meet again, sir?

K. CLARK: All right. Let me see if I've . . .

FRANKLIN: Adelaide raised a question which I think is terribly important. There are so many people who would have been, if I may say so—it's good to be here, but I'm just trying to think how we can be certain that we take the right steps to . . .

REID: Enlarge it.

113. The Center for the Study of Democratic Institutions, a prominent American think tank, was founded in 1959 by Robert Maynard Hutchins, formerly president of the University of Chicago, with the purpose of reexamining ideas. Because the center was a project of the Fund for the Republic, which had a $15 million grant from the Ford Foundation, the center had the resources to provide scholars with a place to do humanitarian research without being held back by lack of funding. The center also occasionally published magazines and pamphlets.

FRANKLIN: —to win them. Let's say that they are voted in in some way. Otherwise they'll say, who the hell do they think they are, to speak or say—I don't know how you do it, but you know, I would have had that reaction if you hadn't invited me.

K. CLARK: Well, John, let me for the moment respond to that with the full understanding that we will probably be coming back to it. As I understood what Anne had in mind in her discussions with Hylan and with me, this meeting was precisely for what happened—a small group of people who knew and respected each other coming together to talk generally about a problem which we felt each of us shared concern. We anticipated that out of this meeting a small group might come the desire for something to follow. But we disciplined ourselves in terms of anticipating what would follow and how. The one thing that we thought that we really didn't want was to have this group "representative" at this time, because you know, I don't suppose a person in this room has not been a part of a representative debate which sometimes is indistinguishable from harangue. You know, we felt that we needed some time to just sit and listen to each other and communicate with each other with the one clear thing being mutual respect, mutual regard and knowing that if there were differences, they would not be differences that would emerge as a desire for posturing or platforming or . . .

Now, I have a feeling that it is sort of important for us to continue that even as we add. I've been—in the last two or three years, I've been in too many attempts at discussions that really became prematurely polarized and you know.

HOLMAN: Quit trying to scare me.

K. CLARK: Now, I think we are free to determine our own timing, our own pacing and our own methods of enlarging for whatever purposes we want.

Now, could I try to summarize what I think I've heard us say by way of where we go from here. It seems to me that we are really coming back to where Bill Hastie started, as a way of one of the first things that was presented—a statement of principles which is our, in a sense, consensus where we all agree to start with such a statement individually—à la Phyllis's suggestion of two pages of summary from each of us as to our goals—the principles which we consider important here and specific steps as to how these principles can be made part of what's going on and where we would like to see our society be. These statements would be sent to us at MARC and we will distribute them and we will try to distill out of them maybe something which represents the collective thinking of all. As I understand what we're saying about this basic statement and the process of trying to arrive at it is that it, in effect, will try to be a model of a rational and ethical approaches to the solutions of difficult social problems, you know. I heard everyone saying that these are not simple—simplistic things that we're dealing with. Well, there's no magic formula, but each of us will try to state as best we can this.

The second thing that was here, that we cannot afford the luxury of just cogitating forever about this. Almost everyone said that there are immediate short range uses of this basic statement or statements which would come out—and that they must be communicated. And we talked about certain ways of short range communication—all the way from publishing these statements themselves in an appropriate form, modifications of this or basis of speeches, talks to various groups, magazine articles, publications of others—different publications and that we will help each other in the possibility of even placing, referring such things, although in this group, there is no need for such help. But I thought I heard underneath what you were saying there was a diplomatic approach to propagating a point of view or points of view that we think need to be goals which we're concerned with.

In this immediate short range communication, Mamie and others have sided with dramatic confrontation, you know, of getting off the defensive, silent posture and some technique and methods for taking initiative in communicating what we believe in and why. And here, it seems to me that the suggestions were a more systematic exploitation of the media—the mass media, television, radio spots and other ways. The Galbraith model[114] was used, but here again, we sort of agreed to exploit and study more systematically how this can be done.

And third, making available materials for use by maybe not a short range—long range, but at least starting to look at—and here I'm

114. I have not been able to determine with certainty what Clark means here. But here is my best interpretation. John Kenneth Galbraith (1908–2006) was a Canadian-American economist. In an article titled "The Political Galbraith," Arthur Schlessinger Jr. writes that the "Galbraith model" holds that the best way to challenge a dominant power is not by changing or abolishing that power but by constructing well-coordinated countervailing powers. In this instance, Clark sees the black separatists as the dominant power, and the black integrationists as the countervailing power. See Arthur Schlessinger Jr. "The Political Galabraith," *Journal of Post Keynesian Economics* 7, no. 1 (Autumn 1984): 7–17.

responding to the emphasis of John Hope that there are some very important issues of truth, validity, you know, as distinct from popular fashions or myth making and this is—this has to be handled not only in terms of the short range communication media exploitation method, but it also has to be handled in terms of materials that deal with the question of the distinction between myth and truth and between fashion and scholarship.

The long range things which I heard were—the most persistent of the ones I heard is the continuing vehicle for presentation of ideas or thought, analysis. We haven't been able to get away from the idea of some form of publication. We aren't agreed as to whether it should be new or whether we should seek to coopt existing publications, but this idea hasn't died, in spite of Adelaide. The problem is whether we call it journal or something else, but the need for something viable and something which—I tried to keep out of my own mind *Partisan Review* or *Commentary* as models—because apparently the group was not ready for a model yet; it only has the idea—but apparently persistent enough for us not to ignore it.

I think Carl gave us the possible handle between what we do with these discussions when they're written and the possibility of that being the basis of looking at a periodical.

We also, in the long range part of—or this wasn't expressed as frequently as the publication, but certainly Bill expressed it at least three times, the need for some kind—not only Bill, but others—some continuing discussion groups or a discussion group from which would permeate and sustain, keep going these other approaches and methods and also continuing, developing and strengthening the contacts with decision makers, not only in the academic institutions, but in government in general.

And then the target groups, sometimes made explicit, but certainly implicit in all of our discussions, and not necessarily in the order of importance, although it does seem to me that the first target group—the one with which we were primarily concerned in terms of this meeting, the Negro students themselves and the whole spectrum of Negro students. I think Eddie and Carl kept coming back to the fact that we can't do anything that will break communication with even the most extreme or, from our point of view, mindless Negro students. I heard from that that we—that our prime target group would be Negro students, without regard to where they are now in their thinking or their tactics, etc.

Nothing would be gained by divorcing ourselves from any part of them, but that we will try to find ways of communicating with all of them.

The Negro community—because we are concerned with the Negro students, in terms of their importance in terms of what happens to our people in 1979—maybe I should say 1984.[115]

The college administrators, decision makers were repeated frequently as an important target group for any number of reasons. If for no other reason than to keep them honest, keep them from playing games with our kids, keep, you know—communicate to them our criteria of the way—and how we know that they're taking our young people seriously rather than setting up stuff that will get them out of their hair.

And public officials—the governmental officials who have surfaced more in the City College confrontation as significant factors in the decision making of the college administrators than anywhere else. And I think it's very good that we have a situation which shows that the college administrator's decisions are not to be seen in isolation from other things. So that certainly is . . .

And of course, the general public.

These are the things which I've heard from certain—the tapes will be examined to see if there is anything which fell within the cracks and Bea's notes.[116]

Then, as it will in all such meetings, MARC's role kept coming up. It seems that there is a role for us now and certainly if no other than to receive and distribute and try to distill into a single document your responses. And, yes, Anne, it will be delegated. We—the role that we will assume, if you want us to—the role of communication among us, coordinating any type of—any second thoughts that may be beyond your written summaries and suggestions. We will continue, because we—that's what we're here for—data gathering, analysis and distribution of what we find as we interpret the problems. We will be open to all suggestions as to how we can serve your concerns. One of the things that we really need is more input from people like yourselves as to how

115. This is a reference to George Orwell's political satire *Nineteen Eighty-four,* which was published in 1949. The novel depicts a brutal totalitarian world where humans are ruled by machinery and under constant surveillance by the government.

116. This is a reference to Beatrice Olsen, who was part of the secretarial staff at MARC that worked on the Haverford Discussions.

we can be more effective in this research, analysis, interpretation of roles.

To the extent that our approach and style are consistent with what might emerge from this group—as a support for your continued activities, we will be happy to make ourselves available for that role.

And publication and publicizing of ideas—we don't have the personnel or facilities for systematic publicizing; but if this group pushes us in this, we will get it. We will get it and we will get it funded and we will make it available to meet your needs. As of now, we have the research potential; we have the coordinating role potential; we have the editorial and publication potential to meet your needs. We do not have the more systematic public education, publicizing kind of thing; but we, if forced to—we will develop it and we will develop it and help.

This is where we are.

FRANKLIN: Ken, I just wanted to ask one question in connection with the editorial and the publication of the resources. You know, I think that a good deal of thought must be given to the format of this conversation, particularly if we want it read by large numbers of people. And I would hope that that might be borne in mind when this material is taken off the tape and when it is combined with the statements that we will make. If somehow this could be worked into a kind of extended discussion with—maybe something I say at one point and Carl picks up and even if it's restructured—even if it's not exactly like you've got it here, and if it—it's got to make good sense and all that, even if we didn't make good sense. And it seems to me that that's important in editorial.

K. CLARK: Now, we have two things now. We have not only the tapes, but we have the statements.

HASTIE: And I think one thing on that same point—it's been said. I think John and Adelaide both stressed it rather late; I'm not saying that critically. It seems to me that it's important, that in the nature of approaching something, it's desirable undoubtedly to start with a small group of this sort where every one knows each other and we let our hair down the way we have. But is there a next stage where perhaps instead of a dozen people starting from scratch, there may be fifty people who perhaps start with the material that was produced by this—are you considering that as a stage?

K. CLARK: Well . . .

HASTIE: If that is—if nothing is communicated to the public, our target audience, before that is done that delays it. But whether that is in addition to some communications to the target audience or whether that is preliminary to it, I am impressed with the importance of that stage in enlarging the group that is communicating.

K. CLARK: What do you think about the idea of having a few people from this group work with us on next steps, procedural matters of this sort, because certainly we don't have the answers to this. One thing we want to do is be sure that each thing that we do is as solid and as well planned as possible and that we don't just inadvertently fall into the harangue bag again.

HOLMAN: Ken, I think what they're saying . . .

WALLACE: Not what they're saying really. If you have any suggestions on next steps . . .

K. CLARK: But what I understand that Bill is saying is, look, what specifically will we do by way of the group and its continuity and expansion. I personally think that there is a role for both, the continuity of this group as a group and the expansion of some aspects of this group. Is that making any sense?

HOLMAN: Could I mention a role that I think that people in this room can play? A group of people who consider themselves activists of one kind or another will be getting together some time from now. You've got the real problem which is a national problem, which is the whole problem of our time and ties in what Eddie's been saying—the question is how many black people of different viewpoints can you get in a room together from—without their killing one another off or producing a stalemate. We're looking for commonalities and as the questions come in from black politicians we're beginning to see some. Everybody is looking now for networks and the identification of resources. Some time ago, I tried to put together a race and education conference and I was told over and over again, there are only two black men in the United States who know anything about education. Ken Clark was one of them. A fellow up at Brandeis or some place was the other one. But as you started checking, here was a guy out there on the West Coast, somebody else in the Midwest, and so on. Most of you travel a lot. It would be helpful, it seems to me, if a sort of talent search and resource identifying became channeled somehow into MARC. That helps you get that extra fifty, one hundred people, that are now out of the exchange. Because there are a lot of good people, bright people, able people that are in the most unheard of places and they don't get fed in. And so you have a young black leader in Newark, Hy, saying that he needed a certain kind of help and perhaps he had to get it from out on the West Coast because he didn't know of any other resource that was closer at hand. I think that that could be fed into you by this group, maybe if they could send some stuff to you—a list of names, a word or two about the person so that you—that's going to be easier, by the way, to get than the list of the black students, because though this is a good idea, you're going to find in many of the schools, there's going to be a great defensiveness.

My final example to show you what this means: Once officials who had been trying to stand up for the right things wanted to know if a list of some black students could be put together, students who would meet with them. I said, well, I know some black students I can call; but I'm out of the list making business. So I called five or six schools and some of the kids that I knew, and the answer I got back was, if this had been some black guy who wanted to sit down with them they might consider it, but they weren't particularly interested in talking with those white officials, besides which, they wanted to get some answers on things like detention centers.

K. CLARK: We've already found it difficult, Carl.

HILL: I'd agree with you on trying to get the detailed profiles on these beautiful kids, but I don't think you will have any trouble, any more than you usually do with black organizations getting the names of the president and secretary.

DRAKE: You can get that from the school because they've had to . . .

HOLMAN: If they're registered as a campus organization, then the school's got them.

REID: Well, Ken, may I go back to the suggestion Bill made earlier. Now, I thought there was something very useful in using the report of this dialogue as a point of departure with a group of—maybe not fifty—but with another group, and out of that there might—well. I think that's something that . . .

K. CLARK: Well, actually, I heard suggestions for using whatever we come out with in written form from this discussion for a number of groups—a number of ways—college administrators, you know, public—and larger—and expansion of this group . . .

WILLIAMS: Two quick points. Since there is such a commonality of experience and shared view here and given the possibility of another meeting like this one, couldn't you use various people here as key men in their respective localities to hold similar meetings. This would give you some distributional and representative aspects.

The other point I wanted to make is in terms of publishing something. I think it's fine to do a transcript, to even rework it some kind of way. For widespread immediate impact, I would suggest a press release which can be followed by something in depth, but something that is concrete, specific.

K. CLARK: A press release after we have our document.

WILLIAMS: After you have whatever is there.

K. CLARK: Yes, but with solidarity.

WILLIAMS: What?

K. CLARK: With solidarity.

WILLIAMS: Yes.

K. CLARK: Was there anything that I left out of the summary?

HILL: I think I would say it's not so much that we shouldn't say what we've said as soon as you're ready to say it, but it's how we say it in terms of how we view ourselves. And we—three or more people can get together and start any kind of institution if they want to. But I would hope that it would be—my only thing was a sense of the significance of the group, but the fact that this is something that we want others to respond to also. This is not the final statement of the issue. And I think this is just a matter of wording so that the person doesn't feel left out, but wants to join.

K. CLARK: That our statement be a model for what we . . .

HILL: Yes. Preamble.

FRANKLIN: I was just whispering to Ralph that perhaps at the end of it would be an invitation to people to respond.

HILL: Yes.

DRAKE: Yes.

HASTIE: A call to others to express themselves.

HILL: Yes. I think.

WALLACE: The way *The American Assembly* does with the little agenda section—further discussions.[117]

ELLISON: Let me throw this idea out. I was just thinking back to

117. The American Assembly, founded by Dwight Eisenhower in 1950, is a national, nonpartisan public affairs forum affiliated with Columbia University. The research and publications commissioned by the American Assembly are used by a wide variety of people, from government officials to everyday community members.

'42 when I sent out a lot of postcards to people in the field of literature—critics and so on, all non-black or non-Negro, saying what would you like to know about us and how—what areas involving the Negro community intrigue you. I got a few answers, but most people were surprised that they should have been asked that kind of question. I think it would be much easier today to put some such question and many people would respond positively. Maybe you might draw up such a list because these people must be made to focus in on this area because they are so conditioned to including us out as they deliberate.

K. CLARK: I want to make explicit the fact that I offered MARC as in fact a sort of staff service group for this group and I would like also to say that in performing this role, we would want to feel free to call on you as individuals or invite a small group to respond to what we're doing in coming to the next step. Phyllis and Hylan and I, I suppose, will assume the major responsibility for coordinating and developing this document or statement and we'll have to lean on you during this stage, you know, up to that point. Hylan, I just volunteered for you.

HASTIE: You want to hear from us within two weeks, right?

K. CLARK: That's right. We will be writing you and reminding you of that—I just volunteered with you, Phyllis and I will assume the major staff responsibility for moving from this step to the next step.

The last question in my mind is the question that Anne asked, namely, when do we meet again or do we postpone that until we have the document?

FRANKLIN: I would say postpone until after.

K. CLARK: Mamie wants to say something and I think she should say it.

M. CLARK: I just think we ought to say what a marvelous hostess we had.

HOLMAN: Including those who kept you up all night last night?

K. CLARK: Well, I am sure that we—the circumstances, the atmosphere, the warmth and Anne with all her graciousness, contributed to what seemed to me to be a very productive . . .

And I want to thank everybody.

HASTIE: I want to reiterate, as I know each one of us would, if we weren't so rushed for time—it's marvelous of Anne to serve so much as the inspiration of this and then be hostess. I think the circumstances under which we met, that have helped so much in making this productive.

By the way, if there is at some time a larger group of fifty to a hundred, I know there are various places, but I just mention it. Temple University has acquired the home, the estate of Albert M. Greenfield, the late financier and is developing that as a conference center. It's not yet large enough for a big conference, but it's already beginning to operate for small groups, a group of fifty, I'm sure they could—it's right in Philadelphia and—but the estate is a magnificent, most comfortable place. I don't know whether you have ever met at a place which had gold plated bathroom fixtures . . .

K. CLARK: On the note of gold plated bathroom fixtures, I think we should . . .

ADJOURNMENT

Statements of the Haverford Group Members

REACTIONS TO THE HAVERFORD DISCUSSIONS ON BLACK SEPARATISM

Mamie Phipps Clark

In the initial stages of the Haverford process,[118] the "dialogue" included descriptions of some poignant, sometimes humorous, but generally depressing individual experiences and thoughts about black separatists, and black and white moderates. Although no member of the discussion group took the "hard line" "black power" approach, there was an apparent diversity of analytical approaches to the problem of black separatism. However, even in the initial stages of discussion there appeared to emerge a loose kind of consensus which offered hope for an in-depth examination of the problem which would lead to formulation of possible solutions.

Here in New York City, from my professional vantage point, it seems that both moderate[119] blacks and whites have, in general, met the confrontations of black and white power groups with a non-strategic "either-or" response. That is, they have "either" given in completely to

118. MARC sponsored discussions on May 30, 31. (This footnote is in the original.)

119. The classification of "liberals" has all but disappeared. (This footnote is in the original.)

the demands, sometimes even with sizeable sums of money, "or" withdrawn from the situation incommunicado.

The Haverford discussions clarified for me the need for a group such as this to examine and refine alternative strategies on several different levels and for many professional and non-professional disciplines.

It was proposed that the group evolve into a "think tank." As such it would have a number of strategies to explore which have already been explicitly posed. There are probably some implicit strategies which will also become clearer as discussions proceed. A salesmanship approach and intellectual persuasion have been proposed as alternative strategies.

My suggestion, inspired by the discussions and by impressions of the local situation in New York is that a new concept of confrontation of black and white militants should be developed as one alternative way to meet the problem. It would be a positive confrontation: a loud, pervasive, nation-wide affirmation of the views of persons such as present at the Haverford meeting. It would develop a strong logical position which could be as militant in the opposite direction of the racist black power concept.

Such a confrontation would be made by a large group of Negroes and would be made by persons of some prestige in a variety of areas of interest. The format should provide that the large group make the confrontation with impact and also that each person in the group would be placed in strategic position to interpret it.

Such a confrontation would not involve negative components such as criticism of the tactics of black or white militants or moderates. It need not address itself directly to these groups. Without meaning to spell it out in detail, the Haverford discussion did suggest to me that such a confrontation would have common denominators for white and black militants and white and black moderates as well.

Since there are alternative levels and forms of strategies to approach the problem of black separatism, there are surely alternative procedures to define in order to achieve these strategies. It has been suggested that the content of the Haverford discussions not be rushed into public print and we would all probably agree with that. What we might discuss at another session would be the possible use of public print and television as strategic to a dramatic, well timed, and effective assault on the urgent problems of black separatism.

BLACK POWER ON THE CAMPUS: GOALS AND PRIORITIES

St. Clair Drake

The 1960 Census listed about 3,500 black Americans as "college presidents, professors, and instructors." Even if the number has doubled during the past decade—and it probably has not—this group of educators constitutes a very tiny proportion of the 18,000,000 Afro-Americans in the United States. There are about 50,000 black Americans with college and university degrees, and a quarter of a million black students are enrolled in college courses. A constant stream of new graduates will join the existing group each year including, fortunately, more individuals from families below the so-called "poverty-line" than ever before. This is a valuable pool of skill and leadership from which the black masses expect much. We shall not disappoint them, for college-trained black men and women have always exhibited a high degree of social responsibility from the days when the first two Afro-Americans to earn degrees finished Bowdoin and Dartmouth in 1836.[120]

Most of our college graduates secured their education in black schools. All of the college presidents listed in the 1960 Census, and virtually all of the professors and instructors, were affiliated with such institutions. The number at "predominately white" institutions has always been very, very small. During the past two years, however, many such institutions have been actively recruiting black faculty and administrative personnel. This move comes some years after programs for increasing the number of black students have been in operation. All of us are aware that the frantic search for black faculty has been a response to the upsurge of the black student movement on "white" campuses.

120. See Horace Mann Bond, "The Negro Scholar and Professional in America," in John P. Davis (ed.), *The American Negro Reference Book,* 1966, Chapter 14. (This footnote is in the original.) Drake's representation of Bond's work, however, is mistaken. Here is what Bond says: "By 1830 at least four Negroes had graduated from college. Edward A. Jones, privately tutored in Charleston, South Carolina, graduated from Amherst College in August, 1826, eleven days before John B. Russwurm (long thought the first Negro to graduate from an American college) took his degree at Bowdoin. Theodore S. Wright, a product of the New York African Free School, graduated from the Princeton Theological Seminary in 1828, and Edward Mitchell, from Dartmouth in 1829" (550).

Every campus presents a unique situation, but there are significant uniformities. The Black Students Union or Black Students Association has emerged as the prevalent organizational structure for focusing protest, for bargaining and negotiating, and for cultivating black solidarity. Leaders of these organizations, varied in degree of militancy and in political philosophies, serve as spokesmen for a heterogeneous student constituency reflecting the whole spectrum of ideological positions and attitudes. Yet, the leaders have won solid support for the demand that courses be included in college curricula that are "relevant" to the quest for self-definition and for service to the black community. There has also been widespread, though not unanimous, support for changes in admission practices so as to increase the inflow of black students, and for more black faculty members and administrators, with insistence upon student participation in their selection. And, in some situations, though not all, there has been a demand for special arrangements to maximize in-group solidarity such as separate dormitory facilities and space for exclusive meetings and social activities; black cultural centers and institutes; classes from which white students are barred; or courses that must be taught by black professors. Consensus has been weakest with respect to this latter group of demands.

These demands sometimes pose serious problems for those black faculty members who share the basic concern of black students for "getting ourselves together" and "taking care of business," but who also feel that frequently not enough attention has been given to the ordering of priorities; who want to insure the maintenance of high standards of scholarship; who are committed to the hard-won rights of faculty tenure and academic freedom; and who ardently hope that patterns of "self-segregation" will be eliminated eventually however defensible they may be in certain campus situations for a limited period of time. They place high value, too, on the right of all students in a university community—white and black alike—to exercise free choice in the selection of programs of study and in the choosing of personal associates without being subjected to embarrassing or punitive group pressures. Black faculty and some of the black student leaders do not always agree on goals, priorities, strategies, or tactics. But there has never been any serious discussion of these differences. There should be.

The black community cannot afford the luxury of *open* conflict between its all-too-few black professors and black students. The time would seem to be ripe for the opening of a *private* dialogue in which areas of agreement and disagreement are explored with frankness but mutual respect. Many of us, as professors, have devoted a lifetime to fighting the battle for "black dignity" and equality of opportunity, through research and publication. Some have also participated in varied forms of direct social action for which they have sometimes had to pay a price. Some of us were involved in the student movement of the 1920's that challenged institutionalized racism on black college campuses, and, then, were in the first wave of black students in the 1930's and 1940's who initiated the struggle against entrenched segregation and discrimination in housing, medical schools, and other facilities on some "predominantly white" campuses and outright exclusion from others. Later, many black college teachers were active in "The Movement." We feel that we have earned the right to express an opinion on current campus issues without being dismissed as "irrelevant" or denounced as "anti-black 'Negroes.'" Not our age or our degrees but our involvement gives us this right.

Such a dialogue would revolve around the "ordering of priorities" within a framework of defining goals, setting targets, and planning for the welfare of the black community on each campus—faculty, students, and non-academic staff; and for fruitful relations with the white segment of the campus community and with the black off-campus community. Questions such as these might be relevant:

1. What targets should be set for increase in number and proportion of black students to white, and black faculty to white, over the next five years?
2. What is the optimum balance between proportion of black students majoring in Black Studies and those pursuing other types of courses?
3. How can curricular arrangements be made so that every black student can integrate some courses into his program that he deems relevant to his own needs and desires as an Afro-American while securing adequate professional or pre-professional training?
4. Do we have any responsibility for trying to attack racism by pressing for the exposure of white students to new curricular content and to black scholars and artists? How important is this goal?
5. Is it possible to devise informal, unofficial arrangements by which specialized needs of black students can be met without institutionalizing and crystallizing separate facilities?

6. How can we insure that changes to meet group needs do not lower academic standards to our own detriment or reduce levels of skill acquisition?
7. How can the widest range of freedom of personal and political expression be assured while maintaining "black solidarity"?

Ralph Ellison

In spite of all the writing I do, and for all of the lectures I give each year, there are many matters which I don't write about; nor, except with my wife and a few intimate friends, do I discuss them. Perhaps this is because they have to do with ideas, emotions and attitudes which grow out of my situation as a Negro American and with those undefined and uncodified aspects of our lives which require the sympathy and insight usually found only among those who have been conditioned and disciplined by our specific group experience. Today such in-group discussion is no mere luxury, it is a necessity; both for ourselves, for our restless youth and for the American intellectual community as a whole. There is no question but that my own participation in our discussions at Haverford had something of the effect of a catharsis. I was cleansed of some of my doubts and confusions and, thankfully, I was stimulated—not by the sound of my own all too familiar voice, but by your ideas and by your passion. If this is to any extent true of the other participants I believe our enterprise was well worth the effort and should be continued on a permanent basis. Certainly it points to the necessity of our no longer working in isolation from one another, and it is clear that we have much to offer that has been missing from discussions in the larger American intellectual community. There is simply no avoiding the fact that there are many aspects of American life which can only be described, analyzed and defined by black intellectuals, for no other group possesses an adequate perspective or so urgent a need.

In summing up what I tried to say in our discussions I would emphasize my personal affirmation of integration without the surrender of our unique identity as a people to be a viable and indeed inescapable goal for black Americans. As a writer who tries to reduce the flux and flow of life to meaningful artistic forms I am stuck with integration, because the very process of the imagination as it goes about bringing together a multiplicity of scenes, images, characters and emotions and reducing them to significance is nothing if not integrative. Further, the object of my fictional imagination is the American society and the

American experience as experienced fundamentally by Negroes and I find it impossible to deal with either in isolation, for they are intricately united in their diversity. The judgments implied by the fictional products of my imagination might well repudiate many accepted American values and definitions of reality, but this by no means infers that the integrative role of the imagination (and of the intellect) is invalid. It does imply that the larger American ideals of freedom are the ultimate ground upon which any literary evaluations of the cost, pain, joy and triumph of being human is tested.

The American people is united in all its regional, class, ethnic and religious diversity by a bond of language. There are many idioms of that language and it is partially the creation of a voice which found its origin in Africa. Indeed, it began to be influenced by that voice long before the American nation was formed. In the beginning was the word and our voice sounded in the language with which the word was spoken. The American language owes something of its directness, its flexibility, its music, its imagery, mythology and folklore to the Negro presence; it is not, therefore, a product of "white" culture as against "black" culture, rather it is the product of cultural integration. And the realities of discrimination and racism notwithstanding, it is a fact that *culturally* the melting-pot has indeed melted and that one of the strongest forces shaping the general American culture has been what I call the Negro-American idiom.

I am calling attention to the cultural pluralism of American life because until the present college generation that pluralism as expressed in the art, folkways and style was an important source of Negro American optimism—just as that optimism was a support of the general faith in the workability of the American system. Our elders recognized their presence and influence in areas of American life from which they were physically barred, and while the American house was of many mansions they knew that despite racial discrimination there was something of themselves dwelling in most of them and not merely as servants. Sometimes they made hue and cry over the theft of their substance and their style, and sometimes they were silent but they saw themselves in all the movements of American life no matter how confused the scene. For them the problem was not that of identifying with the scene but of having others give public recognition to their contribution. Certainly there was no question of trying to withdraw in a pique and of surrendering their investment in the experiment.

Today that sense of having shared creatively in the common American experiment is under an assault by passionate young blacks who have lost their mooring in tradition. They are romantic, earnest and ignorant, a state for which I believe that we as intellectuals are responsible because in pursuing our specialties we have failed to interpret the past and define the present and project the future in ways that are available to the young. Far too frequently black youth has been forced to depend upon intellectuals of other groups for interpretations of their relationship to the larger society. In fact other groups of intellectuals have given more time to the task than we ourselves. Often they appear so obsessively concerned with defining our life styles, character, traditions and values as to reduce us to silence and pliable inaction. Frequently they seem motivated by a desire to manipulate our image for political and economic purposes of their own, and some have taken the concepts of Negro sociologists and turned them against us, creating thereby much confusion and great resentment. But whatever their motives, there is the fact that they are functioning as intellectuals, and it is their legitimate task, as it is ours, to explore the wholeness of American life and the inter-relationships between the various groups which compose it.

That they have coopted our role is a criticism of ourselves, for we have failed to address ourselves effectively to many of the broader problems of American life, and we have failed to follow up our often creative analysis of specifically Negro American problems into the broader areas where they inevitably lead. In other words, we often forget that the only way to be an effective Negro intellectual is by being a most perceptive and responsible *American* intellectual. I believe that the state of black youth points to our failure and if we have failed them, then we have failed American youth generally. For all their talk of black separatism—really another version of secessionism, an old American illusion which arises whenever groups reach an explosive point of frustration—and for all their stance of alienation, they are really acting out a state of despair. They are frightened by the existence of opportunities for competing with their white peers on a basis of equality which did not exist for us. They suffer traumatically from the shock of sudden opportunity. The shackles have been struck from at least one of their ankles and the skin is sensitive to the turbulent air and the illusory possibility of absolutely unrestrained movement. Actually they are in the position of pioneers who must enter an unknown territory armed only with the knowledge and skills which they've brought with them from the past, but instead of plunging in and testing themselves against the unknown, they choose rather to argue with the deficiencies of the past and to direct accusations against their parents. They accuse us of lacking manhood and courage and they have declared themselves a new breed, which perhaps they are. One thing is certain, they have thrown us a challenge and I believe that we should meet them head on. I don't think that we should be put in the position of apologizing for our backgrounds, values or goals but I do think that we must provide a forum wherein the unwritten wisdom of the group can be intellectualized and passed on to those who are sincerely seeking for answers and orientation.

Finally, I hope that this group continues in some form but I hope that we won't rush our discussions into public print.

FOR THE HAVERFORD DIALOGUE

John Hope Franklin

It is very important that in these days of heated debate we do not lose sight of the fact that the integrity of the field of Afro-American Studies rests on its validity as an intellectual discipline and not on its importance as a rallying point for some abstract proposed reordering of society. If it has value in the reordering of society, as I very much believe that it has, its claim must be argued from the position that it tells the truth and does not engage in myth-making. The ground for Afro-American Studies is weak, if not altogether untenable, if it operates on the premise that persons of African descent possess some mystical qualities that are denied to others. That is what the white racists have been arguing for generations, except that they have insisted that these mystical qualities brand persons of African descent as inferior. The argument is no more forceful or successful when it claims that these mystical qualities endow persons of African descent as superior.

The prime purpose of Afro-American Studies is to provide a body of knowledge about the activities of a sector of the American population that has been deliberately ignored or neglected in most studies of American life and history. The effort to build up such a body of knowledge and the effort to purvey that body of knowledge, whether in writing or teaching, cannot be the sole possession of any group, even if that group is the one most significantly involved. Real knowledge should be universal both in its acquisition and in its dissemination. The principal qualifications of those involved in the quest for such knowledge should be their commitment to truth and the appreciation of its value in creating a better intellectual and social order.

It is a marked display of disdain for the importance of Afro-American Studies when educational institutions at any level place a moratorium on excellence and on high standards of teaching, research, and the performance where Afro-American Studies are concerned. Crash programs in this area that are not carefully developed and executed are as susceptible to miseducation, distortion, and failure as similar efforts would be in other areas. Such programs do not enjoy the full confidence and support of their sponsors and whose integrity are not fully recognized are immediately placed in an intellectually indefensible position that, in the long run, will contribute to their ineffectiveness as a part of an academic curriculum. Responsible advocates of a wholesome, healthy pursuit of truth cannot countenance compromise and evasion in the area of Afro-American Studies.

William H. Hastie

During the late 1960's an alarming number of Negroes have tended uncritically to accept and encourage racial separatism in our country as a desirable and potentially rewarding pattern of American life. This trend must be halted and reversed, for it can lead only to greater bitterness and frustration and to even more inferior status than black America now experiences.

Almost a hundred years ago, first by force and intimidation and somewhat later by segregation laws, the majority whites in the south and elsewhere succeeded in imposing racial separatism as a law enforced pattern of post civil war political, economic and social life. While this imposition was hateful to almost all Negroes it was not until the 1940's that a continuing drive, spearheaded by blacks and supported by an ever increasing number of whites, succeeded in making major breaches in the wall of separatist laws which kept most blacks out of the mainstream of American life. Amazingly, by the 1960's practically all of this structure of laws sanctioning racial segregation had been destroyed. This has happened in education, in regulation of voting, in access to public facilities, in freedom to marry, and all other areas that had been controlled and restricted by racist laws. Thus many believed that the 1960's would see black America and much of white America, freed of racist laws, united in a climactic drive to eliminate from our society racist practices, behavior and patterns of thinking and living which still persisted after they were no longer required or encouraged by law.

At the same time, American Negroes have been migrating north and into cities. Fifty years ago, the majority of Negroes, poor, untrained and disinherited, lived in rural areas. Millions of them, still poor, untrained and disinherited, have since moved into large cities. This black migration into the core of our cities has continued and accelerated and at the same time there has been unprecedented development of new residential areas in our outer cities and in suburbs beyond the cities. But access to most of this housing has been and even now, despite new fair housing laws tardily enacted, continues to be in fact inaccessible to most Negroes. Millions of whites have dispersed into new communities away from the center of our cities while millions of blacks, including most of the poor, untrained and disinherited, have concentrated in old and overcrowded center city ghettos. This distortion and prevention of normal population movement, probably more than anything else has retarded the realization of a substantially integrated society which might otherwise have developed with the destruction of legal barriers. Instead, it has fostered the development of a deprived desperate subculture of poverty-stricken and all but hopeless black city dwellers. It also has spawned a new attitude toward separatism among many Negroes.

This is not to say that other factors have not been operating. Young blacks like young whites have become increasingly distrustful of, even cynical about the values of white society which tolerates so much poverty in the midst of extraordinary national affluence, which will spend lavishly for international war but only grudgingly for the domestic well-being of the disadvantaged, which spawned the white racists who murdered Martin Luther King, Medgar Evers[121] and other less well known blacks and whites whose only wrong was aggressiveness in fighting racism. But the other side of the coin shows a black society that

121. Medgar Evers (1925–1963), a field secretary of the NAACP who specialized in recruiting and encouraging youth in civil rights activism, was assassinated in 1963.

is no better in its aping of white materialism, in its accommodation of hucksters, hustlers and other operators as predatory and cynical as their white counterparts, in its spawn of sick violent men who murdered Malcolm X just as viciously as whites murdered Martin King, and who continue to disfigure the black community with sporadic homicidal guerilla strife among rival separatist groups.

Thus, revulsion against the vicious and indecent aspects of white society is no justification for glorifying and building a black society which in itself mirrors and at times intensifies the same evils. The only really better society of the future to which we can hopefully look forward and for which we can meaningfully work is a better total society in which present major evils, racism prominent among them, are substantially corrected.

Many blacks now reason that the black ghetto has become an ineradicable feature of American urban life.[122] Accordingly they have set out to glorify a separate subculture as a desirable base for community life and for developing black political and economic power and the human potential of black people generally. Too many young Negroes, particularly black college and university students have conceived of their education as merely preparation for living in a black ghetto substructure and for the role of better exploiting the economic, political and humanistic potential of that subculture.

Of course sensitive and concerned young people should work as best they can to help make the life of the poor and untrained ghetto dwellers more rewarding, to relieve their economic plight and to mobilize their political power for effective self help. But this should not blind them to the fact that the ghetto subculture is in itself stultifying and self-defeating. No one, least of all young students should view it as something to be perpetuated. Rather, beyond ameliorating ghetto life, the basic direction and drive of effort should be toward bringing blacks fully into the main stream of American life. Young Negroes of college age have the double opportunity of bringing themselves physically, psychologically, economically and culturally into that main stream and at the same time concerning themselves with the plight of their less fortunate brothers.

Unfortunately, many college administrators, teachers and students

122. For Hastie, the goal is the "the elimination of the ghetto" (182).

who are white find in the misguided drive of black students calling for and glorifying separatism an easy escape from responsibility for making black students fully a part of campus life and helping them to make the most of their educational opportunities as preparation for life and service in the general community. They must share the blame for separatist trends in college life and education.

In summary, while ghetto life must be improved, this must be recognized as only a palliative, though a necessary one, in a period during which blacks and whites increase their efforts toward the elimination of the ghetto and the dispersal and integration of blacks within the total community.

While personal pride and self confidence must be developed as essential to human advancement, arrogance and race hatred accompanied by rejection of all that cannot be labeled black must be avoided as dangerous and self-defeating evils.

While education featured by the development of knowledge, skills, interests and concerns appropriate to human advancement in the 20th and 21st centuries is as fundamental for blacks as for whites, the notion that the major thrust in the education of blacks should be directed at training for ghetto life in a black subculture must be rejected as a hideous and unrewarding waste and misdirection of human talent.

To think and act intelligently, aggressively, generously and compassionately, with a view to a better total society, not to think and act belligerently black with a view to a separate society, must be the commitment of our young people who desperately want to fashion and to live in a better world.

Adelaide Hill

It is ironic that the subject of Afro-American Studies should have reached a level of public clamor before Afro-American intellectuals have in fact commented on it. Is it because with the possible exception of the church, almost all institutions within black society have been merely imitations of, or entirely determined by the preference and values of white society on this subject and comment would seem pointless? Or maybe it is because the black intellectual as a person is really an invisible man, unknown to white society, ignored by the black masses and insecure within himself. Truly, some black intellectuals have felt so insecure as to avoid the responsibility of having an opinion on Afro-American Studies. This lack of comment has left the topic of Afro-American Studies without a framework for growth and "non-negotiable" demands of the younger militants without an ideology. It should be obvious that the time for comment is long overdue.

Perhaps more than any other large and powerful society, the United States has had difficulty permitting the reality of existence to affect the viability of her myths. The "American Dream" of the equality of all men has in reality meant the dominance of some men, usually White Anglo-Saxon Protestants, over other men and the preference of the standards of some men, usually White Anglo-Saxon Protestants over those of others. The reality is more complicated for even the desirability of pluralism as an ideal seems tarnished against the myth of the melting pot. The ambiguities and paradoxes that stem from this do in fact play havoc with the values of education for the society as a whole. Fluctuating cycles and varying schools of thought should discourage any dogmatic judgments, in any philosophy of education, Afro-American Studies included.

The position of the Afro-American in American society and the education he needs must be viewed within a larger context of these uncertainties, fluctuations and changes. Here too there is the conflict between the myth and the reality, between the expectation of equality and the fact of inferiority. How then to design a workable pattern of education—education for what goals—to develop what kinds of persons—and on whose terms?

Afro-American Studies if they are to have any lasting merit must be designed, evolved is perhaps a better word, to answer these questions. And the questions themselves must be directed toward the future of the total society with the expectation of the Afro-American as a full and equal member of it. Only the uninformed question the existence and reliability of sufficient documentation to warrant Afro-American Studies as an object of scholarly pursuit. To lack information, when it is there, after almost 350 years in this country and in the New World speaks more of the selective scholarship of white scholars than of black scholars. Ignorant too is any argument that the richness of these experiences can be completely absorbed into the traditional courses within our schools and colleges. The broadening of knowledge dictates the expansion of disciplines and of course within disciplines. Societies and institutions have always existed, but sociology as a science or discipline has emerged within the memory of those still alive—there are equally familiar examples from the field of science and medicine.

Afro-American Studies should take its rightful place in the body of knowledge available to all those who seek a complete education. It goes without saying that Afro-American Studies, as with all knowledge, must be built on truth—recording accurately the experience of the past, analyzing precisely the present in order to educate students for the world of the future. There should be room for those scholars who seek only to understand the statics of a situation as well as those whose concern it is to understand the dynamics of a situation, with a commitment to change it. The unavoidable consequence of being a social being identifiable by race, sex and culture is that the subject matter of the social sciences either includes or excludes a particular individual or group. It is either about him and his way of life or it is not. In either case there may be equally important reasons for studying it. Accordingly, Afro-American Studies obviously means something different to Afro-Americans than it does to other people. While the feeling may differ, the acquisition of the knowledge of Afro-American Studies does not differ. The techniques of scholarly inquiry are available to all who seriously seek to acquire them. Bias, rhetoric, careless documentation are harmful to all scholarly research and Afro-American Studies is no exception to this rule.

However, scholarship and the communication of knowledge do not occur in a vacuum—they occur within the restrictions of organized society where there is always the possibility, even the probability, of dominant and subordinate relations between the scholar and the subject of his inquiry. Nowhere has this been more obvious than in the relation of studies about Afro-Americans and the position or role of Afro-Americans themselves. Historically, with some significant exceptions, such interest as there was in Afro-American Studies was manifest by Afro-Americans who nevertheless often found the opportunities for research grants, publication outlets and travel denied them. Now, in the wake of the sudden fashionableness of Afro-American Studies there is a struggle to participate in this field on the part of non-Afro-Americans. Any efforts made by Afro-American scholars to assert their historical monopoly in this field or on the part of black students to prefer education in Afro-American Studies only by Afro-Americans are viewed at best without understanding and at worst as suspect. Suddenly the objects of the studies, Afro-Americans themselves, refuse to continue to relate to the scholars' search in a subordinate position or to acquiesce to demands for control, direction or even equal participation by the dominant group in this area. This seems to me to be a phase in the relation between the races, an epoch, which will surely pass but *must* occur. It does place considerable responsibility on Afro-American scholars and students alike not to have it remembered as a period of distortions, new biases and pointless rhetoric. Hopefully, it will be remembered as a period of creative and exciting developments from which the academic results and the Afro-Americans as a group will be reciprocally strengthened and thereby contribute to the overall strength of the entire society.

M. Carl Holman

I came to Haverford with no preconceived sense of agenda and, though I have spent a good part of my life on one campus or another, I found it difficult to look at the black student movement or black studies except in relation to other pressing problems originating outside the campus gates.

Back in the early 1960's as the student movement began, a majority of the older and supposedly wiser heads on some campuses were convinced that the sit-ins were a mistake and were certain to slow down or reverse such racial progress as had been previously made. We are now passing through a period when a new generation is questioning that other college generation both on the grounds of its tactics and its goals. If there is a significant gap between black student leaders of the early and the late 60's, small wonder that the present crop of black youngsters in college and high schools, and those who are now decades away from their own student experiences often see the world and themselves quite differently. In part the argument between the generations is an argument about values—about the relative importance of certain things. It goes beyond matters of dress and decorum to what is really wrong in this country; and beyond the proper tactics for setting things right, to the serious questioning of whether any real change under the present system is a genuine possibility. To the degree that older black Americans have an opportunity to argue out or try to understand the spokesmen of this black student generation (many of whom, like their elders, are self-elected), it will be necessary to establish some common ground of mutual trust which may be even more important than the more frequently invoked standard of "relevance."

The fact is that many young blacks are simply unwilling to believe that their elders can possibly share their own deep concern about the disjunction between what America professes to be and what it is. It may be that, as some Negro adults maintain, many of these students are seeking refuge in the cocoon of self-segregation because they are afraid to face up to certain challenges. On the other hand, some of the students are questioning the sanity of parents who seem not to be deeply frightened at what the young see so clearly and impatiently: a nation which successfully spends billions to place men on the moon while hungry children await the outcome of debates over the difference between starvation and malnutrition. They see a nation whose urban dwellers are literally, if slowly, dying of man-made smog; where the election of a handful of black mayors is still front page news; where a war very few Americans seem to want continues to offer an unfortunate minority of youngsters, many of them black, the unhappy gamble of killing or being killed thousands of miles from home.

But it is not necessary, of course, to go to Vietnam to encounter violence. It is not even necessary to leave the campus. I am as dubious about force as an instrument in change on the campus as I was when I led a student strike all too many years ago. But isn't it troubling to note how much was made of the un-fired guns at Cornell,[123] as over against, say, what guns in other hands did at Orangeburg and at Texas Southern?[124] No pictures of the burning cross at Cornell—and in the news story on estranged blacks at another Eastern college, no reference to the brawling and obscene behavior of some white athletes at a black-

123. On April 19, 1969, the Afro-American Society of Cornell University took over Willard Straight Hall in response to acts of prejudice on campus, culminating in the burning of a cross outside the Wari House Cooperative. The AAS remained in Willard Straight Hall with guns for protection from a violent fraternity until the following day, when their demands for a black studies program and better protection from acts of racism on campus were met. Nobody died or was severely harmed.

124. On February 8, 1968, three African American students were killed and an estimated thirty people were injured at a riot on the campus of South Carolina State in Orangeburg. The riot was caused by the refusal of the All Star Bowling Lanes to integrate. The riot at Texas Southern University on May 16 and 17, 1967, was caused by police arriving at a previously peaceful protest with weapons, gas, and dogs. Students had been objecting to discontinuation of the Friends of SNCC organization on campus, the firing of the organization's adviser, and the poor quality of education they were receiving. One policeman was killed, and two others, along with one student, were wounded.

sponsored campus program. Our selective indignation plays its part in making precocious cynics of young Americans, black and white.

Black students, of course, are not alone in their susceptibility to the temptation not only to speak for all Afro-Americans, but to prescribe patterns of behavior for their fellow blacks on and off the campus. Liberationist militancy—like some brands of conservatism and liberalism—has already developed its share of authoritarian orthodoxy. One of the special problems of being black in this country is that more than the usual number of other people are eager to tell you what is good for you, and to go to considerable effort to see that you take their advice. The myth that black people not only badly need to be thought and spoken for, but actually find this congenial dies hard—even among one's black brothers and sisters. I rather suspect, however, that those black Americans who are beginning to emerge from decades of brainwashing by whites, are not good long-term prospects for a new course of treatment at the hands of other blacks, whatever their ideological credentials.

We have all seen the excesses, the exaggeration, the commercialization even, of "Soul." But it seems to me undeniable that something is going on among young blacks (and a good many older ones) which cannot be dismissed as mere posturing, or chauvinism, or panic-stricken flight from reality. There *is* a genuine, if often confused, black consciousness and an increasing sense of what Martin Luther King called "somebody-ness" abroad among the largest racial minority in this pluralistic land. To say that there was more of this in 1960 than was seen and felt among Negroes in the previous decade, or that there is more of it today than was around when the sit-ins and Freedom Rides boiled up out of the South, is not to suggest that a sense of personal and group worth and purpose was absent among blacks from the days of slavery into this century.[125] Indeed, one of the healthiest

125. The first Freedom Ride, sponsored by CORE, occurred on May 4, 1961, and was designed to determine whether southern states were heeding court orders to desegregate interstate transportation systems. Thirteen riders—six Caucasian and seven African American—divided themselves among two Greyhound buses with the intent of reaching New Orleans by land, but after the riders were beaten (with little protection from police) and their buses mobbed and firebombed in Alabama, they were forced to fly to New Orleans. With the help of Robert Kennedy, a group of SNCC students volunteered to finish the ride for them under similar

signs of our times is the reaching back to retrieve earlier models of pride, solidarity and courage. Just as one of the unhealthiest signs is the tendency so to distort our history on this continent as to make it an irrational hop-skip-jump from Attucks,[126] to Douglas, to Malcolm, to whoever happens to be the militant-of-the-moment. All credit to those who protest this wrenching of our total reality as both bad history and ultimately bad strategy. We deserve nothing less than the full richness and diversity of our heritage, its pluses and minuses, from its African roots to the present. But there are those of us who can remember well enough when white Americans, with some help from strategically placed Negroes, fed thousands of black children a very thin diet of models typified by Booker Washington.

Though I perhaps feel less reverence than I should for what sometimes passes for sound curriculum and good teaching on both majority-white and majority-black campuses, I am willing enough to grant that some of the black studies proposals I have seen may turn out to be no better and may well be as bad as the worst of current pedagogical fare. I am not sure that as foreign languages, African languages can be any worse taught or taken any less seriously by American students than have the European language "requirements" students commonly speak of as "finishing" or "getting off." Unless we are talking about professional training (and some recent studies suggest caution even here) it may be risky to insist too strongly on the test of utility for black studies at the college level, considering how little correlation we can assume between much of what is now taught on our campuses and what is used effectively in the workaday world. If the argument shifts to the culture-bearing value of education, then there are serious deficiencies in our present imbalanced educational diet which some infusion of black studies might well help to offset. My hope would be that fads and fakery would ultimately be shaken out in the course of the same sharp

---

terrible conditions. The students were thrown in jail at the end of their ride, but in the process they inspired many other Americans to join them in the fight for desegregation.

126. Crispus Attucks (c. 1723–70) was a man of African and Native American descent who led an armed crowd to confront British soldiers who had harmed a young boy on May 5, 1770. This triggered the Boston Massacre. The soldiers opened fire after one of them was hit by a piece of wood (allegedly thrown by Attucks), and Attucks was killed.

questioning which may eventually rid us of some of the more sanctified myths and irrelevancies of traditional higher education.

It will take some hard thinking and some determined efforts at bridging class and generational gaps to make what can be an historic opportunity of what may otherwise become a series of profitless internecine attacks and counter-attacks. And we are a longer way still from the time when race can honestly be said to be an irrelevancy in our national and personal lives. Hylan Lewis and I long ago agreed that if some convergence around certain social goals could be achieved, absolute unity might be foregone as both unattainable and probably unnecessary. It is troubling, no doubt, to see young people from a group already woefully short of doctors and other professionals questioning whether they should be educated for those professions at all, for fear they will be educated away from their people. No debate about the unwisdom of this attitude, however, is likely to be as effective as the opportunity to know and work with professionals who for some years have been demonstrating their pragmatic concern for "the brother in the street."

We seem to be entering upon another of those national periods of uncertain duration when repression is on the rise. Justice is suddenly too "soft" a word, and the majorities are weary of the problems of the troublesome minorities. Our institutions—colleges and universities included—are too often paralyzed or indifferent as the society of which they are a part proceeds to create a sub-class without the paper credentials to get and hold a job, the means of qualifying to run for elective office—or in some places even to vote, the power to insist that they have some choice in the matter of schools, housing, and the kind of justice that is available to them on the streets and in the courts. In such times, breakdowns in communication and mutual support among those who stand to lose most is especially dangerous. I hope that Haverford will prove to be an important step toward mending the breach.

BACKGROUND AND SIGNIFICANCE OF "BLACK STUDIES" PROGRAMS

Saunders Redding

There is no single generative force behind this sudden frantic rush to develop so-called "Black Studies" programs in American schools and institutions of higher learning. Several circumstances account for it, and I would like to remind you of some of them. I am reluctant to put them in any order of priority or even of chronology, for in the first instance, so far as I am aware, no psycho-social study has been made to measure the degree of influence of one circumstance or factor as against another; and in the second instance the circumstances, the factors, the events came into being at so nearly the same time that dating them has no importance except for the statistics-minded historian. Nor do they lend themselves to quantitative analysis.

One of the circumstances that comes first to mind is the Black Nationalists movement in Africa, and the liberation of certain areas of that continent from white colonial domination. Two of the African Nationalist leaders—Nkrumah of Ghana[127] and Ezekiwe of Nigeria[128]—had been educated principally in black colleges in the United States.[129] They had some claims on the affection and respect of black Americans, who were not slow to recognize these claims, and, indeed, to accept and honor the men who made them as heroes, even before the freedom they struggled for was completely won.

The circumstance that comes second to mind was the quiet reassessment of history—and particularly of southern history—that scholars of the calibre of John Hope Franklin, Rayford Logan,[130] Ken-

127. Kwame Nkrumah (1909–1972) was the prime minister of the Gold Coast from 1957 to 1960, and, when it gained its independence in 1957 and was renamed the Republic of Ghana, he became its president. The people of Ghana overthrew Nkrumah in 1966 after he began to suppress other political parties and assumed complete control of the country's armed forces and the Convention People's Party, a political group he formed in 1949. Nkrumah was a major proponent of Pan-Africanism.

128. Benjamin Nnamdi Azikiwe (1904–1996), a Nigerian statesman and Igbo nationalist, became the first president of the Republic of Nigeria in 1963. He was overthrown in 1966.

129. Azikiwe and Nkrumah both graduated from Lincoln University, in 1930 and 1939, respectively.

130. Rayford Whittingham Logan (1897–1982), a history professor, author, and editor, received a Ph.D. from Harvard, and then a law degree from Howard in 1972. He penned several scholarly texts concerning African American history, including *The Betrayal of the Negro, from Rutherford B. Hayes to Woodrow Wilson* (1965), *The Negro in the United States, a Brief History* (1957), and *W. E. B. Du Bois: A Profile* (1970). He also served as a consultant to the NAACP and the American government.

neth Stampp,[131] Benjamin Quarles,[132] and C. Vann Woodward[133] were making at about the same time that Africa was taking shape as a part of the so-called third world. Actually, of course, a reassessment of American history had been going on for more than a hundred years, and was actually organized as a scholarly endeavor with the founding of the Association for the Study of Negro Life and History by Carter G. Woodson in 1915;[134] but mainly, if not only black scholars were involved, and no one paid much attention to black scholars in those days; or when academicians of the stripe of Ulrich Phillips,[135] Bancroft[136]

131. The historian, professor, and author Kenneth Stampp (1912–2009) received his Ph.D. in history from the University of Wisconsin, Madison, in 1942. Stampp wrote numerous books that challenged commonly held beliefs about the South. In 1956 he published *The Peculiar Institution: Slavery in the Antebellum South,* which argued that plantation owners were not benign and paternal figures, as was generally believed at the time.

132. Benjamin Quarles (1904–1996), an author and professor, received his Ph.D. in history from the University of Wisconsin in 1940. He is known for his research and books on the part African Americans played in the founding and early years of the United States. A prolific writer, he authored many books, including *The Negro in the American Revolution* (1961), *The Negro in the Making of America* (1964), and *Black Abolitionists* (1969).

133. C. Vann Woodward (1908–1999), a historian, professor, and author, received his Ph.D. in history from the University of North Carolina in 1937. He focused on race relations and the South and taught at various schools, including Yale. He published many groundbreaking books, including *Origins of the New South, 1877–1913* (1951), *The Strange Career of Jim Crow* (1955), and *The Comparative Approach to American History* (1968).

134. The Association for the Study of Negro Life and History (now the Association for the Study of African American Life and History) was founded by Carter G. Woodson in 1915. It is still pursuing its mission to research and spread information about the culture and accomplishments of people of African descent. The ASALH started Black History Month. Woodson (1875–1950), an educator and writer, received his Ph.D. from Harvard University in 1912. He was a teacher, a school principal, and a professor, and the author of many books on African American history. Because of this, he is often called the Father of Black History.

135. Ulrich Phillips (1877–1934), regarded in his time as an expert on the history of the South, received his Ph.D. in philosophy from Columbia University in 1902. Phillips did extensive research about plantation life in the South, collecting an impressive number of firsthand accounts (diaries) on the topic, and finally published his findings in the form of a book, *American Negro Slavery,* in 1918. The book painted slaveholders in a largely positive light.

136. Hubert Bancroft (1832–1918) published *The Works of Hubert Howe Bancroft,* an extensive history of the west coast of the United States, Central America,

and Dunning[137] did pay attention, it was only to repudiate them and their work. Franklin, Stampp, Woodward, and the rest, beginning in the late 1940's, were not easy to repudiate. Woodward's *Origins of the New South,* Franklin's *From Slavery to Freedom,* and Stampp's *The Peculiar Institution* discredited much of what had been written before as historical gospel.

A third circumstance I would remind you of is the Supreme Court decision of 1954, which had several results among which it is extremely difficult, in the time we have, to discriminate between cause and effect. One result of that decision was to broaden, even if only a little, the areas of black-white integration and black-white competition. Before then, with the exception of the Armed Forces, where integration was partially achieved, there was only token integration and competition. After that decision, tokenism was no longer acceptable to blacks.

And finally, I would have you recall the organized resistance of blacks to segregation and discrimination: the sit-ins, the bus boycotts, the pray-ins, and the wade-ins; and I would have you recall that black Americans were not alone.

Now the point I wish to make is that if all these circumstances, factors and events were creating a "new" Negro self-image, they were at the same time compelling a good number of whites, especially among the young, to take a fresh look at themselves, at the society in which they lived, and at the institutions that supported the society. But taking a look is one thing, and doing something about what you see is an entirely different thing. And only a handful of whites were capable of the latter, or had the will, or the courage—and those who were capable, and had the will and the courage were frowned upon by the vast majority, and for many of them the only out was the drop-out, the withdrawal, the trip—safe in the knowledge that they could drop-in again;

---

and Mexico. The majority of *The Works* was written by paid but uncredited writers. Bancroft donated his collection of books, maps, and pamphlets detailing the history of the West to the University of California.

137. William Archibald Dunning (1857–1922) was a historian who earned his degree at Columbia University in 1881. He is famous for having founded the Dunning School of Reconstruction, which depicted former slaves as overreaching and white Northerners in the South as carpetbaggers. Scholars such as Du Bois, C. Vann Woodward, and John Hope Franklin discredited some of the key ideas on which Dunning's work was premised.

that, being white, all they had to do was stay off pot and LSD, put on shoes again, get a bath and a haircut, and they would be back in.

But black Americans could not drop out of a society of which they had never been a part, and of course they could not drop in. More and more of them began to feel that they had to make their own society. More and more of them repudiated integration as a goal. The extremists among them wanted to go all the way to a black uni-racial state. If in a multi-racial state they could not attain pride and dignity as black people, then they would create a society in which pride and dignity would be theirs by virtue of their blackness, black is beautiful. And history, including the events of day before yesterday, proves it. So they turned to black history, black literature, black culture.

That then, greatly oversimplified, is the background. What is the significance? The significance lies in the fact that knowledge that is not shared is useless. It lies in the fact that satisfying the demands of black students for "black courses" will open up to white students areas of knowledge about which most of them have been willfully kept in ignorance, or, perhaps even worse, about which the truth has been willfully distorted. And all this leads to the final statement I wish to make:

Except when we put it in the context of Africa, there is no such thing as "black studies"—no black history, language, philosophy, physics, chemistry, ethics, etc. in the context of the United States. There *is* such a thing as *American studies,* and in courses such as American history, literature, sociology, economics, the ideal is to structure into these courses the substantive facts about black Americans. I can conceive, also, of special courses and seminars that might deal pretty exclusively with black Americans—for instance, a seminar in "The Social Dynamics of the Ghetto," or a course in "Labor and Management and the Negro Community," but one would be a course under the rubric of *American Sociology* and the other would be under the rubric of *Economics* and such courses can be multiplied and brought in under other rubrics as needed, as under *American Literature,* a course in "Ghetto Rhetoric: Language and Meaning."

These and other courses should not be restricted to black American students. One of the difficulties of our present American situation is due to the ignorance of white people about Negroes. Moreover, any degree of segregation is anathema. Nor should such courses necessarily be conducted by black teachers, of whom, anyway, there are not enough to go around: and just to bring in somebody to teach because he's black puts us in danger of reducing standards so drastically as to work to the harm of education in general and black students in particular. I go along with Bayard Rustin.

Phyllis A. Wallace

When future historians attempt to assess the campus upheavals of the late 1960's they may be puzzled by the fact that one group of persons of keen perception contributed little to the resolution of the conflict. I believe that these scholars have a responsibility to themselves, to black and white students of present and future generations and to all concerned with the survival of institutions of higher education. Their responsibility is to help redefine goals and to project new patterns of behavior and action.

Much of the discussion at Haverford was eloquent, and I shall not attempt to write my own manifesto. I would like to catalogue some crucial follow-up activity:

1. A brief statement (manifesto, credo, declaration, etc. and of no more than three pages) of the consensus from the Haverford Conference should be prepared *immediately* and disseminated as soon as possible.
2. Perhaps an additional fifty scholars should be invited to sign this statement. Each person attending the Haverford Conference would be asked to suggest several names. The signers would include representatives from predominantly black and white colleges and universities as well as few who by reason of their achievement in other areas have credibility in the academic community.
3. The signed statement could be released to the American Council on Education, American Association of University Professors, foundations, important newspapers and journals (including the ethnic press), radio and TV, and boards of trustees of selected universities. All of this should be compiled *before Labor Day.*
4. After the release of the statement the great debate could begin with a larger group of black scholars, black students, white administrators, etc.
5. MARC should seek funding for this on-going project. Essentially it would be necessary to compile a roster of black student leaders at universities around the country. One or two of MARC black summer interns could initiate this part of the project now.

6. MARC could serve as the neutral meeting place for black scholars and black students to communicate with each other.
7. Some loose regional network could be established with black scholars from several parts of the country periodically submitting reports.
8. If MARC accepts the role of facilitator it must be prepared to assign at least one person on a full time basis.
9. After nine months the program could be evaluated and a determination made on whether it was advisable to continue it, or the entire operation could be spun off to some other agency.

Robert C. Weaver

Perhaps in large measure because I could not attend the final session of the Haverford meeting, I find that I have a degree of ambivalence about the subject. Also, I believe that this is a reaction to the dogmatism and certainty of some who speak for different points of view. And, too, I am confident that part of my difficulty lies in the fact that many of the terms used in these discussions are rarely defined.

Within this context, there seem to be certain concepts that are pertinent. The first is the necessity to differentiate between issues and tactics. The issue is clear-cut. This nation has neglected and discriminated against its black people. Efforts to secure their full participation in the mainstream of society have had only partial success and have had little meaning for a large segment of Negroes. Many of the latter are now demanding that they have a meaningful role in their affairs.

Among youth this is especially pressing. And its impact is accentuated on the college campuses where a growing number of alienated black young people, who feel excluded from middle-class America and, along with other youth, challenge accepted, dominant values. The colleges and universities which these black youth attend are not prepared to provide what seems to be meaningful education to a new population having new, unfamiliar, and sometimes unique needs.

Because established institutions and established programs seem unresponsive to the needs of many black students, they reject them. In their place some of the black students call for separatism as a goal and confrontation as a tactic.

The second issue, therefore, involves value judgments relative to the method of meeting an undeniable problem. Here, it seems to me, one cannot be dogmatic. The traditional programs and approaches have not been without results, but they have not reached many Negro Americans. Thus, there is a tendency for those who have benefited to champion traditional programs and methods, while those who have been neglected are prone to repudiate these approaches. Black Studies programs (which cry for careful and comprehensive definition), if they are academically sound, must probe into this matter and attempt to define the true situation.

Perhaps the most basic issue is that of goals. Do we want to establish a separate black society; and if so is it a permanent goal or a temporary arrangement which is achievable now and will be effective in ultimately facilitating black people's full participation in this nation? And if the latter position is espoused, is it viable, or does the acceptance of separation create institutional patterns and vested interests that give it permanence? Here again, I would hope that Black Studies will provide the facts, analyses, and discussions which will offer the basis for sound evaluations.

Such studies, too, would be helpful in evaluating tactics. They might well recognize the short-run efficacy of confrontation and also question its longer-run implications. Or it would be appropriate to explore the possibility of merging some of the features of each approach.

Implicit in what has been said above is the realization that the Negro has been affected by the total society at the same time that he has affected that society. Thus, any sound consideration of his problems and status must be developed within the framework of the larger society in which he has functioned and will continue to function, to some degree, at least.

If we are to arrive at sound objectives, programs and tactics, it seems to me that we need to encourage continuing dialogue. To act meaningfully, those of different points of view must develop the capacity to listen to each other, recognizing that no segment, or no one point of view, is endowed with enduring, absolute validity.

APPENDIX I

Biographical Sketches of the Haverford Discussions Participants

Kenneth B. Clark (1914–2005), an educational psychologist who received his Ph.D. in 1940 from Columbia University, became the first African American tenured full professor at City College of New York and the first black president of the American Psychological Association. With his wife, he did groundbreaking research using black and white dolls to document how segregation damaged black children; the findings were used in the *Brown v. Board of Education* case. He authored *Dark Ghetto: Dilemmas of Social Power* (1965) and *Pathos of Power* (1974).

Mamie Phipps Clark (1917–1983), an educational psychologist who received her Ph.D. in 1943 from Columbia University, conducted experiments that demonstrated that there are no mental differences between black and white children. She copublished articles with her husband, Kenneth Clark, and their work was cited in the *Brown v. Board of Education* case.

St. Clair Drake (1911–1990) coauthored with Horace Cayton *Black Metropolis* (1945), an extremely influential study of race and urban life in Chicago. Trained as a sociologist, he became chair of black studies at Stanford University in 1969. He authored numerous books, including *Our Urban Poor: Promises to Keep and Miles to Go* (1967), *The Redemption of Africa and Black Religion* (1970), and *Black Folk Here and There: An Essay in History and Anthropology* (1987–90).

Ralph Ellison (1914–1994) published *Invisible Man* in 1952, which won the National Book Award in 1953. He also published groundbreaking essays, collected in *Shadow and Act* (1964) and *Going to the Territory* (1986). From the 1950s through the 1980s, he was one of the most influential and respected writers in the United States.

John Hope Franklin (1915–2009), a renowned historian who received his Ph.D. from Harvard in 1941, published many books, including *From Slavery to Freedom* (1947), *Reconstruction: After the Civil War* (1961), and *The Emancipation Proclamation* (1963). In 1995 he was awarded the Presidential Medal of Freedom. As a professor, he taught at Howard University, Brooklyn College, the University of Chicago, Cambridge University, and Duke University.

William H. Hastie (1904–1976), the first African American federal judge, received his Ph.D. in juridical science from Harvard Law School in 1933. He became dean and professor of law at Howard University, where one of his students was Thurgood Marshall.

Adelaide Hill (1919–), now Adelaide M. Cromwell, received her Ph.D. in sociology from Radcliffe College in 1952 and was director of the Afro-American Studies Department at Boston University. She authored numerous books, including *An African Victorian Feminist: The Life and Times of Adelaide Smith Casely Hayford, 1868–1960* (1986); *Apropos of Africa: Sentiments of Negro American Leaders on Africa from the 1800s to the 1950s* (1969); and *Dynamics of the African/Afro-American Connection: From Dependency to Self-Reliance* (1987).

M. Carl Holman (1919–1988) received M.A. degrees from Yale University and the University of Chicago. A poet, he received the John Billings Fiske Poetry Prize and a Rosenwald Fellowship. He was a leading strategist of the civil rights movement, and he headed the National Urban Coalition from 1971 until his death in 1988.

Hylan Lewis (1911–2000), a sociologist who received his Ph.D. from the University of Chicago, published *Blackways of Kent* (1955), a groundbreaking study of a segregated southern town in the late 1940s.

J. Saunders Redding (1906–1988) authored numerous books, including *To Make a Poet Black* (1939), *Stranger and Alone* (1950), and *The Lonesome Road: The Story of the Negro's Part in America* (1958). Redding was one of the most influential and powerful black academics in the United States. He was the first African American to hold an endowed chair at an Ivy League university (Cornell) and was considered the dean of African American studies from the 1950s through the 1980s.

Anne Cooke Reid (1907–?) received her Ph.D. in theater from Yale University in 1944. In 1934 she founded the first black summer theater in the United States, in Atlanta. A professor of drama, she chaired Howard University's first drama department from 1944 to 1958.

Phyllis A. Wallace (1920–1993) received her Ph.D. in economics from Yale in 1948. She authored *Black Women in the Labor Force* (1980), *Women in the Workplace* (1982), and *Pathways to Work: Unemployment among Black Teenage Females* (1974). She was the first female tenured professor at MIT's Sloan School of Management.

Robert C. Weaver (1907–1997) received a Ph.D. in economics from Harvard in 1934 and was the first African American to hold a cabinet-level position: he was the first secretary of housing and urban development (1966–68).

Eddie N. Williams (1932–) was vice president for public affairs and director of the Center for Policy Study at the University of Chicago. In 1972 he became the president of the Joint Center for Political and Economic Studies, the premier black think tank in the United States.

APPENDIX II

Haverford/Hastie Group Meetings

First Meeting MAY 30–31, 1969

Title: Haverford Discussions
Location: Haverford College in Haverford, Pennsylvania
Participants: Kenneth B. Clark, Mamie Phipps Clark, George Dalley, St. Clair Drake, Ralph Ellison, John Hope Franklin, William H. Hastie, Adelaide Hill, M. Carl Holman, J. Saunders Redding, Anne Cooke Reid, Robert C. Weaver, Phyllis A. Wallace, Eddie N. Williams

Second Meeting OCTOBER 8–9, 1969

Title: Haverford Follow-Up Conference
Location: International Hotel, John F. Kennedy Airport, Jamaica, New York
Participants: Kenneth B. Clark, Mamie Phipps Clark, George Dalley, Ralph Ellison, William Hastie, Adelaide C. Hill, M. Carl Holman, Hylan Lewis, Dixie H. Moon, Beatrice Olsen, Alfred Prettyman, J. Saunders Redding, Phyllis A. Wallace, Franklin H. Williams

Third Meeting MAY 28–30, 1972

Title: Haverford Group Meeting
Location: Metropolitan Applied Research Center, Inc. (MARC), New York City, New York
Participants: Kenneth B. Clark, Mamie Phipps Clark, George Dalley, Bernard Gifford, William Hastie, Hylan Lewis, Catherine Martin, Dixie H. Moon, Beatrice Olsen, J. Saunders Redding, Mrs. Saunders Redding, Anne Reid, Joan Tormey, Kitty Terjen, Phyllis A. Wallace, and Bernard Watson

Fourth Meeting MAY 16–18, 1975

Title: Meeting of the Hastie Group
Location: Metropolitan Applied Research Center, Inc. (MARC), New York City, New York
Participants: Kenneth B. Clark, Mamie Phipps Clark, Bernard Gifford, William Hastie, Adelaide Cromwell Gulliver, M. Carl Holman, Hylan Lewis, J. Saunders Redding, Robert C. Weaver, Franklin H. Williams

APPENDIX III

Kenneth B. Clark Letters

November 2, 1967

Dr. Homer A. Jack
Director
Unitarian Universalist Association
c/o Robert E. Jones
245 Second Street, N.E.
Washington, D.C. 20002

Dear Dr. Jack:

I received the material you were kind enough to send to me and I have thought a great deal about our conversation. This letter is an attempt to summarize my thinking about the problem posed for the Unitarian Universalist Association by the demands of the Black Caucus and it is also an attempt to analyze as coldly as possible whether I can play a constructive role in helping the board of directors of the U.U.A. arrive at just, rational, human and democratic decisions on this matter.

The most important first step for me is to make perfectly clear my own position on matters of race relations in America. It would be dishonest for me to pretend that I do not have firm value positions on this matter. Anyone who knows me and knows of my work knows that I am committed to a struggle for a racially integrated American society. I believe that racial segregation in its subtle or flagrant forms is dehumanizing to both Negroes and whites. I believe that racially segregated communities perpetuate intolerable forms of social pathology. I believe that racial segregation and discrimination in employment is pivotal in perpetuating the total pattern of family instability, dependency and neglect of human beings, particularly of Negro children.

Given these beliefs, which are backed by evidence, reason and morality, I am unable to accept any ideology, plans, or programs which I believe directly or indirectly contribute to the perpetuation and intensification of any form of racial segregation in American life.

My study of the Black Power movement and my reading and analysis of the materials which are related to the Emergency Conference on the Unitarian Universalist Response to the Black Rebellion lead me to the conclusion that the demands made by the Black Caucus are specific manifestations of a new racist thrust. The method of the Black Caucus, the rationale, and its specific suggestions and demands make clear the fact that a certain group of Negroes have come to the conclusion that racial integration in significant areas of American society, including the church, is an impossible goal. In rejecting this goal, they are explicitly and implicitly now asking for a racially separatist system. The fact of a Black Caucus and the demand for a permanent Black Affairs Council, are clearly racially separatist developments.

If the U.U.A. were to concede to such demands and give official sanction to an organization such as a Black Affairs Council or Black Unitarian Universalists for Radical Reform, it would be taking a regressive step, which the Methodists, in giving up their central jurisdiction (all Negro), abandoned within the last few years.

While I can understand the depth of frustration out of which the Black Power movement comes, and understand also the fact that the masses of Negro people justifiably are revolted by verbal civil rights "victories," tokenism, and the pervasive moral hypocrisy which perpetuates dehumanizing American racism, I am personally convinced that the Black Power and Black Caucus method of reacting to these realities is self-defeating in that it tends to intensify rather than to remedy this violent disease of American racism.

Given this perspective, the question arises whether I can play a constructive role in helping the U.U.A. deal with this problem as it is presented to it by the Black Caucus form of confrontation. It would follow from my analysis that I would suggest that the first step in any attempt at rational discussion and constructive resolution of the problem posed to the Association would be for the board of directors of the U.U.A. to reexamine its own value positions and goals on the matter of the American racial problem. I cannot in good conscience ask that the U.U.A. accept my values and goals and reject those of the Black Caucus. I can only assert that the reactions of the board of directors to the specific demands will certainly reflect the fundamental position of the board on matters of race. If the U.U.A. and its board of directors are committed to the goals of an integrated America, an America in which the fact or the fiction of race becomes irrelevant in the enjoyment of the rights of American citizens, then it would seem to me that it could not be logical to attempt to obtain those goals by intensifying race and by making it the relevant factor in seeking to obtain the goals of racial democracy.

If, on the other hand, Unitarian Universalists are ambivalent, and are prepared to abandon or to postpone indefinitely the difficult struggle for the attainment of an integrated America, then it would seem consistent to entertain seriously the inherently racist demands of the Black Caucus.

I would be prepared to suggest also that if the goals of the U.U.A. *are* consistent with racial integration in America, that it might be possible for it to examine carefully the demands of the Black Caucus, and select those which seem rationally consistent with these goals and reject, without apology, those which seem unrealistic and rationally and morally inconsistent. I am not suggesting that this is easy. Reason and unswerving adherence to moral and democratic goals are particularly difficult to maintain when they are being emotionally attacked, particularly when there appears some justification for their rejection. But it is precisely at those times when these values and goals must be most vigorously defended if they are to be preserved.

You and your steering committee must know that the only possible role which I could perform at a meeting with the board of directors in a discussion of this matter would be one in which I made clear my own position, one in which I asked them to examine as thoroughly as possible their position and one in which I asked of them that they have the courage to make decisions on the basis of a clear articulation of their values, their goals, and programs for action which are relevant. I could play no other role which could be consistent with my own self respect and my own standards as a professional.

It is quite likely that such a role is not consistent with the passion of our times. It may be that the deep sense of guilt and racial ambivalence on the part of rational and liberal whites in America, and probably the deeper sense of frustration, anger, and bitterness on the part of a growing number of Negroes contribute to the irrelevance of those voices which continue to ask for unswerving allegiance to reason, morality, and human dignity.

I cannot accept with equanimity a call for racial separatism coming from human beings with dark skins any more than I can tolerate such calls coming from human beings with lighter skins. Both groups of human beings to me reflect the pathos, the despair, the anguish of unfulfilled lives. It is no more just to acquiesce to the demands of the one than to those of the other—particularly when they are the same in effect. Justice can be served only by remaking our society so that it realistically fulfills the requirements for dignity for all human beings. This demands that Negroes, whites, and all others join forces, speak together, work together, argue with one another, and fight the formidable forces of irrationality and immorality as allies.

It has been argued that one should be more attentive and responsive to the racist demands of the Black Power movement because this is necessary to build a racial pride and dignity which must precede serious racial justice in America. I do not accept this for a number of reasons. First, a similar argument could be offered in support of the racism of white segregationists. One could accept even the most cruel and flagrant manifestation of white supremacy as essential to building the dignity and pride of otherwise deprived and insecure whites. Second, I do not believe that any genuine pride in race or nationality can be built upon the realities of racial degradation, the realities of economic deprivation, the realities of criminally inferior racially segregated education, the realities of the total pattern of pathology inherent in racially segregated housing. Genuine pride and dignity for whites and Negroes can come only when an affluent society such as ours makes available the necessary financial and intellectual resources to bring about the massive social and economic changes essential for social justice. We have the resources; so far we have lacked only the commitment. And third, I personally question the validity of pride based on color of skin, whether it be white or black. Such a pride seems to me at best tenuous and at worst destructive of the potential of a human being to develop a more fundamental basis for pride and dignity.

To deal with the Black Caucus with standards and criteria of reason, maturity and general acceptability that are different from those which would be used by the board and the Association in dealing with any other petitioning or dissident group would be a most insidious form of racial condescension. This form of racism would be no more tolerable or acceptable offered in the name of guilt or sentimentalism than if offered in the name of frank and traditional forms of racial bigotry. The obscenity of the New Politics–Black Caucus charade cannot be repeated by an Association which prides itself on bringing reason to religion. A rational approach to the meaning of God and a humanistic view of man and society demand that one acts to redress rather than to imitate the horror of Chicago.

Sincerely yours,
Kenneth B. Clark

May 14, 1968

Dr. Edward H. Levi, Provost
University of Chicago
Chicago, Illinois

Dear Dr. Levi:

In response to the telephone conversation in which you asked for my opinion of the demand of some Negro students for an all Negro dormitory at the University of Chicago, I believe that this problem is of such grave importance as to require a carefully thought through response. I am therefore writing you this letter to attempt to summarize in writing my thoughts and feelings.

First I should make it clear to you that my negative response on the telephone was not a spontaneous "off the top of my head" response. As you can see from the enclosed copy of a letter which I sent to the Unitarian-Universalist Association, I have been thinking for a long time about the problems inherent in the demand of some Negroes for "self-imposed" forms of racial separatism or voluntary segregation. Recently, I watched with concern the negotiations between some Negro students and the administration at Northwestern University which culminated in a decision—so I am advised—on the part of the University to accede to the Negro students' demands for an all Negro dormitory.

As a psychologist I try to understand the depths of frustration and bitterness out of which these racial separatist demands arise. Given the fact that American society has played cynical games with the legitimate aspirations of Negro Americans for racial justice and have offered, at best, either the condescension of tokenism, evasion or, at worse, southern cattle prods and bombings and northern liberal backlash, I understand the impatience of Negroes—and particularly the youth—and their unwillingness to continue to have faith that reason and appeals to conscience will lead to the attainment of racial justice during their lifetime. They are unwilling to continue to seek an affirmative definition of their humanity through appeals to and the willingness of whites to accept them as human beings. In effect, given their assessment of the moral capacity of white America, an increasing number of human beings are turning their backs on racial integration as a practicable approach to the goal of racial justice and as the basis for personal dignity for themselves.

In understanding this, however, I do not accept or agree with the variety of demands which some Negroes are making for racially segregated facilities and institutions. I particularly do not agree with the demands for racially segregated educational institutions or facilities. My studies of this problem have convinced me that all forms of racial segregation institutionalize racism and thereby intensify the basic American disease. Furthermore the consequences of voluntary or self-imposed racial segregation are as detrimental—at times more insidiously so—as that of involuntary segregation. In fact, one might argue persuasively that so called voluntary racial segregation is merely a thinly disguised reaction to imposed segregation—an attempt to protect oneself, to escape, from the more flagrant hurt inherent in imposed racial segregation.

It would seem to me rather obvious that the function of any educational institution which fully understands and accepts its role of freeing human beings of petty provincial constrictions of the human mind—freeing human beings of irrational fears and hatreds and freeing human beings of the gnawing burdens of myths and superstitions—could not tolerate being a partner to any institutionalized forms of racism.

I am aware of the fact that historically American educational institutions have been flagrantly and insidiously contaminated by racist considerations. I know that our colleges and universities have in the past, and also at present, defaulted in assuming any assertive leadership role in helping to free America of the costly burdens of racism. But I cannot accept the fact that they must retrogress under the pretext that some Negro students are now demanding racially segregated dormitories or other college facilities. How would college officials react if white students demanded all white dormitories? I am afraid that the answer to this disturbing question must be seen behind all facades and liberal rationalizations by the unseemly alacrity and acquiescence with which they react to the Negro students' demands.

Aside from the moral, educational and legal (which I shall allude to later) problems which are raised by these demands for all Negro dormitories, there is the important human problem raised by the question: What about the Negro student who does not want to live in an all Negro dormitory—who does not want to be categorized on the basis of his race or color while seeking an understanding of the commonality of the human predicament? Is he to be forced by the university to live under conditions which affront his sense of his own humanity and individuality? Will the university be an accessory to his being coerced or intimidated into showing a solidarity or unity with his fellow Negroes under threat of ostracism, name calling or worse? Is this an atmosphere conducive to reflective thought and free inquiry? Above all a university must be a place where the rights of the individual to intelligent, rational, systematic probing must not only be cherished but protected. This, I believe, is the meaning of "academic freedom." The university's involvement in the setting up of an all black or an all white dormitory for its students would be a profound violation of academic freedom. It would be a mockery of the goals of education and could only occur in a society which was so severely ill with the disease of racism and its symptoms of guilt, hostility and ambivalence as to be in severe crises of survival.

Not being a lawyer, I cannot write with a great deal of assurance concerning the legal and constitutional implications of these demands. What little I do know about civil rights constitutional litigation and law (together with my own stated biases) lead me to believe that any university or college which sets up an all Negro dormitory violates the letter and the spirit of the *McLaurin* decision and also the *Brown* decision of the United States Supreme Court. In the *McLaurin* decision the court was quite clear that the University and its governing board could not segregate or isolate Negro students on the arbitrary basis of race without violating the equal protection clause of the United States Constitution. I do not believe that this basic principle is inoperative merely because the victims ask for the segregated facilities. The important issue, it would seem to me, is that in granting such demands for racial segregation, the university as an agent of the state or public, is acting in violation of the Constitution without regard to the source of the request. If our universities and colleges do not deal with these matters with more assertive educational leadership then it will be necessary to bring this problem before our courts. A taxpayer suit might be necessary to prevent this type of racial retrogression in our educational institutions.

For all of the above reasons—and others which are much too visceral for me to express with any pretense of coherence—I am personally unalterably opposed to any educational or other public or quasi-public institution classifying or in any way categorizing its students or personnel on the basis of the irrelevant and arbitrary factor of race or color. I am opposed to all Negro or all white classes, dormitories, schools or colleges. The fact that Negro nationalists are now joining white supremacists in demanding such racially segregated facilities merely means to me that the cancer of American racism has metastasized and that our societal prognosis is indeed grave. Those of us who still believe in the positive potential of human beings and that educational institutions must reinforce these positives cannot contribute to the disease but must try to cure the patient even when such cure might require the painful remedies of courage and clarity.

Sincerely,
Kenneth B. Clark

May 15, 1969

Dr. Theodore M. Newcomb
Department of Psychology
Ann Arbor, Michigan 48104

Dear Ted,

This is not an easy letter to write. As you probably guessed from my telephone conversation this morning and from having known me for more than 25 years, I can become so concerned, so disturbed by what I believe to be important problems of social justice and mutual respect among human beings that I often become incoherent and unable to express my feelings logically and systematically.

The problem of Antioch's support of the Afro-American Institute and the controversy with the HEW as to whether Antioch's support of this racially organized and exclusionary facility on its campus did or did not violate Title VI of the Civil Rights Act is to me a serious matter involving racial justice and dignity, and the role of the college and university in helping to free the human mind and body of primitive passions. As you know from my previous letters to you and to President Dixon and from our series of discussions, I have been, not only disturbed, but vigorously opposed to the college's decision to participate in any form of racial exclusion.

I opposed this for the same reasons that we fought together in the school segregation cases which led to the Brown decision. I continue to believe, as I know you do, that racial prejudice, discrimination and segregation are damaging to the human personality without regard to the racial rationalizations or excuses offered in support of such practices.

There is absolutely no evidence to support the contention that the inherent damage to human beings of primitive exclusion on the basis of race is any less damaging when demanded or enforced by the previous victims than when imposed by the dominant group. There is absolutely no valid basis by which educational institutions can or should make any distinctions on the basis of race or color. Some argue that blacks and whites must be separated because they represent different cultures and that cultures, like oil and water, cannot mix. Segregationists have argued so for generations against integrated transportation, drinking fountains, integrated schools, and intermarriage—maintaining that mixture would lead to mongrelization of the races. Such racial distinctions are arbitrary, dangerously ignorant, and cruel. They are destructive and inimical to all of the goals of serious education. In this regard I am in complete agreement with the editorial in the New York Times of Wednesday, May 7, 1969, which said among other things that HEW did "a serious disservice to the cause of racial integration by authorizing Antioch College to operate an all-Negro black studies institute." I am not, however, particularly surprised that practical and political men would find such justification consistent with their political needs to seek to accept a patently racist arrangement by subterfuge.

To exclude someone of one race—or to admit that it would be appropriate to do so—on the grounds that his background or experience are irrelevant, that they render him unable to achieve is precisely what white segregationists have been doing to blacks for centuries. Yet this seems to be the burden of rationalization at Antioch for a black separatist policy. Yet, it is whites who need a black studies program most of all.

The white liberal for his part who concedes black separatism so hastily and benevolently must look to his own reasons, not the least of them perhaps an exquisite relief. To encourage or endorse a separate black program not academically equivalent to the college curriculum generally, indeed to endorse any such program, is to reinforce the Negro's inability to compete with whites for the real power of the real world. It is no excuse to justify the deed by citing the demand.

The history of the Civil Rights movement, the pattern of evasion since the Brown decision 15 years ago prepared me for this HEW type of logic and evasion of the fundamental moral and legal implications of this problem. What I am *not* prepared to accept is continued association with an educational institution which is an accessory, if not an instigator of this type of game-playing with the lives of human beings and with the life and stability of society. I am personally not prepared to continue an association with Antioch College in which as a member of the Board of Directors I am, and must be considered educationally responsible for and a participant in what is to me, a shoddy evasion of the moral and educational responsibility which a college must assume or frankly admit that it is indistinguishable from the political areas of our society.

I believe that above all under times of tension, stress, and pressures to conform to the shouting demands of the populace, colleges must have the courage to stand firmly for the rule of reason and for those principles and values considered indispensable to serious education. I do not believe that Antioch, in acceding to the demands for a separate facility for its Negro students, has showed this type of courage. I do not believe that Antioch, in permitting some of the more hostile Negro students to coerce and intimidate other Negroes and whites by quashing vocal dissent, has showed the courage necessary to maintain that type of academic climate which permits man that freedom of inquiry, freedom of thought, and freedom of dissent which are essential to the life of the intellect.

Colleges and universities must be the custodians of the rational and intellectual approach to the study and eventual solution of difficult and complex human problems. To succumb to any form of dogmatism, to institutionalize the irrational is to fail in fulfilling this important obligation. I am convinced that Antioch has not only violated this sacred obligation by its approach to the Afro-American Studies Institute, and by permitting the existence of and financially supporting the racially exclusionary Unity house on its campus, Antioch has also tarnished its own glorious traditions of stubborn resistance to the fashionable. It was this history which made me profoundly proud to be identified with Antioch College.

In permitting a group of students to inflict their dogmatism and ideology on other students and on the total college community; and in being silent while some students intimidate, threaten, and in some cases physically assault the Negro students who disagree with them, the Administration at Antioch has not only defaulted in its responsibilities, but, I believe has made a mockery of its concern for the protection and development of human dignity without regard to cost.

Therefore, Ted, for all the above reasons and many more which are tied up in my being, I cannot continue the pretense of membership on the Board of Directors at Antioch and, hereby, send you my resignation, to take effect immediately.

Cordially,
Kenneth B. Clark

Afterword: The Mission

Alfred E. Prettyman

In his announcement of the change of name for the Institute on Urban Problems, founded in 1967, to the Metropolitan Applied Research Center, Inc., Kenneth Bancroft Clark said, "Hopefully, through usage, we will be known as the MARC Corp."[1] And indeed MARC became an exemplar of informed activism and applied research, as illustrated in part by its support of the Haverford Group.

The confidential third and final draft of MARC's mission statement was sent to Clark for final approval by Jeannette Hopkins on July 4, 1968—not a coincidence.[2] This draft became the basis of a small brochure setting forth in its opening paragraphs the goals and assumptions of "The MARC Experiment":

> MARC seeks to serve as a catalyst for change and as an advocate for the poor and powerless in American cities. MARC has no precise model: it is more a process than an institution. Its goals are defined by the needs of contemporary urban society; its effectiveness or failure is determined by the extent to which it meets—or fails to meet—these needs.
>
> The MARC experiment is an attempt to determine by systematic exploration whether trained intelligence can be mobilized as an effective form of power for positive social change. The MARC Corporation is an independently-funded consortium of persons with experience, knowledge, and skills in the fields of social science, law, and municipal and public affairs, who are committed in the attempt to influence social policy.
>
> MARC cannot gauge its own efforts by customary measures of organizational activity or even of productivity; its only test will be evidence of improvement in the conditions under which lower-status persons are required to live.

1. Box 309, Folder 6, Kenneth Bancroft Clark Papers, Manuscript Division, Library of Congress, Washington, D.C. (hereafter referred to as KBCP LOC). My thanks to Patrick Kerwin of the Manuscript Division for his ready assistance.

2. Ibid. Hopkins was Clark's longtime advisor and editor.

> The MARC Corporation program includes:
> *Research*
> *Analysis*
> *Strategy development*
> *Intervention.*
>
> Its staff will undertake the monitoring of governmental services and programs to ensure that the rights of the poor and of lower-status minority groups are not ignored or shortchanged, and that their share in the economic and political benefits of the society is not lost or pre-empted by others because of their lack of power to protect themselves.
>
> When social exploitation is made possible by others because of the lack of coherent and concrete information, MARC tries to gather and present the relevant data in a meaningful pattern.
>
> When lack of communication between Negro and white communities impedes positive social change, MARC tries to analyze the causes and to suggest ways to ease alienation.
>
> When intervention and direct action are required, MARC tries to develop effective strategies and to test them.
>
> When social programs fail—its own as well as others—MARC tries to understand and report the reasons for failure and the criteria for effectiveness in ways useful to social activists, policy makers, students of social dynamics, and the concerned public.
>
> MARC assumes that the self-interest of the city and the nation as a whole—not merely the self-interest of the ghetto and of the poor—depends on improving the living conditions of the poor, and eventually on abolishing poverty. The poor, by virtue of being poor, are in many respects powerless and cannot be expected to provide the only energy mobilized in their behalf. All groups—not the poor alone, nor Negroes or Puerto Ricans alone—are responsible for finding the means to save their cities.

Such was the principled context in which the work of MARC was conducted. Its ethos was a natural constituent of the environments in which all of the Haverford and Hastie Group meetings took place and intrinsic to the integrity of every participant. Both the MARC mission and the analysis the *Haverford Discussions* provides are still relevant today.

The eagerness of the Haverford Group participants to be of help to both their younger critics and college administrators was apparent from the beginning. As a participant observer and editor of the transcripts for all of the discussions, I took notes at the evening session that opened the October 8–9, 1969, follow-up meeting. Clark then observed that it was clear to him from his visits to campuses that not only did "students really need us . . . college administrators also need informed interlocutors." Adelaide Cromwell Hill observed that some of the black studies centers on campuses were tied to community needs programs, some were parts of academic programs, and some had no clear connections with the community or the academy. Judge William H. Hastie, Chief Judge of the U.S. Court of Appeals, Third Circuit, Philadelphia—the first African American man to hold such an office—proposed examining the deficiencies of college programs that had brought about the ingress of black studies programs and how those deficiencies might be remedied by new courses, new approaches, or changes in current courses.[3]

An "intergenerational dialogue" was pursued by each of the participants in venues of their choosing, *not* through a singular group position paper. For his part, Judge Hastie chose his address to the 62nd Annual Convention of the NAACP in Minneapolis on July 7, 1971, to speak of "The Black Mystique Pitfall":

> . . . During the late 1960s, an alarming number of Negroes have tended uncritically to accept and encourage racial separatism in our country as a desirable and potentially rewarding pattern of American life. I state categorically that this trend must be halted and reversed, for it can only lead to greater bitterness and frustration and to even more inferior status than black Americans now experience. . . .
>
> . . . Revulsion against the vicious and indecent aspects of white society is no justification for glorifying and building a black society which in itself mirrors and at times intensifies the same evils. The only really better society of the future to which we can hopefully look forward and for which we can meaningfully work is a better total society in which present major evils, racism prominent among them, are substantially corrected. . . .

3. From my summary handwritten during that evening meeting, for which there was no tape recording, Box 380, Folder 4, KBCP LOC.

> . . . The serious thing is that racial mystique, with its overemphasis on racial differences and its attendant hostility toward other racial groups, is destructive of that sense of our common humanity and the willingness to make common cause for human betterment which whites and blacks so badly need. Any increased drawing apart from whites in any institutional aspect is self-defeating and harmful to all of us. It is not less harmful because some blacks say they want it that way.

Hastie ends his speech as follows:

> My concluding observation, particularly addressed to separatists, is this. For too long in America, whites have been up and blacks have been down. We are trying as never before to correct this racial disparity. In the process, whites must free themselves from false pride in their whiteness. And many of them are doing so. But it will not help for blacks, aping the worst characteristics of whites, to acquire false pride and arrogance in their blackness. Kenneth Clark, a very wise and thoughtful black American made the essential point better than I can when he wrote:
>
> > "Nor can one build a solid pride on the quicksands of emotion, anger, rage, hatred—no matter how justifiable. Genuine pride—the pride that makes life worth the struggle with some hope of serenity—must come from solid personal achievement, from sensitivity and concern and respect for one's fellow man, from compassion and the willingness to struggle to give some substance to one's own life by trying to help others live with confidence in the possibility of positives. Pride, like humanity, is destroyed by one's insistence that he possesses it."
>
> Let us face our problems and work for their solution in that spirit.[4]

We seem now to have come full circle, with the sometimes roiling debate over the notion of "post-blackness," an alternative to the assumption that blackness has a fundamental signification that is pejorative, and therefore self-limiting to anyone for whose identity it is a modifier, whether or not they accept it as such. This notion is particularly meaningful for artists across a spectrum of arts who have found

4. *The Crisis,* October, 1971, vol. 78, no. 8 (Box 440, Folder 4, KBCP LOC).

its embrace liberating in rejecting the assumed embedded signifiers of "imitative" or "predictable" in *blackness*. There are, of course, many artists, as well as other professionals—whether of an older generation or not—who find this a self-engendered, if not ludicrous, perspective. It is a new mystique.

In his recent book *Who's Afraid of Post-Blackness? What It Means to Be Black Now,* Touré says of the old mystique,

> I think it's our awareness of being Americanized and our deeply conflicted emotions about that—our righteous unhappiness with America—and our intense desire for a tangible connection with an alternate national identity that led us to Afrocentrism. We have craved a relationship with Africa, we have needed to be from and connected to some other place because our relationship with this country is very problematic and we feel unrooted here. But Africa, too, is an unrequiting lover because it is a long-distance lover—long-distance temporally. By that I mean we haven't lived there in a very long time. We may retain Africanisms that run deeper than our consciousness can grasp, but our relationship with Africa is wrapped in an overly romantic notion, like a love for someone we no longer know. Or like messaging a body part that's been amputated.[5]

Yet we are, he argues—rightly, I believe—quintessential Americans who now more than ever have the institutional, economic, and political power to change America. Such a perspective engages in the challenges set forth by the participants in the Haverford Discussions and the succeeding Hastie Group. And I am certain that it would resonate with Dr. Kenneth Bancroft Clark.

5. Touré, *Who's Afraid of Post-Blackness? What It Means to Be Black Now* (New York: Free Press, 2011), 193–94. He continues this line of thought through page 199.

Works Cited

Baraka, Amiri. "A Reply to Saunders Redding's 'The Black Revolution in American Studies.'" In *Sources for American Studies,* ed. Jefferson B. Kellogg and Robert H. Walker. Westport, CT: Greenwood Press, 1983. Pp. 15–21.

Bennett, Lerone, Jr. "The Black Establishment: Who Are Its Members?" *Negro Digest,* July 1964, 81–96.

Berry, Faith. Introduction to *A Scholar's Conscience: Selected Writings of J. Saunders Redding, 1942–1977.* Lexington: University Press of Kentucky, 1992.

The Black Aesthetic. See Gayle.

Black Fire: An Anthology of Afro-American Writing. See Jones and Neal.

Black Separatism: A Bibliography. See Jenkins and Phillis.

Brown, H. Rap. *Die Nigger Die! A Political Autobiography.* 1969. Chicago: Lawrence Hill Books, 2002.

Brown, Sterling A. "Negro Character as Seen by White Authors," *Journal of Negro Education* 2, no. 2 (April 1933): 179–203.

Carmichael, Stokely, and Charles V. Hamilton. *Black Power: The Politics of Liberation in America.* New York: Random House, 1967.

Clark, Kenneth. The Papers of Kenneth B. Clark. Library of Congress, Manuscript Division. Boxes 318, 319, 320.

Cruse, Harold. *The Crisis of the Negro Intellectual.* 1967. New York: New York Review of Books, 2005.

———. *Rebellion or Revolution?* New York: William Morrow, 1968.

Du Bois, W. E. B. *The Souls of Black Folk.* New York: Penguin Group, 1995.

Ellison, Ralph. *Going to the Territory.* New York: Vintage Books, 1995.

———. *Shadow and Act.* New York: Vintage Books, 1995.

Gates, Henry Louis, Jr. "'. . . and bid him sing': J. Saunders Redding and the Criticism of American Negro Literature." In *To Make a Poet Black,* by J. Saunders Redding. Ithaca: Cornell University Press, 1988.

Gayle, Addison, Jr., ed. *The Black Aesthetic.* Garden City, NY: Doubleday & Company, 1971.

Glaude, Eddie S., Jr., ed. *Is It Nation Time? Contemporary Essays on Black Power and Black Nationalism.* Chicago: University of Chicago Press, 2002.

Jackson, Lawrence P. *The Indignant Generation: A Narrative History of African American Writers and Critics, 1934–1960*. Princeton: Princeton University Press, 2011.

———. "Irredeemable Promise: J. Saunders Redding and Negro New Liberalism." *American Literary History* 19, no. 3 (Fall 2007): 712–44.

Jenkins, Betty Lanier, and Susan Phillis, eds. *Black Separatism: A Bibliography*. Westport, CT: Greenwood Press, 1976.

Jones, LeRoi, and Larry Neal, eds. *Black Fire: An Anthology of Afro-American Writing*. New York: William Morrow, 1968.

Lackey, Michael. "Moses, Man of Oppression: A Twentieth-Century African-American Critique of Western Theocracy." *African American Review* 43, no. 4 (Winter 2009): 577–88.

———."Redeeming the Post-Metaphysical Promise of J. Saunders Redding's 'America.'" *New Centennial Review* 12, no. 3 (2012): 217–43.

Mannheim, Karl. *Ideology and Utopia: An Introduction to the Sociology of Knowledge*. New York: Harcourt, Brace & World, 1966.

Mills, Charles W. *The Racial Contract*. Ithaca: Cornell University Press, 1997.

Myers, Bob E. "Shades of Black: African American Undergraduate Life at Northwestern University." Northwestern University Office of Admission, circa 1991. Office of Admission General Files, Northwestern University Archives, Evanston, IL.

Redding, J. Saunders. "Black Chauvinism and Black Culture: A Modest Dissent." *Brown Alumni Monthly*, September 1978, 12–17.

———. "The Black Revolution in American Studies." In *Sources for American Studies*, ed. Jefferson B. Kellogg and Robert H. Walker. Westport, CT: Greenwood Press, 1983. Pp. 8–14.

———. "Negro Writing in America," *New Leader* 43, no. 20 (1960): 8–10.

———. *No Day of Triumph*. New York: Harper & Brothers, 1942.

———. *On Being Negro in America*. Indianapolis and New York: Charter Books, 1962.

———. *A Scholar's Conscience: Selected Writings of J. Saunders Redding, 1942–1977*. Ed. with an introduction by Faith Berry. Lexington: University of Kentucky Press, 1992.

———. *Stranger and Alone*. Boston: Northeastern University Press, 1989.

Said, Edward. *Orientalism*. New York: Pantheon, 1978.

The Spirit and the Intellect: Haverford College, 1833–1983. Ed. Gregory Kannerstein. Haverford, PA: Haverford College, 1983.

Washington, Booker T. *Up from Slavery*. New York: W. W. Norton, 1996.

Index